Losing Lisa

Ally Garbutt

First published in Great Britain in 2022

Editing, design, typesetting and publishing by UK Book Publishing

www.ukbookpublishing.com

ISBN: 978-1-915338-25-9

LOSING LISA

This story is based on a true story and most names have been changed to protect individuals.

The information in this book is correct, accurate and based on true facts substantiated by evidence. The author is not liable for errors, inaccuracies, omissions or any other inconsistencies of any type, whether such omissions result from negligence, accident or any other cause.

It is a story of horrendous domestic violence and abuse, narcissism, indoctrination, coercive control, brainwashing, THE SUICIDE OF MY DAUGHTER LISA and the devastating effects of parental alienation.

The impact of parent and child being separated through parental alienation will no doubt have long lasting psychological and emotional effects on all those involved.

As an adult, woman and mother, the life I have endured during the worst times of the abuse suffered, has left me with debilitating medical and psychological conditions which will last a lifetime; this includes PTSD.

The thought that my two innocent young adolescents will potentially suffer with long term damage from the isolated and controlled life they have endured at the hands of their father, truly breaks my heart.

ACKNOWLEDGMENTS

I dedicate this book to my late daughter:
Lisa Marie, my angel in heaven, whom I love and miss beyond words.

24 June 2006

Lisa & Nikki!

ACKNOWLEDGEMENTS

My two oldest sons:
You two have truly been my life savers in more ways than one, you really are my heroes and I love you so very much.

My two youngest children:
Temporarily lost to us through parental alienation, I love you with all my heart and miss you every day.

To my daughters-in-law and my four precious grandchildren, *I thank you for all your support and all you do for me; my grandchildren are the light of my life.*

I thank all my amazing friends *who have supported me and been there for me at my absolute lowest, too many to name but you all know who you are, and you all mean the absolute world to me.*

My heartfelt thanks to the trauma surgeon Dr. Deborah Goldfield and Mr Jamie Gibson *for attending to Lisa at the scene, you were truly amazing.*

I also thank North Yorkshire Police *– you have been brilliant.*

Stowe family law: *Theo, Kate, Gill, Michelle and all the staff who became my 'family' for more than two years, you were and still are amazing.*

Miss Julia Nelson barrister:
I couldn't have done it without you, thank you from the bottom of my heart.

Ally Garbutt

Foreword

I am simply just a woman who met the wrong person; I am a mother who just loves her kids; I am a person who strived to keep her family together against all odds; I was a naive, young bride and mother who could never have been prepared for the hand which I was dealt in life.

I have written this book to hopefully address and help other people like me in a situation where you believe it is impossible to escape; a prison where you are wearing invisible chains; where you are constantly wondering what you could have possibly done so wrong to deserve this treatment; a mother racked with guilt at the thought of breaking up her family; a woman whose voice becomes silent for her own protection; and most of all a person who has absolutely no self-worth and accepts this to be normal.

My absolute wish is to eradicate domestic abuse, coercive control and parental alienation from this world – these acts KILL many thousands of people every year; we all need to be aware and speak out for victims of these despicable crimes who have no voice!

Chapter 1

In the beginning

It was Christmas Day 1977, it was just a normal, happy day celebrating with my two younger siblings, Anthony, 13, Jane, 11, and my mum and dad in our home town of Leeds, West Yorkshire, England.

I was 15 years old and still at secondary school about take my O Levels. We were a very close-knit family and had a lovely, stable, happy childhood; my mum was an education welfare officer at the time and my dad worked for a roofing company.

I remember after we had eaten our Christmas dinner and still feeling elated with all our presents, they sat us down and told us that Dad had been promoted at work which meant he was to be relocated to Darlington. My brother and sister listened excitedly, but at this very moment, my whole world fell apart. My Life was in Leeds NOT Darlington!

"What about my friends?" I said. "What about school and my job at the restaurant in Harehills?" Also: "My ballet?" I had done ballet for years and years and was a principal dancer in many of our performances – I couldn't give ballet up; I was doing really well, having gone through all the grades with excellent results!

My parents were surprised at my reaction – they assumed that I would be as excited as Anthony and Jane were. After many long discussions it was decided that I would stay with my neighbour until I finished my exams. This was great news to me as Carol, my neighbour, was my best friend; we were punk rockers and regularly would go to Leeds Poly and other venues, where we would attend concerts like The Clash, Billy Idol, 999 and The Stranglers. I would go from my house to hers looking normal and respectable, assuring my parents we were going to the cinema, but in my hand was a carrier bag of ripped shirts from the charity shop covered in writing, safety pins for our ears and of course black eyeliner for our faces – the transformation was so good that my dad drove past us while we were walking to catch the bus one evening, and he didn't recognise me.

I remember bumping into Elvis Costello one Saturday, on Briggate in town, and he asked me if I wanted a back stage pass. I politely declined, which I now regret, but at the time I was not a fan of him or his music; he was also considered to be "straight" in the punk world and I couldn't betray my love for punk, could I?

Carol's mum was a single parent and was out most evenings, giving us free rein to have parties. We would invite punk bands to Carol's house and have amazing parties. I couldn't imagine living anywhere else – this was the seventies, punk rock era in Leeds, I was 15 and having a great time, I didn't like school much so I would bunk off and go into town with Carol and Geraldine (another friend); we loved going into Schofields store and putting make-up on in the cosmetics department, hanging out in Virgin Records then getting the bus back in time for the end of school.

I had a part time job on Saturday evening in the Embassy restaurant in Harehills and was earning £8.00 for 4 hours' work, which was good money back then – but I would also have to give that up to move to Darlington!

It was quite a scary time to live in Leeds in the seventies – a girl called Jane from my school had been murdered by Peter Sutcliffe, "The Yorkshire Ripper" on a Saturday night in June in Chapeltown, just around the corner from where we lived. The very same evening that she was murdered, I was working only a few metres away in the restaurant. He had already murdered two women and Jayne was his third victim; he had been targeting prostitutes, and he assumed that Jayne was one – she was just an innocent 16 year old on her way home from a night out with her boyfriend and was just a year older than me. It haunted me for years, knowing that he was so close and that it could have been me walking home from work after midnight if the manager hadn't given me a lift home; just the thought that he was murdering her about the same time that we left the restaurant just around the corner still sends shivers down my spine today.

Meanwhile, my parents had fallen in love with a small city called Ripon in North Yorkshire; this was the compromise they had made, rather than live in Darlington. I had never heard of this place but their excitement had me intrigued. I caught the 36 bus from Leeds to Ripon every Friday after school, and the first Friday I came to Ripon, my parents met me at the bus station. We proceeded to walk towards the market square. It seemed very quiet to me and so far removed from my home town of Leeds, so we arrived on the square, and my mum was buzzing.

"What do you think, Alisha, isn't it lovely?" she said.

"I will let you know when we see the town centre," I replied, feeling deflated with my new surroundings.

"This *is* the centre," she said…

Well, I went into a full-blown tantrum at the thought of living in what I considered to be a *tiny village* compared to massive, busy, Leeds.

"I CAN'T LIVE HERE!!" I shouted. "THERE IS NOTHING HERE!"

"Let's show you the new house we have bought, you will love it," she said excitedly.

She was right: they had bought a large semi-detached Victorian house. It was a huge, 5-bed, 3-bath house with a beautiful large garden, cherry blossom trees, apple trees, a fish pond and a beautiful flower garden; it was truly idyllic and I did fall in love with this impressive house. *It* was gorgeous, but I still wasn't convinced about this tiny city!

I was glad when Sunday came so I could get the 36 bus back to Leeds, which will always be my hometown where I grew up.

June 1978 I finished my exams which meant it was time to say goodbye to my life in Leeds and make a new life in Ripon, I tried to be positive but while my parents were at work and my siblings were in their new school making friends, I felt lost. My brother and sister quickly made friends while I moped around in a strange house in an alien city. I even rang my friend Cooky and asked if I could live with her and her family in Adel, Leeds. Her mum promptly said, "No!" This was really upsetting for me. I was desperate to get back to Leeds. I needed another plan but it's not easy when you have just left school and have no money.

It was obviously annoying my mum that I was moping around doing nothing, so she told me to get a job but I couldn't face the thought of going for interviews. One day she said there was a vacancy for a checkout operator in the local supermarket and I should apply! Not my chosen career, but I needed to earn money, so off I went dressed in my black velvet jacket and white shirt, long floral skirt, looking very smart. I got the job there and then, I didn't know if I was happy or not. So June 1978 I was working full time in Morrisons supermarket earning £19.00 per week. My new life began from this day and I loved it; I made lovely friends and had great times. We worked all week to party all weekend and we had so much fun, Leeds didn't seem so high up on my agenda anymore.

A very good looking guy came in to see me regularly at work and eventually asked me out, giving me a piece of paper with *D FONZ* and his telephone number on. His name was Denis. I remember thinking he was full of himself but very good looking. He was five years older than me, he was the brother of a girl I worked with so I felt at ease to go out with him. He would take me to the local pubs, of which there were many for such a small place. He was amused that I drank Babycham, but that's the only drink I knew. "Why don't you drink lager and lime like everyone else?" he would say to me. "Because I like Babycham, thank you," I snapped. Secretly I felt quite posh drinking Babycham, and didn't want to follow everyone else like a sheep. We had a short, rocky relationship but remained friends until he sadly died a few years ago.

Soon after, I met my first love, Nick. I really loved him but he was influenced by his mother who took an instant dislike to me based on the fact that I was from Leeds, I was blonde and liked to party; she favoured his previous girlfriend Poppy from a well-respected local family and a 'girl next door appeal'. He was confused and went from me to her, her to me. In the end we parted company amicably and he later married Poppy, who still remains a dear friend of mine to this day.

I was still enjoying my working life. I had been there almost a year now and my social life became more intense. I spent a lot of time with my best friend Yvonne – we were inseparable, we worked together, partied together and spent hours on the phone when we were apart. Now I was starting to like Ripon after all, we were having a great time going to barn dances, parties and night clubs; it started to feel like home at last. I even planned to go on holiday with Yvonne, Kim and Pam (three friends from work) to Spain for a week in a couple of months' time, my first holiday with friends; I was so excited. Lloret de Mar was the resort we chose in Costa Brava. I was so happy right now.

July 1979 and our girls' holiday was upon us – Lloret de Mar, here we come! I was so excited to go on this girls' holiday; when our plane landed in sunny Spain it was such a great feeling. During the flight Kim suffered severe pain in her side. I remember we were all laughing and she was begging us to stop laughing as it made *her* laugh which caused her excruciating pain. She seemed fine when we landed so we didn't think much about it again. While travelling to our hotel, the rain came down. I have never seen rain like this before. We took cover in a nearby cafe and watched the rain bounce high off the pavement while eating our burgers swilled down with half a lager – I had by now graduated from my previous tipple of Babycham. The rain didn't dampen our spirits – we were determined to have a great time, whatever the weather. That evening we discovered a nightclub just around the corner from our hotel so we spent most evenings in there.

The second day we put on our bikinis and lay on the sunbeds by the pool even though it was a cloudy day with very little sun, but I had bought this lovely knitted bikini, it was cream with coloured beads on the straps and the bottoms (amazing what we remember); we were all the colour of bottled milk at the end of the day. I soon realised that it was not the most practical beachwear as when it became wet, it stretched beyond belief, making it embarrassing exiting the pool, clinging onto my bikini for dear life while I had a captive audience, mostly testosterone-filled Spanish males.

DAY 3: We hired bicycles – not sure whose good idea that was; we were cycling on the main road which in itself was very challenging with all the potholes, not to mention the saddle sores we all had. Along the way we came to a small shop with the biggest punnets of strawberries I have ever seen, outside on a wooden table. Again I'm not sure whose good idea this was, but we all sat on a nearby wall and ate the whole punnets of strawberries, hence my close relationship with the toilet in our room back at the hotel a few hours later – while I was sat on the loo with terrible stomach pains, I was vomiting in the nearby bidet. Still, this did not stop us from going to the nightclub later that evening.

DAY 4: Barcelona, here we come. We went on the organised trip to the bullfight – Kim and Pam seemed more keen than me and Yvonne, but we went anyway. It was a huge stadium, we took our seats and watched the most horrible, distressing event I had ever seen in my life; my heart was breaking for that poor bull. I was so glad when we left. I vowed never to go watch bullfighting ever again.

DAYS 5&6 seemed to merge into one; the weather was wet and miserable so I had a good idea. "Look, none of us have got a tan, we can't go back to work, whiter than we came, we will be a laughing stock, so why don't we go to the shop and buy some false tan?" I said, feeling very smug with myself. (Back then the false tans were not what they are today.) "Yes, that's a good idea," Pam, Kim and Yvonne agreed, so off we went to buy a shed load of false tan. Back at the hotel we were eager to apply the tan. It was one which took time to develop, so, tan applied, make-up on and the nightclub here we come. The next morning Yvonne, who I shared a room with, took one look at me and laughed until she cried, but I was laughing as much at her – we were both stripey and patchy with stained hands, knees and elbows; the bed sheets weren't much better either. We just lit our usual morning cigarette before heading down to breakfast and saw that Kim and Pam hadn't exactly applied theirs evenly either.

"We are going home tomorrow and look at the state of our tan!" Yvonne said – but it was alright for her, she worked in the cash office in the warehouse where no-one would see her; but me, Kim and Pam had to sit on the checkout in full view, serving customers. We loved working on the checkouts where we would all start putting customers' shopping through the checkouts at the same time, shout "GO" then race through the shopping to see who would finish first to be the winner. This was our favourite pastime until a customer reported us to the manager, who was NOT impressed at all. That was our first verbal warning, but we carried on doing it, but just more discreetly.

THE LAST DAY. Packed and ready for the plane home, Kim again complained about the pain in her side. She had mentioned it while riding the bike, but we chose to ignore her complaints. However, on the plane she was holding her side while we were all crying with laughter at our streaky bodies. On arriving home, Kim was taken to hospital with acute appendicitis and underwent immediate surgery. All we kept saying was "what will the surgeon think of her tan?"!

Not long after our holiday, on a lovely sunny day, Yvonne and myself decided to go to a local village fete (any excuse so she could drive her car). There was a cricket match in the next field to the fete, lots of people were there, kids were taking part in the running races which were on the grass marked out with chalk, tombola stalls, welly throwing etc; everyone seemed to be happy.

We walked over to the tug of war, and my eyes feasted on this gorgeous, dark haired, ripped guy called Graham. He had also spotted me and our eyes locked; instantly there was a chemistry between us. I even said to Yvonne, "Wow, look at him, he's gorgeous, I'm going to marry him." I was only 16 years old. Later that evening in the village pub, I saw Graham from afar and he was already staring at me. The physical attraction was immense between us; we flirted and kissed outside the ladies' toilet where he had been waiting for me.

"Where do you live?" he said. When I told him, it just so happened to be around the corner from him, so he offered me a lift home, I declined as I was staying over at Yvonne's house.

"I've fancied you for ages," he said. "I see you walking to work on a morning, I wolf whistle at you from a roof I'm working on, you have the most gorgeous legs," he said. Well I was so flattered and felt like I was walking on air. *Is this really it,* I thought to myself; I couldn't stop thinking about him. I bumped into him a few days later, we sat and chatted on a nearby wall, he was extremely flirty with me, telling me how much he fancied me and asked me out. "WOW," I thought; I was ecstatic inside but played it cool and said "maybe". We arranged to meet the following evening in a local pub. I arrived first and he was nowhere to be seen. I remember thinking, well it was too good to be true, so I resigned myself to being stood up until a hand from behind slipped around my waist and a delicate kiss landed on my neck – he had arrived, albeit late... We chatted all evening and he asked me back to his bedsit. I was so attracted to him physically, so I did go back with him and stayed the night. It was lovely, he was very attentive and we both enjoyed our first night of passion. This was it, I was in love, besotted and on cloud nine.

My 17th birthday, August 18th, 1979, was only three weeks away, I was looking forward to seeing Graham. My birthday came and he totally spoilt me, he took me out to dinner, bought me lovely gifts and most of all, he made me feel like I was his whole world. I was so happy at this point.

Graham asked to take me out the following Saturday night, to which I eagerly agreed. "Great I will pick you up at 7pm," he said. The day soon arrived and I spent ages getting ready, having a long bath, putting on make-up, doing my hair, and most importantly applied enough hairspray to it so that it was the texture of cardboard, almost like wings at the front of my head – sounds gross, but it was the fashion in the 70s.

The time had arrived for Graham to pick me up, there I was sat at the dining room window waiting and waiting and waiting; meanwhile my mum was very vocal with her disgust towards Graham and upset looking at me waiting with tears rolling down my face. I waited until 10pm then went up to bed distraught. At 11.30pm there was a knock at the door – "Graham is at the door," my mum shouted to me. I came down and listened to his apology and the reason he had left me waiting all night. "I've been bushbeating and working," he said. I didn't doubt him, even defending him to my parents, saying that he was working hard to earn money for our future, but my mum said it was unacceptable that he had left me waiting the whole night without any contact. She was right, and unfortunately this was just the beginning of things to come.

Chapter 2

I had surgery coming up as I am deaf in my left ear due to contracting measles when I was 6 years old so I have always been a regular patient at the doctors and hospital (it was so embarrassing when my mum, who was a teacher by now, came to my school many times and told all the teachers that I should sit at the front of the class due to me being deaf) – my friends would mouth words to me from then on to my annoyance...no wonder I hated school!

I was told that the three tiny bones behind the eardrum were not vibrating sound because they had all been fused together and my eardrum was perforated. The surgeon explained that he would make three new bones and make a new eardrum from a skin graft. I had been offered hearing aids many times but chose to be deaf rather than wear one of them massive plastic boxes behind my ears – not a good look if you wanted street cred. I was 17 years old and my only concern was that they didn't shave my hair off during the surgery, but they explained that they could go into the ear canal and my hair wouldn't be shaved. This surgery had a success rate of 60%, great; I had every faith that I would get my hearing back.

The night before surgery my parents came to visit me with my brother and sister, but all I kept doing was looking at the door of my hospital room waiting for Graham. Nothing else mattered to me. I could see that my parents felt my disappointment that my boyfriend had not come to visit me, but a while after my parents left, Graham appeared and stayed with me for only a short time. I asked why he was so late and he said he didn't want to see my parents, which I failed to understand at the time, but my mind was on my surgery and I didn't want to probe into the reasons why he was so rude. I remember being wheeled into surgery one minute and the next thing I remember was waking up, asking the girl in the next bed to me for a mirror. She didn't have one, so I just lay in my bed until I could ask a nurse. As I lay there, I felt a cool breeze on one side of my head, I reached up and felt my skin, and some hard, wiry like string sticking out of my head and a patch which was completely numb. "OH MY GOD, I'M BALD!" I screamed. They had promised not to shave my head. I was really upset so I got out of bed, dropped to the floor as I was still sedated, was picked up by a nurse and put back in to bed. "Can I have a mirror?" I asked. "I'm not sure it's such a good idea at the moment, wait until you come round properly," she said quietly.

"Oh no, I'm not being fobbed off," I thought, so off I stumbled to the toilet, looked in the mirror and saw a bald patch with a great long scar of very ugly stitches sticking out of my head. I went back to my bed and cried to the girl next to me. I was mortified, and to add insult to injury, it was an unsuccessful result: I was still DEAF.

I was spending more and more time with Graham and it was a volatile relationship – one minute we were love's young dream, the next we were screaming at each other. I noticed that as time went by, I became more reluctant to argue my point, I became scared and would give in to Graham rather than let him get so angry with me. I had never seen a temper as vicious as Graham's in my life.

18th August 1980, my 18th birthday, my parents had bought me a green Princess Vanden Plas car, it had polished wood trim inside, leather seats and a radio cassette player. I was overjoyed and couldn't wait to drive. I took driving lessons and passed my test first time. I was so elated and couldn't wait to share my news with Graham. When I arrived home, parked up my car outside my house and started to take off my "L" plates, I heard my mum coming down the drive.

"Alisha, don't be so despondent, you can always take your test again, not many people pass first time, it's not the end of the world," she said, trying to be tactful.

"What are you on about?" I said to her, a little pissed off that she thought I had failed my test. "*Actually,* Mother, I have passed my test, thank you for having so much faith in me," I said sarcastically.

"Oh Alisha, that's brilliant news, I'm so pleased for you. It's not that I didn't have faith in you, it's just rare to pass first time, that's all, I'm really proud of you," she said apologetically.

"*Well then, how lucky are you having a rare Daughter?!*" At this, we just burst out laughing.

I was eager to drive my car, so I drove into town feeling like the cat that got the cream. In the meantime Graham had called after work to my house, and my mum couldn't wait to tell him that I was out driving in my car.

"Mum, I wanted to tell him!"

"I'm sorry, I couldn't help it, I'm so excited for you. I got you a little present for passing your test first time." She was more excited than me! She produced a bag with a gift set of 'Charlie' perfume, bubble bath and moisturising cream, all in a lovely pale blue shiny cosmetic bag. I was so happy right now; I loved my mum – I always wanted to be like her, she was beautiful and intelligent. I remember when I was six years old, I had a day off school and my mum was going shopping with her friend in Leeds, I watched intently as she applied her make-up, she had lovely green eyes and the most perfect lips, gorgeous, shiny, long dark hair. I just stared at her thinking she must secretly be the "Pretty Polly" model, pictured on all the ladies' tights as she was her double and the most beautiful woman I had ever seen.

"Thanks, Mum, this is lovely, I love it." At this very moment, I felt really happy, loved and lucky.

I drove to Graham's bedsit, excited to tell him my news, He was so angry and aggressive to me, I was shocked and didn't understand why he was shouting at me; I thought he would be happy for me.

"OH, THAT'S IT NOW, YOU WILL THINK YOU ARE GOOD SWANNING AROUND IN YOUR CAR, GOING OUT WHEN YOU FEEL LIKE IT, YOU WILL LOVE BEING INDEPENDENT, OUT ALL THE TIME! YOUR MUM AND DAD BOUGHT YOU THAT CAR TO SPLIT US UP!" he screamed at me.

I left distraught and drove home only to be greeted by my mum demanding to know why I was so upset. I couldn't tell her because she would tell me to leave him and I was very much in love with him, so I made up an excuse which she knew wasn't true. I was still upset but I excused his behaviour and assumed he was exhausted from work; however, the reality was that he was unbelievably insecure which would become more and more apparent in time.

A few weeks later, a work colleague announced she was leaving and returning to her home town of London. I asked if I could have first refusal for her one bedroom rented flat. I was so excited looking around this damp, mouldy, freezing, dirty flat, but it would be a home for me and Graham and that's all I was concerned about. My parents hated him, they said he was rude, arrogant, selfish, disrespectful and argumentative. He would have full blown arguments with my mum over politics, which he knew nothing about; my mum was a member of a political party, she was well educated and very intelligent, she was a university lecturer and was the first woman to gain a first class honours degree in sociology at Bradford University, but Graham seemed to have a problem with my mum; he would criticise her opinions constantly. It made me feel uncomfortable having to listen to them arguing and I was torn in two, but I was making my new life and my loyalty (displaced as I now know) was with Graham, just like my mum's loyalty was to my doting father – after all, my parents were my role models, they had a very loving, long, respectful, equal, successful marriage, and I wanted to emulate this and be as happy as they were.

Graham and I moved into the flat in September 1980 with absolutely nothing; we had makeshift tins with labels; rent, electric meter, food, etc. People were really kind, we were given a second hand bed, second hand sofa, my dad came and decorated but my mum was mortified when she came to see it – I had left a beautiful, massive, 5-bed, 3-bath Victorian family home, to live in absolute squalor just up the road. By this time, my parents, brother and sister, nanna and some of my friends had raised concerns about my relationship with Graham, they said I wasn't myself and I seemed timid, scared and insular; my life with Graham had just begun and I had no idea what lay ahead...

Graham had talked about us setting up our own business – he was a joiner by trade and worked for a local joinery firm making timber windows, so May 1981, we started our joinery business. I carried on working full time so we had an income, I would then finish work, come home and help prime timber windows at our workshop, and quickly learnt how to do bookkeeping. I was enjoying life, we seemed like the perfect couple; we both worked hard and had amazing times together. He would say to me, "We don't need anyone else, just me and you is all we need."

I just felt that he was being protective over me and that he would wrap me up in his love, and I felt like I had found the idyllic life with the man I loved deeply.

November 1981 I thought about marriage. My only passion in life, if I didn't make it to be a ballerina, was to get married and have a family. Apart from his outburst over my driving test, we were happy; we discussed it and it was me who asked him to marry me. I wanted to get engaged on Christmas Eve. I had already seen the ring I wanted, it was exactly the same ring as Princess Diana's, yellow gold, Oval sapphire with diamonds around the stone. I was so excited; he agreed that it would be romantic to get engaged at Christmas, so that was the plan.

A couple of weeks later, Graham took me out in his car for the day. We had a lovely time, but on the way back home, suddenly, out of nowhere he started getting very angry and shouting at me because he said I was looking at a guy while we were out. The control had already started, but I failed to identify it as emotional abuse. But while in the "trap" of mental and physical abuse, I mistook it for love and denied that the abuse was happening in order to feel loved, not recognising this to be the start of an extremely abusive, controlling, narcissistic relationship. I was strangely flattered that he was so jealous – I was obviously delusional and in denial that this behaviour was unacceptable.

"He must really love me if he's so jealous," I thought, but he was raging by now and smashed his car into a parked car near our flat. He instantly said it was my fault and I found myself apologising. He then screamed at me:

"YOU CAN FORGET ABOUT THE F***ING RING YOU WANTED, I NEED THE MONEY TO REPAIR MY CAR NOW!"

I have no idea why I was so keen to marry this scary man who could easily get angry with me over nothing, but I was still eager to get engaged on Christmas Eve, so he suggested to go and find a second hand cheap ring in town or wait until he could save up, which he said would take months and months. So I opted for a £70.00 second hand, tiny, diamond, solitaire ring.

The next few weeks were so lovely: we would light our coal fire in our rented flat, snuggle up on our very worn, hand me down sofa, watch our black and white portable TV which my nanna lent us. When it was just us two, Graham seemed the happiest. He would squeeze me so tight and say, "I want you all to myself, you are all mine." I misjudged this for love, but now realise it was the beginning of control.

December 1981, it seemed to snow forever. One night Graham was out drinking with his college friends in York, I visited my family just a few metres away for a couple of hours, then returned home to the flat.

I snuggled in bed with lots of blankets on and wore my dressing gown as it was freezing cold. I could see my breath each time I exhaled. I was just dozing off when I heard the key in the door and Graham muttering to himself. I immediately threw the covers off and took my dressing gown off, laid naked, albeit freezing cold, expecting him to ravish me. He came into the bedroom. "Wow, look at you, how lucky am I? Alisha, you are amazing, look at your gorgeous body." He came over to the bed and stroked my leg from my foot to the top of my thigh. "Your legs go on forever," he whispered. His hand glided over my hip and down in to my, then, very tiny waist, then traced my back up to my shoulders, then suddenly grabbed my neck... "What have you been doing tonight?" he said coldly. I pulled the covers back to cover me and said I had been to visit my parents. At this he flew into a violent rage, shouting at me.

"WHY COULDN'T YOU JUST STAY IN, YOU ARE ALWAYS AT YOUR F***ING PARENTS' HOUSE! JUST BECAUSE I WENT OUT, YOU THEN HAVE TO GO OUT!" He then grabbed my arm and dragged me to the front door, opened the door and pushed me outside. I was naked and fell in the snow, I was crying and begging him to let me back in, banging on the door to get help from the other tenants, but this made him more angry. I was shaking and crying.

"Please let me in, I'm freezing cold, please, please, I'm sorry for going to see my family, please let me in," I cried.

He started laughing and saying, "It's not that cold, stop being a drama queen," then opened the door and let me in. He was still laughing at my shaking, naked body. I was freezing so he put his arms around me and said that it was just a joke and he would warm me up. He then became really loving towards me and cuddled me, while he tried to convince me that it was just a silly prank and I should laugh it off like he did. I was desperate to get engaged on Christmas Eve, so I dismissed his behaviour as being trivial, even starting to think, it was my fault for going out earlier to see my family.

Christmas Eve 1981, Graham put this tiny ring on my finger and I was just happy to be engaged and looking forward to planning the wedding, the ring wasn't as important to me as the meaning of it, so I was happy wearing it, even though many people were shocked at the meagre content of this tiny, second hand ring.

We decided the following year, 28th August 1982, would be a good day to get married – it was bank holiday weekend and 10 days after my 20th birthday.

Christmas Day arrived and I was ecstatic to find that Graham had got me a gorgeous, cute little black kitten, I called him Ziggy, he was adorable, everything seemed so good now.

I was excited to tell my family that I was getting married. Graham had already said to me, "Your parents can pay for the wedding seeing as they are the bride's parents, and when you see them you can tell them that we are getting married in August so they have time to save up."

I had no idea why I was so appeasing and so under his control, so I repeated this to my parents who immediately knew that these words were not coming from me; this was so out of character. From this day they pleaded with me to leave him, they could see the change in me and they were afraid, but I knew better. I told them it was up to me and it was my life and to stop 'interfering' in my life. They did back off under duress; they loved me and saw danger signs everywhere, signs that I didn't recognise to be domestic abuse/narcissism/coercive control/violence/manipulation/gaslighting and isolation, but this was just the start. My Mum would say...

"I don't like the way he OPERATES, he's either really, really nice, or absolutely EVIL." I knew exactly what she meant by that, but didn't admit that to her.

From January 1982 until August 1982 it was a whirlwind of working and planning the wedding. It flew by with no hassle or cross words; with the help of my mum and his mum, I ordered my dress, booked the cathedral and posh hotel for the reception, white Rolls Royce was booked, flowers and photographer were sorted and everything was perfect. I was so excited for my big day.

My grandmother died just weeks before my wedding; we were devastated. It was my dad's mum, she had gone blind in her thirties from glaucoma, so he had a very close bond with her as he looked after her for many years. It was heartbreaking to see my dad crying so much. His father had died when he was just 14 and his brother died in the early seventies so he was very close to his mum, just being the two of them.

Saturday 28th August 1982, it was a gorgeous, hot sunny day, we had a photo shoot in our lovely back garden. It wasn't long before the wedding car arrived at my family home, my dad looked so proud and after he gathered up my train as we got into the wedding car, he held my hand tight and said to me: "You look stunning, Alisha...are you sure you want to go through with this?"

"Are you joking?" I said. "Why are you saying that on my wedding day?"

"I just want to make sure you are happy."

"Dad, I *am* happy."

"Okay, good," he said. There was a long silence, I felt physically sick, I knew deep down that I wasn't sure. My heart started to pound out of my chest, I felt dizzy and scared, surely I should be excited on my wedding day, but maybe it was wedding nerves and perfectly natural.

We arrived at the Cathedral shortly after, the wedding march started playing and my dad linked my arm walking slowly down the aisle in the amazing Ripon Cathedral. I was in awe of this beautiful building.

He whispered in my ear, my good ear, "You can turn back now, Alisha, it's not too late."

I remember saying, "No I can't, Dad, look at all these people here." I carried on walking to the altar, telling myself, everything will be okay. Our eyes met at the altar, Graham smiled at me saying I looked gorgeous, and I was relieved and felt more relaxed. We said our vows to each other and after the ceremony we proceeded to the reception venue. The day was lovely, I felt like a princess, I was so happy.

We then honeymooned in a caravan in Cornwall, a wedding gift from my parents. The journey was adventurous, we had an old grey van which was decorated with tin cans attached to the bumper by a long rope, 'JUST MARRIED' sprayed all over, and a smelly kipper in the engine thanks to the best man; it started to stink half way to Cornwall, so we promptly stopped and disposed of the disgusting smelly kipper in a nearby bin, but continued the journey with the noisy cans trailing behind us on the road to most people's amusement. The honeymoon was good, but I didn't feel completely happy like I expected to... Echoing in my mind were the words of my parents, and their obvious dislike of Graham – this bothered me hugely.

When we arrived back home from honeymoon, it was September, and we both continued to be busy with the new business and looking for a house to buy, so life was on the up. Only a few weeks later, my nanna died at 59; she had a heart condition. My mum was devastated, we were all close to her as she came to live with us for the last couple of years of her life. I couldn't believe that both my grandmothers had died just weeks apart – I never had a grandfather so I now had NO grandparents at 20 years old.

Chapter 3

Graham had seen a mews cottage for sale in Ripon, not far away from the flat we rented. It was £11,000, and we had made enough money to get a deposit together, so moved in to our own home in Spring 1983. We renovated the whole place and it was stunning; the business was thriving. I got a new job in retail while still doing the bookkeeping for our business and life was looking good, we were earning good money and enjoyed expensive restaurants, days out, and a fairly lavish lifestyle. I felt so lucky that we were living such a full and happy life.

In the autumn of 1983, I started to feel broody and we decided to try for a baby.

On 23rd December, my parents' 22nd wedding anniversary, I rang them to tell them that they would be grandparents in August the following year. I was so happy, I felt so lucky, my parents were delighted. I enjoyed the whole nine months of my pregnancy, me and Graham were so happy. My baby was due 8th August, but that day came and went, so did the next day and the next day, I was getting very frustrated by now, I was booked in for a C-section on the 14th August. Sunday 12th August, my parents invited us out for lunch, we had a lovely Sunday roast at a village pub, but I soon started to feel unwell. Later that night I started with labour pains, and the next day 12.37pm Monday 13th August our beautiful baby girl was born naturally. She was perfect, weighing 7lb4oz, lots of black hair, and gorgeous big eyes. I felt amazing, I was elated, very tired but I couldn't take my eyes off her, she was gorgeous. Graham didn't seem as happy as I imagined he would be; he just said, "I will ring everyone up and tell them the news, but I will tell them not to visit you until tomorrow because you are too tired."

He then left to go home for some rest, and would be back for the evening visiting time. I never really gave it much thought, I was so in love with this beautiful, perfect baby; I just stared at her. Within an hour, I was surprised to see my mum and dad looking so delighted, carrying lots of baby girl gifts. They said that Graham had told them not to visit me until tomorrow, but my mum said, "We rang the hospital and they said it was fine to visit and there was no way that we were waiting to see our newborn grandchild, we had to come straight here to see you both, we couldn't wait." They fell in love with my beautiful daughter, they were over the moon.

Later that evening, Graham came in holding a bouquet of flowers, but his faced dropped when he spotted cards, flowers, balloons and baby gifts at the side of my bed.

"I TOLD THEM NOT TO VISIT YOU UNTIL TOMORROW!" he shouted. "WHY DID YOU TELL THEM TO VISIT YOU?"

The nurses looked over, saw my tears rolling down my face and came over to comfort me, they explained to him that my mum had rang and it was the nurses who told them they could visit their newborn granddaughter, and I was awake and absolutely fine, they were so excited to visit.

After the nurses left, he was so abusive, saying to me, "Anyone would think it was their f***ing baby, they have ignored me, now they have seen the baby BEFORE my mum and I'm fuming that they didn't listen to me! I hope your mother doesn't think she can come round to see the baby all the time, or I will tell her to F**k off!"

After he left, I was inconsolable, this was the best day of my life so far and now it felt like my world had just shattered. I held my baby close and apologised for her father's disgusting behaviour.

I whispered to her, "I love you more than words can ever say, I've waited my whole life for you and I am so sorry that only hours into your life, you have been exposed to your daddy being angry with your mummy, my beautiful baby, please forgive me." I wiped my tears from her tiny head, kissed her, then cried myself to sleep. I found out years later that Graham had gone out drinking that night to 'wet the baby's head' and voiced his disappointment of having a baby girl to some of my friends.

My mum was so excited that she had a granddaughter, which really angered Graham, as he only ever wanted boys. I loved being in hospital, the midwives were so lovely and I felt relaxed so I stayed in for five days. I wanted to call our little princess, Nina, but when Graham came to visit, we discussed names and agreed on LISA, and I said MARIE for her middle name which he agreed to. I liked the name Lisa Marie, but my mum's middle name was Marie and I was worried that he would think that I had called her after my mum, which wasn't the case. Sure enough my mum was delighted when we told her the names we had chosen and said she was flattered that we chose her name. This became a bone of contention between us, and he accused me of being underhand and deceitful. It was becoming clear that he was jealous of the relationship between me and my family, and worst of all, me and Lisa Marie. He would constantly criticise my family and tried his utmost to turn me against them all, the constant negativity towards my family deeply affected me and I became emotionally distant from them just to make my life more bearable. Lisa did spend a lot of time with my parents; they spoilt her and doted on her.

When Lisa was two years old, my parents announced that they were moving to a small holding 45 miles away. I was gutted and immediately started to feel lonely – Graham worked all week while I cared for Lisa at home. I still did the accounts from home but most of all I was loving being a mum to my beautiful little girl, Lisa. "This is it," I thought, I'm destined to be a mother. I loved motherhood and became broody again; we discussed this but decided to move to a bigger property first, but meanwhile we bought a couple of garages with the profits we were earning from the business. We let them out to a local building company for many years, which helped us climb the property ladder quickly.

One evening we had some friends of ours come to see us, they had a baby girl (Holly) the same age as Lisa and we had been friends since Graham had met Paul while being in the retained fire brigade. (Graham looked so sexy in his fireman uniform.) We were sat chatting, then Paul suggested for him and Graham to go out for a drink while me and Emma stayed behind and caught up on our lives. Graham and Paul had been gone for a couple of hours and arrived back at 10pm approx, after a good night, Paul suggested that me and Emma should go out for a drink while he and Graham babysat. I immediately knew that Graham would absolutely disapprove of me going out without him, so I made up an excuse that I was too tired to go out, but Paul insisted and Emma was keen to go out too. I looked over at Graham and saw a familiar look on his face that made me go cold – the words he was saying did not match the look on his face and I really knew that I would be in trouble if I went out.

"Get yourself out, Alisha, it will do you good," he said in a patronising manner. I was financially dependent on him, and used that as an excuse to stay in, but to look reasonable to our friends, he again reiterated it: "Go on, you and Emma go and have a good time, I will give you some money." He became very insistent and Emma was practically out of the door raring to go out. Graham took two £10 notes from his wallet and put them hard against my hand with his teeth tightly clenched. I reluctantly went out with Emma.

We had a couple of drinks in the first pub we went past and I started to feel more relaxed and put to the back of my mind Graham's disapproval. We were really enjoying ourselves and Emma suggested going to the local nightclub; again I was dubious, I didn't want to make my situation worse by arriving home late, but it was a rare night out for both Emma and myself so I agreed to go. I paid the £3.00 to get in the club, we then bought a couple of drinks and I was feeling good to be out; we decided to dance, so left our bags under the table where we were sat with some other people. We danced and had a lovely time, but when we got back to our table, I picked up my bag to buy another drink, only to discover that a £10 note had been taken from my purse, I was really upset and decided to leave, so Emma and myself made our separate ways home.

As I was walking home, I started to feel anxious, remembering Graham's mood when I left.

I was soon home, put my key in the lock but couldn't get it in. I looked in the keyhole to see a key in the back of the lock – this was way before mobile phones, so I knocked on the door. It was about midnight, so I assumed he was asleep. I waited then knocked again. I heard footsteps coming down the stairs to let me in. Graham opened the door slightly ajar preventing me from going inside.

"Give me one good reason why I should let you in?" he said with cold eyes and his fists clenched. I was at a loss of how to resolve this, should I be brave and say:

"WELL ACTUALLY, I LIVE HERE, SO STOP BEING SUCH AN ARSEHOLE AND LET ME IN MY BLOODY HOUSE NOW!"

But NO, that would just make him more angry, so I said in my pathetic, pleading voice...

"Please let me in, it's cold and dark. Please, Graham, just let me in…"

"Okay," he said. "Give me my money back that I gave you."

"I spent £10 and had a £10 note stolen from my purse while me and Emma were dancing."

"Oh," he said, as he let me in.

"Great, that was easy," I thought.

He locked the door behind me as I turned to climb the stairs, and suddenly, I was winded by a very hard punch to my back as I fell into the stairs; he then grabbed my hair, dragging me up the stairs, down the landing while kicking me in the ribs. I was being dragged along the floor by my hair into our bedroom; my head hit the radiator along the way. I was screaming, I felt the warm blood running down my face, I was shaking with fear wondering what was coming next. There was a large chunk of my hair in his hand, I was shaking and crying begging him to stop. He did then stop. He looked at me with no expression and just said, "That's what happens when you disrespect me. Don't ever do that to me again," he said.

"What do you mean?" I said.

"You know *exactly* what I mean, going out, dancing and probably flirting, you slag!"

He couldn't bear the thought of me looking at another man; worse still he thought I now belonged to HIM, and dare another man so much as speak to me he would fly into an almighty rage; his jealousy and insecurity was beyond normal.

If only he knew that I only ever had eyes for him. I really don't know how I was so blind and weak, but I just longed for my very own happy family.

"I didn't flirt, I have done nothing wrong," I said with tears streaming down my face. He didn't say another word as we climbed into bed, back to back with a huge space between us. I was trying not to make a noise while I was in agony with my ribs and my head was pounding. A sharp pain seared through my leg as Graham kicked me hard with his heel while saying "Whoops my leg slipped".

I didn't sleep and was amazed that Lisa slept through the whole episode oblivious to what was happening, which I was so thankful for. I lay awake all night frozen to the spot. Morning came, Lisa woke up, and I went to get her but couldn't pick her up, my ribs were so sore. I heard the front door slam and was immediately relieved that Graham had gone to work. I struggled to function properly. It felt like a bad dream, but I had my beautiful baby to look after, so I took painkillers and carried on with my day. Normally Graham would call home for lunch, but I was willing him not to.

After lunch there was a knock on the door. I knew it wasn't him. I shouted from the window, after seeing it was my mother-in-law, who I had a good relationship with, "Come up, the door is open." I don't know how I thought I could hide my injuries from anyone. She came up and immediately went to pick Lisa up. She glanced over at me and said, "Oh no, what's happened to your face, you look like you have been in a fight. Shall I look after Lisa while you have a rest?"

I winced in pain with my ribs then burst into tears.

"What's wrong?" she said.

"Oh nothing, it's fine, I'm just tired."

Then she noticed a large bruise on my leg. I felt so embarrassed and ashamed when she said, "Did Graham do that to you?"

How does she know? I thought, I can't tell her what happened, would she believe me? Would she tell him that I told her? I didn't know what to say – it was her *son,* after all.

"His father was violent," she said. This immediately gave me the green light to admit what had happened.

"Graham has started using his fists," I said, crying.

"Leave him, he will end up nasty like his dad," she said.

His OWN MOTHER said that to me. I was shocked!

"I have nowhere to go to," I said.

"You could go to your mum and dad's up in the Yorkshire Dales."

How could I tell them? I was so embarrassed, I felt ashamed. How would Graham react? What would my parents say? All these questions swirling around in my head. I told her not to tell him about our conversation, to which she agreed.

I decided to do absolutely nothing. I didn't have the strength to confront this; it might just be a blip and I was sure that we could be okay.

Teatime came, I fed and bathed Lisa and put her to bed. I cooked a meal for me and Graham, ran a bath to ease my aching ribs, climbed out of the bath after a long soak, took more pain relief then heard the door close. Up came Graham.

"Something smells good," he said. "And you smell even better. How are you feeling today?"

"In a lot of pain," I said; he was acting like nothing had happened.

"I know how to make you feel better." Then he put his arms around me as if I were a child; he was gentle and started to rub my back, and said I would feel better after we have a cuddle!

"Let me get my dressing gown on then," I replied cautiously. We sat cuddled up on the sofa, but I was in pain.

"I'm in too much pain to cuddle," I said, pulling away.

He was trying hard to make idle conversation, but I was too hurt and upset to respond; he was being really nice and saying lovely things to me. "I'll make you a nice cup of tea," he said.

Maybe I am being a bit cold towards him, he is making a big effort after all, I thought. I wanted everything to be happy, but I just couldn't forgive what he'd done last night. My mind was racing, I couldn't think straight, it was so confusing with the mixed messages. I did adore Graham, he was the love of my life.

"Come here, you know I fancy the arse off you, don't you?" he said but soon started to get agitated at my lack of conversation, taking it personally.

"Oh, be like that then, here I am being nice to you and you have a face like a smacked arse and can't be bothered talking to me. I don't know why I bother," he said.

"I don't feel well, I'm in pain and still upset about last night."

"Oh dear, why are you bringing that up, that was last night, come on, Alisha, snap out of it," he said.

It was getting late and I was tired so I went to bed.

He got into bed and started to kiss and caress me, but I didn't respond; I felt cold and empty.

"Come on," he said, "stop sulking, you mean the world to me, Alisha, you know that. Maybe I over-reacted last night, but let's just forget it and move on."

He held me tight in his arms whispering how he fancied me like crazy and found me really sexy and gorgeous. I was still sore from the previous night, so I pushed him away saying that I was sore and just to leave me alone until I recovered. He carried on, ignoring my request, and started to become aroused. He lay on top of me, with my ribs aching.

"No, come on, Graham, not tonight, I'm not feeling good."

"It's okay," he said, "it will be fine, you know you want it really."

"Look, please get off me and maybe tomorrow night would be better."

He just carried on as if he hadn't heard me. I struggled to get him off me but he was a very strong, muscly man and I was a very slim 8st woman. The more I struggled, the more it hurt. I just lay there with silent tears rolling down my cheeks until he had finished.

Is this right? I thought to myself, is this rape? I felt physically sick, I wasn't sure whether it was considered to be rape between husband and wife or not. He calmly got off me without saying a word and went to sleep. I was left feeling violated, embarrassed and ashamed. These feelings were beginning to feel familiar to me now.

Back in the eighties, domestic violence/abuse was not treated as a crime. It wasn't taken seriously like it is today., so I just accepted things as they were. I didn't want to bother anyone with my problems, I always put on a brave face to protect my family.

Slowly, I became more and more isolated and I lost myself along the way. Socially I began to realise that any fun times we had, were always on his terms, always *his* choice of restaurant, venue or holiday, I just went along with him and enjoyed our times together.

He started to criticise the house cleaning, running his finger along the door frames when he returned home from work, calling me lazy if the flat wasn't immaculate. I just wanted to please him and have a happy family life, so I would make more effort to do more, even though I was completely exhausted.

It's in my nature to be placid and appeasing. I hadn't been exposed to confrontation growing up and I just knew that it made me feel anxious and afraid, so I did my utmost to eliminate it from our relationship as best as I could, which ultimately made it easy for Graham to take full advantage of my "weakness" – after all, he had already exposed himself as a narcissistic control freak, which at the time I wasn't familiar with. If only I knew then how he could devastate so many lives.

It is so confusing living with domestic abuse and it's hard for people outside to understand the power and control they have over you; it's a pattern of 'hoovering' and 'gaslighting'; you are so downtrodden that you become their prey almost.

Chapter 4

We sold our mews cottage in spring 1987 and made a good profit on it which enabled us to buy a lovely detached bungalow in a lovely area. By now in the business, we had ventured into uPVC windows, buying machinery to manufacture the products. We rented a workshop and the business was booming. We continued to enjoy our privileged lifestyle, nice cars, lovely holidays, gorgeous bungalow which we extended and renovated. In July 1987, one summer's day I was strimming the 5ft high weeds in our new garden shortly after moving in, when I suddenly became unwell and nearly passed out. "Maybe I'm pregnant," I thought, so I bought five pregnancy tests just to make sure I wasn't wrong. I came home from the shop with my home tests and was so excited when the two blue lines appeared. "Yes," I said to Lisa who was nearly three, "you're going to have a baby sister or brother." I was ecstatic and couldn't wait to tell Graham, when he came home. I was eager to break the news and he was really pleased; our life was good now.

At 12.30pm on Thursday 11th February 1988, weighing 7lb15oz, our first son was born. Graham was ecstatic and so was I; our family seemed complete. Lisa was besotted by her little baby brother. She loved to dance to Michael Jackson, so when we asked her if she could think of a name for her brother, she quickly blurted out, "Michael Jackson", so we called him Jack.

How lucky I felt with my lovely family. Graham would take Jack everywhere with him. Our life was hectic, building up the business, having two small children, renovating our bungalow. We were doing really well and were proud of our achievements. We had now sold the garages in Ripon, which gave us enough money to buy a commercial property with residential accommodation above it in Harrogate. This would become an extension of our business. We used the shop to sell windows and glass from, and rented out the five bedsits above.

Graham had kept racing pigeons as a child and had the passion to race pigeons again. We soon lowered the tone of the street when he built the shanty town of pigeon lofts from scrap pieces of timber. The garden was an eyesore of pigeon lofts and hundreds of smelly pigeons, but it became his passion and he loved racing them; he was successful and won trophies in abundance. I would dice with death on a morning with the wagons on the motorway while I was stupid enough to train his pigeons at 6am, while he cleaned them out and had food prepared for their return – I had little choice in the matter; he was an expert at manipulation, persuasion and guilt tripping if you didn't oblige. Pigeon racing became his obsession; it took up the majority of his time, training, racing, and building horrendously scruffy pigeon lofts the whole length and width of our garden which I had no say in whatsoever; he did exactly as he pleased without any consideration for anyone else. He was extremely selfish and I was beginning to see that the person I fell in love with, didn't really exist – it was all an act to hoover me in, make me believe that he loved and adored me, made me believe that I was his world until he had me in his "trap" then he didn't need to keep up this false persona any longer, he didn't need to play this game anymore; he had me and he knew I would strive trying to get back the non-existent person whom I had fallen in love with.

I did accept the pigeons for his sake as it was a passion of his. I helped him by writing out pedigrees, ring numbers before a race, and with pigeon sales. It wasn't my passion and I didn't particularly enjoy the view of pigeon lofts from our kitchen windows – I would have much preferred a pretty garden with flowers and nice garden furniture, even a hot tub; but it wasn't even an option as far as Graham was concerned – he wanted to keep racing pigeons, so that was that.

Just 15 months later our second son was born at 4am on 14th May 1989 weighing a healthy 8lb 10oz. This was by far the easiest labour and birth; he was perfect with blonde hair and deep blue eyes. We were so happy.

"Let's call him Kevin," Graham said.

"Ummm, NO, I don't think so, why not Andrew?" I said, so it was agreed that we would call him Andrew, but only a couple of weeks later, I had gone off the name Andrew and preferred Lee, so he was registered as Lee.

One day I was in the front garden with Lee in my arms while Lisa and Jack played happily on their bikes. As I looked over the road, I saw a removal van. I really hoped we were getting some nice neighbours, preferably someone my age with small children who could potentially play together and a young mum who I could befriend, and as I was eagerly looking for the new neighbours, a heavily pregnant woman appeared from behind the van. I instantly recognised her and was delighted that I knew her – it was Anj, married to Ripon's equivalent of Paul Newman. I promptly got Lisa and Jack, and crossed the road to go and see her.

"Hi Anj, I can't believe you are moving here over the road from me."

"OMG, Alisha, I didn't know you lived here, how are you?" she beamed.

"I'm good, thanks, when is your baby due?"

"Imminently," she replied. "When I'm done unpacking a few boxes, why don't you come round for a cuppa, it will be nice to have a catchup?"

"Great, I will pop back after lunch, if that's okay?" I said, feeling really happy that Anj and Tom were moving in so close.

This was to be the start of a very close friendship between us. She already had a little boy slightly younger than Lisa called Ben and it wasn't long before her second baby came along – Josh, the double of his dad, lucky boy. Our kids attended the same school, they played together at home; I was either at her house, or she at mine; it was so lovely to have such a close friend on hand.

The worrying element of this is that me and Anj were in such close contact, I was really aware that she would see signs of domestic abuse, but I didn't want to sever our closer bond because she had become so important to me and our kids were best friends, so I deliberately would spend more time at hers than mine.

Over the years that we were friends and neighbours, Anj had noticed a number of incidents, even though I desperately tried to disguise them. One day she came over to see a big hole in the kitchen window and glass all over the worktops where Graham had thrown a teapot through it. I was so embarrassed, I just played it down and blamed it on a clumsy accident, but she was more astute than that; she had picked up on Graham's behaviour previously and she was respectfully supportive to me which I really appreciated. Anj loved Lisa and spent a lot of time with her while I had the boys over to play. It was a very special friendship.

A few years later, Anj and Tom moved away and we lost touch for approximately 20 years, but a few years ago, just after I had left my marriage, we bumped into each other in Ripon, which was amazing; we instantly connected and are now once again good friends.

I told her recently that she was the only person ever that knew about the domestic abuse I was suffering, and she was clearly shocked, but she never disclosed it to anyone out of loyalty to me.

Everything was going great. Graham decided that we should treat ourselves to a new car each, seeing as the business was doing so well. He opted for a lovely blue, brand new BMW, and I chose a new white, Astra convertible with a black roof. I loved my car. Me and Graham seemed to have got through our rocky times, we seemed to be really strong and happy now until summer 1992. We had booked a family holiday in the south of France for 10 days' camping. It was very hot and Graham seemed to be preoccupied on the journey. We didn't speak much on the drive to France, and I did most of the driving which I found quite stressful, while Graham drifted in and out of sleep. I pulled over and asked him if he would drive, as I was tired, so he drove for a while. It had now started to get late; we had been travelling for hours and hours, and Graham wanted to pull over in a layby and sleep in the car overnight with the kids. I suggested a B&B as I didn't think it was appropriate to sleep in a car in a foreign country with three small children. He didn't agree and insisted that we pull in to sleep in the car...the conversation became heated and he became very abusive and suddenly clenched his left fist and from the side with a straight arm, he punched me full in the face. The blood was pouring from my nose, and my lip immediately swelled up and my teeth were broken. I remember looking to the back seats – the boys were sleeping, but Lisa looked horrified with her massive brown eyes full of fear. I told her not to be scared, that mummy and daddy just had a little argument. My heart was breaking at the thought of how Lisa must have felt, seeing her daddy punch her mummy in the face. The next day we arrived at the campsite. I tried to hide my face from the welcoming rep, but she immediately saw my swollen lip and the dried blood on my face; however, to my relief, she didn't comment.

I was very quiet on the holiday, thinking I just wanted to go home, but we made the best of it for the kids – nevertheless it was very strained between us.

I was being abused, controlled, manipulated and isolated. I had become distant with my family and friends because it seemed to displease Graham if I dared to have good relationships with anyone else; he seemed jealous of my relationship with them. I understood how he felt as his family life was abusive – his mother had left Graham's dad when Graham was only 14, leaving him and his sister with their abusive father. Maybe he felt like his mother had abandoned him? I found out years later that he had said to my nanna that he wished I didn't have a family.

He would accuse me of being flirty if any man looked at me.

"You are someone who everyone would like to fuck but not marry," he said one day out of the blue. This deeply affected my confidence and self-esteem.

I was becoming concerned that we seemed to be withdrawing from people. We both worked in the business. My main role was accounting, PAYE, VAT etc, but I could also manufacture uPVC windows and make double glazed units. I occasionally went out to sell to customers, but Graham didn't like me venturing out from under his control – a male customer might speak to me, or God forbid flirt round me.

I was starting to feel like a different person on the inside. I became careful of how I should word things; it was like constantly walking on eggshells, but what option did I have? I had my babies and it became normal life. Sadly I became accustomed to it, almost conditioned.

I was desperate to make our life happy, and we did have some amazing, happy times without a doubt. We were very affectionate to each other and he would constantly tell me that we were forever and he would always love me; he would reel me in, "hoover", "suck" me in when it suited him. I just drifted along with our life thinking everything was okay, everyone had their arguments, didn't they?

Summer of 1993 Graham suggested that we go away for the weekend, just us two; he said he wanted to spend more time together as a couple. I was really pleased that he seemed to be getting more romantic. My parents were happy to look after the kids for the night, so it was sorted – he booked a night in a B&B in Blackpool. I loved the Pleasure Beach, we had an amazing day, we laughed, we were loved up, and we explored all of the sights. In Blackpool Tower we had a couple of drinks and some food, planned future events and holidays, even a move was mentioned – it was just a perfect day. We went back to our B&B about 7pm, changed and came into the bar where the entertainment was on in the form of a band. The music was Motown and it was a brilliant atmosphere, the bar was buzzing with people dancing and singing. We sat with our drink listening to the music, when Graham got me up to dance; we danced and danced, it was such a lovely atmosphere. Graham said he needed to sit down but I wanted to keep dancing, so I danced, like everyone else did. I then went up to Graham at the table and danced for him, kissing him and he was pulling me close saying how sexy I looked. I then went and danced on the dance floor for a few more songs, looked over to Graham and saw he was looking annoyed, so I went over to him and asked if he was okay.

"No, I'm tired and ready for bed, so let's go up to our room," he said. I was agreeable to this; it had been a lovely day and I was ready to sleep.

He was eerily quiet, but I just thought he was tired.

"It was a great day, wasn't it? I really enjoyed it, I'm so glad we came," I said.

Graham didn't reply.

"Are you okay?" I asked.

"I would be if you didn't dance like a slag in front of all them men!"

"WHAT?!!!!!! I danced with you most of the time, I don't know what you mean. It was just me dancing, doing NOTHING wrong!"

"Exactly, you don't know when you are doing wrong, you left me sat down while you danced provocatively in front of everyone, making a fool of yourself. I was embarrassed," he said.

As we climbed into bed, he started to become aroused. I reciprocated as I brushed off what he had said about the dancing – "it's just the drink" I thought. Suddenly he flipped me over onto my front and proceeded to anally rape me. I screamed for him to get off me, but his cold reply was "If you behave like a slag, I will treat you like one".

36

"GET OFF ME NOW!" I screamed, and mustered up enough strength to break free from him.

We lay in silence until breakfast but I just walked straight out of the B&B into the town, sat on a bench in a daze, wondering what to do. I looked up to see him looking around for me but kept my head down. However, he soon spotted me and came over to me sheepishly.

"What you doing here, come and get some breakfast," he said in a soft, apologetic voice.

"I'm not hungry, I just want to go home."

I cried the whole way home while he was telling me to stop crying as my eyes were all red and what would my mum think?

"I don't care," I replied. I felt broken, lonely and confused. My head was spinning with different scenarios, and it was exhausting, the absolute feeling of love that I had for this person had changed into fear and confusion.

I would imagine that I had an invisible barrier around me and he couldn't get through it so I would feel safe and secure, but the sad reality was that NO-ONE could protect me from this life!

Chapter 5

Within a couple of years Lisa was now 11, and was to sit her 11+ exam, and we were approached by the BBC who were looking to film a documentary with five families from our City. It was called "THE KNOWLEDGE", it was raising a debate regarding grammar school education v Comprehensive education. It followed the five 11-year-olds through the results, interviewed them about their future goals and what they thought to the 11+ test, Grammar school and the comprehensive school over the road. The film crew were in our house filming me opening the results letter. I read it out on camera and Lisa was overjoyed to hear that she had passed for the Grammar school.

The first year at the Grammar school was hard for Lisa academically, but she managed and worked really hard. She soon discovered that she was an extremely good cross country runner and very quickly she was competing all over the country. She was spotted by a coach who approached us, asking if we would be interested in her running in his running group. It was decieded that she would like to accept this offer. Her chosen career was now to be a PT instructor and she worked extremely hard to achieve this. She ran in the English schools at Cheltenham and started to enjoy her time at the Grammar school.

When Lisa turned 13, she seemed to become subdued. I would find her in her room crying but she wouldn't tell me the real problem.

"I don't fit in anywhere," she said. " I have a friend who is hassling me all the time."

Then she said, "I have horrible thoughts."

"What horrible thoughts?" I asked her.

"I HATE Dad," she said, "and I want to kill him."

I was horrified and told her that sometimes people do feel like this if they are hurt, trying to open up the conversation.

"He is horrible and nasty," she said...

"MUM, he doesn't love me, you know. He really doesn't love me. Why are you with him, he's horrible," she said with uncontrollable tears. She was 13 years old, very bright and astute, so this was extremely concerning to me and I asked Graham why she would say these things and his explanation was...

"When I take her out running, I can see her heart isn't in it, so I push her for her own good. She fell in the mud and hurt her leg, so I shouted at her to get up and carry on running. That's what it takes to be good at something; it is tough love, Alisha, she needs it to succeed in life," he explained.

Lisa never accepted this as an explanation and became more distant and insular. She had started to write diaries and although she liked her friends at school, she didn't like the controlled environment of home. "It's like being in a prison," she said. "All my friends are allowed out after school, except me."

"It's important that you study hard, Lisa, time for socialising will come later on. Your friends will only be up to no good anyway," her dad would tell her.

By now, it had become normal for the kids to see our arguments and the violence he inflicted on me. Lee had become scared of his dad, blaming his moustache, although he later confessed that the facial hair had no bearing on why he would cling to my apron strings and follow me around constantly – it was pure fear of him. Jack had been Graham's favourite, so he didn't seem so affected.

There were obviously lots of love and laughter in between, which made it more bearable. I just put more time and effort into the kids.

Graham was more interested in his racing pigeons (and as I later found out, living a double life), than me and the kids.

As long as we were in Graham's isolated bubble with no outside interventions, then he was happy. I started to feel like he was spinning a web for where we would all end up being trapped in.

While in this controlled, abusive world, I become embroiled in a state of mind where it almost becomes acceptable and normal. It's only when I have escaped that I can disclose and expose the abusive life I lived, when I stand back as a "free" woman, it hits me like a brick, the shock of the life I lived with so much abuse sends me into a panic state, it's literally like waking up from a 40-year nightmare, the guilt, the self-hatred, the fear, the loss and the realisation of someone I loved treating me so badly is the biggest wake-up call; and once it has been recognised, it becomes difficult to come to terms with what happened behind closed doors, and the longer I am free the worse it becomes; flashbacks, nightmares, panic attacks become prevalent in my life and it feels never ending, but not only have I suffered domestic abuse, violence and control, it actually gets a lot worse.

Chapter 6

When Lisa turned 15, she got a couple of part time jobs, one in a supermarket and cafe. She worked really hard and became very independent and tried to break away from our "controlled" family life. One evening she asked to go to the local shop, but took a couple of hours. She had met a friend and they had been smoking, so when she arrived home, Graham could immediately smell smoke, confronted her and she denied it. She was just a typical 15 year old girl. He immediately viciously, physically attacked her while she sat in the chair. I screamed at him to leave her alone – this was unbearable to witness. I comforted her but I could see that this was the turning point in her life to break free. Only a few weeks later Lisa went out with her friends from work, and I got a phone call from her boss who said that Lisa seemed to get very drunk very quickly and she was worried about her. Graham was due home from playing cricket this day and saw Lisa staggering about outside a local pub. He pulled up and demanded she get in the car to go home. On arriving home he told her to go to her room and he would deal with it the following morning, but within minutes there was a scream and a loud bang. We ran into the kitchen where her brothers were and saw that Lisa was lying at the bottom of the stairs, blood squirting everywhere. She had got a Stanley blade from school and had slit her wrists. Graham immediately started to scream at her "You selfish bitch", then proceeded to kick her while she lay bleeding on the floor. Me and her brothers stopped him and took Lisa to A&E

where she was stitched up. A doctor wanted to talk to Lisa alone, but Graham forbid it. She later told me that it was a cry for help. I tried to persuade her to get some kind of counselling from an independent person whom she could open up to, but she refused, fearing that she might spill the fact that she was living in an abusive situation and was worried that there would be repercussions from her father.

We booked a skiing holiday to Andorra in 1999 with my brother, sister-in-law, my mum and dad. Lisa, Jack and Lee were really looking forward to their skiing holiday. We all had a lovely week skiing and they were keen to go again; they had become really competent skiers by the end of the week and were doing the usual sibling things like racing down the slopes at high speed and generally having a fantastic time.

The next few months passed by and we found out that Lisa had been smoking cannabis with her friends. I was in denial, I knew nothing about any drugs.

Again she reiterated that the wrist incident and the drugs had been a cry for help. She also said to me that there was something she had to tell me but couldn't. I tried to get her to open up, encouraging her that she could tell me anything.

"I can't tell you," she said. To this day I have no idea what it was she needed to tell me, and I will now NEVER, EVER know!

Lisa had left the Grammar school with very good results, she was happy and relieved – she had worked so hard and it had paid off. We had a celebration for her, we were so proud of what she had achieved. She could now go to 6th form in the knowledge that she had the results she'd hope for.

Mother's Day 2000, Lisa, Jack and Lee came into my room with breakfast, cards and presents. I could see that Lisa looked very sad and noticed that Graham glanced at her with a cold look on his face.

Only a week later, I came home to find that Lisa had left home. I panicked and immediately went to tell Graham. We drove around the streets and contacted her friends to try to find her. One friend said that Lisa had told her that she was going to her grandma's. This was correct: she had moved in with my mother-in-law but Graham was fuming, thinking that it was my parents who had taken her in behind our backs. We drove up to my parents', who had no idea where Lisa was, then drove to his mother's flat.

"Have you let Lisa come here to stay behind our backs?" he shouted at her.

"Well, you were nasty to me," was her reply. Which translates as "Yes I have"?!

"I WILL PISS ON YOUR GRAVE!" he screamed at his mother.

"Wait until it's your turn," she said to Jack and Lee sat in the rear seat of the car. I was totally shocked and was just concerned about Lisa, but I now know what she meant by her words. He didn't have the ability to be "nice" to more than two people at a time, hence he had always fallen out with one or two of us and we all had our *"Turn"*.

We had no further contact with Graham's mother again.

We ran a local football team of which both Jack and Lee were members. Jack had started secondary school at the local comprehensive and just a year later Lee passed the 11+ exam and got a place at the Grammar school. Lisa was now attending the 6th form 12 miles away to do sports studies. She seemed a little lost in life, but I was in regular contact with her.

Graham had turned his back on her since she'd accused him of abuse via a solicitor's letter, so Graham threw himself into work and started karate with Jack and Lee, having very little contact with Lisa.

Jack, at 11 years old, was playing with Lee upstairs in their room, when he heard screams from downstairs. Jack looked concerned and turned to Lee who said, "Oh it's just mum and dad fighting again, leave them."

But Jack raced downstairs and saw Graham punching me while I lay on the floor. Jack shouted for him to leave me alone and get off me with no success, so he grabbed his dad and tried to pull him off me. This was the day that Jack changed. Graham hit him hard across the face, knocking him to the ground. Jack was dazed and I shouted at Graham to get out. Jack had always been his dad's favourite, but he had betrayed him in the most scary way and Jack would never trust him again.

In the meantime, I had seen an advert for a vacancy as a sales negotiator on a new housing estate just down the road from where we lived. I discussed with Graham that potentially this was a great opportunity for me to have my own earnings and open the doors for the expansion of our business, being in the building trade.

Graham seemed to be becoming very distant and worried. We talked about the problems we were having, financially we were starting to cut back, our commitments were too great, paying a huge mortgage on the property at Harrogate, our home and other commitments, so we decided to cash in an endowment policy to release some funds, which eased the situation.

I applied for the job with absolutely NO experience in the real estate industry. There were three interviewers and had been over 50 applicants, I was told. The interview went really well, and it was confidence building for me.

Later the same evening, I received a call from the housing company who were really excited to inform me that I was a successful candidate and had got the job as a sales negotiator. I was in disbelief – being dragged down, and constantly demeaned and belittled by Graham had made me doubtful, insecure and with no self-esteem. I was so excited that I was capable of being employed, but not only that, they had faith in me...ME, who was mentally on my knees. This gave me a massive boost. It was an immediate start, with a week's training in Stockton. I accepted the position and felt proud of myself; we arranged the training dates and start date and I would soon be working on the new housing estate minutes from home – it seemed like the dream job for me, I was on cloud nine.

Graham came home an hour later and I was bursting to tell him my news.

"Hey, guess what, Graham?" I eagerly said to him as he entered the house.

"What? I can't guess," he said impatiently.

"I got the job on the housing estate down the road, I can't believe it, it will be so convenient and such a good job for me and for our business," I said without drawing breath.

He looked really shocked and said, "Well you haven't accepted it, have you, without speaking to me first?"

"You knew I was going for the interview, yes I have accepted the offer, there is one week training in Stockton, then I will be working just down the road selling houses, the money is good, the hours are great..."

"Hang on! You CAN'T GO TO STOCKTON FOR A WEEK'S TRAINING, HOW WILL YOU TAKE THE KIDS TO SCHOOL?" he said angrily.

"I'm sure that we could manage for one week, it's literally five days, then back on our doorstep," I explained.

"NO NO NO NO!!!!!!! It's NOT possible, you are saying that a job is more important than the kids!!!!!" He shouted.

"Not at all, it will benefit us all as a family, I love my kids more than anything, it's only a week and long term it would benefit us all." I tried to reason with him.

"Ring them back and say that you can't possibly accept the job, you have three kids to transport to school daily," he said in a smug voice – but he'd had no objection to me working in our business only hours before giving birth and returning back within only a couple of weeks!

I was devastated to say the least, this was massive for me and deep down it felt like an opportunity to have my own space and freedom, which is exactly what he was trying to prevent at any cost... maybe we should sleep on it, he might be more accepting in the morning. He made it clear that he was NOT receptive to my new job opportunity and NEVER would be, he was so insecure and jealous that he couldn't bear me being away from his control. At the time, I failed to recognise this, I mistook it for over-possessiveness, and bizarrely it made me feel wanted and loved, when in truth, the reality was so much more sinister than that, as I would eventually find out.

Chapter 7

Graham's mother had told Lisa to leave her flat as they had had disagreements about Lisa inviting her friends around, but his mother lived mainly in Durham with her then boyfriend, so was very rarely there.

We discussed the possibility of Lisa going to stay with her aunt in Scotland and start a new life away from the negative influences she faced in her home city. She was keen to try and make it work in a new town, so we put her on the train from Harrogate to Aberdeen where her aunt would pick her up. Lisa seemed to be happy in the first week – I rang her every day to make sure she was okay – but after only two weeks, her aunt said she couldn't cope with having a teenager and several dogs in the house (sadly she had never had any children of her own) and wanted her to return home. Lisa didn't want to live back with us, and neither did Graham, so I approached my parents and asked if she could stay with them. She had a very close bond with my mum from the close contact they had had when Lisa was a baby, so it was arranged for her to move in when she arrived back from Scotland. My mind was at rest now knowing she was in safe hands.

Lisa seemed happy and settled at last. She got herself a full time job at the local builders' merchants, which she loved, and worked at a gym part time. She soon met her then boyfriend, John, and moved into a shared house with him. I'm not sure that this was the best idea as there were lots of parties and drugs – her friend Taylor, only 18, had a stroke due to taking drugs which scared Lisa. Taylor made a full recovery, though, and went on to university, married and become a mother.

Lisa had become a very strong, independent woman. She could be volatile and confrontational at times and had some fights within the groups of friends she had, but on the whole, she was a kind, caring, loving girl.

By 2002 our business was doing really well again. We bought a commercial premises on a local industrial estate and things seemed more settled. I persuaded Graham to have another baby – I have no idea why I was so broody and desperate to have another baby when the other three were nearly grown up, but I had the strongest yearning. He reluctantly agreed and I fell pregnant quite quickly, only to have a miscarriage at eight weeks. I was devastated but wanted to keep trying, again I conceived but only to lose this pregnancy in my 10th week. I had a D&C, I couldn't understand why this was happening to me. I spoke to Lisa about trying for a baby and she was completely against the idea.

"WHY? Why the hell do you want another baby? Why don't you do aerobics or some other hobby like most women your age do? You are too old. Is it because Jack and Lee will be leaving soon and you don't want to be alone with Dad?" she said.

"No, I'm just really broody and feel so strongly that I want another baby," I replied.

"You are crazy, Mum, you really are."

Another blow: I miscarried again, surely there must be something wrong with me, how can this keep happening? But soon after, I conceived again and was under close watch from Northallerton hospital; this pregnancy was going really well, I had a good feeling about it.

Lisa's eighteenth birthday was approaching. I talked to Graham about buying her a car, I knew she had recently passed her driving test, but he thought it would be a better idea to buy her lots of alcohol and drugs. I then realised that Lisa was right – he was cruel and horrible; this was his daughter's 18th birthday. I said to him that he was just being facetious and we should buy her a car. He expected me to back him up, even if I didn't agree with him, and on many occasions I would, only through fear.

I was adamant that Lisa should have a car, so we bought her a little white Fiesta, I bought pink champagne, a bouquet of flowers and tied ribbons all around the car. She had no idea about this. She came to see us at lunchtime and she cried tears of joy at her lovely new car; she was over the moon. Hopefully this would give her a new lease of life and freedom.

That evening we took Lisa, her then boyfriend John, Jack and Lee to a local Chinese restaurant for a celebratory meal, which was lovely. Lisa was still elated from the surprise gift of her car.

It wasn't long before her car was vandalised and she was devastated, but Graham and Lisa's boyfriend repaired her damaged car. However, she had decided to sell it and buy another one.

Her relationship with her boyfriend in the house share had become strained and they split up not long afterwards, so she left and moved into another house share not far away.

She threw herself into studying and Open University courses on sports and nutrition. I was in close contact with Lisa most of the time, but Graham didn't want a relationship with her any longer.

She seemed to be getting on with her studies to be a qualified personal trainer and seemed more settled.

She obtained:

- AS in sports science
- YMCA Gym instructor award level 2
- YMCA exercise to music award level 2
- Health science access course
- Nutrition and weight management level 3

- Advanced gym instructor award level 3
- YMCA training in different environments.
- YMCA clients' lifestyle and fitness assessments level 3
- YMCA sports conditioning level 3.

She taught studio classes for adults and children, she did boxing, running, skiing, cycling and trained long distance runners.

I was now hopeful that Lisa would be more settled and positive having achieved her goals.

Chapter 8

I was heavily pregnant now with my fourth baby but still working full time.

Graham wanted me, Jack and Lee to help him in the factory to catch up with some orders which were due out. I was really tired so when we arrived, I said I needed a sit down for a while, so we all had a sit down in the canteen. We were chatting about the excitement of a new addition to our family, we were discussing names and George was decided upon if it was a boy; we couldn't decide on a girl's name. We also chatted about the ski holiday Graham had booked for him, Jack and Lee to France within the next few weeks, which they were looking forward to. While Lisa would stay home with me while they were away in case I went into labour early... Chatting over, we all went down to the factory to do some work, and while down in the factory, I'm not sure what it was regarding but there was some dispute between myself and Graham which ended up with him striking me. I fell to the floor and he lifted a heavy tape measure to my head. Luckily Jack immediately ran over and grabbed it from Graham. I ran upstairs but Graham followed me; I managed to run back down the stairs and he pushed me down the last couple. I fell on the concrete floor, and by this time I was seriously worried about my baby. I managed to run out of danger and immediately booked a detailed, private scan in Leeds soon after to check that the baby was okay. Everything was fine at the scan, which was a huge relief to me.

I worked until 05 March 2003, and the next evening at 7.30pm I gave birth to a beautiful, perfect baby boy weighing 10lb; he was huge and slightly jaundiced. Jack and Lee were overjoyed with their brother and Graham was over the moon – three sons, his dream come true, baby George had been born, and he adored his new son. Lisa was very emotional when she saw George for the first time, but I think by now, she had started to feel alienated from us; she had moved to Harrogate but hadn't settled very well.

Jack and Lee were besotted with their baby brother and would change, bath, dress and cuddle him constantly, I hardly got a look in; but it was so lovely to see George being doted on by his big brothers and big sister.

I returned back to work within a few weeks at Graham's forceful 'request' – he built a playpen in the office so I had a place for George to be. It was harder than I imagined. I was breastfeeding one particular day and suddenly a builder walked up to reception and pressed the bell which interrupted my feeding. I put George in his Moses basket with his belly half full, and went to the counter to serve the builder. He was eager to chat to me and make idle conversation, so I got a bit impatient and said I would write out a contract etc and as I looked down to fill it in, all I saw was my naked breast leaking milk in full view of this builder. "No wonder he was happy making idle chit chat with me, he was ogling my tits," I thought. I quickly tucked myself in and continued without reference to the embarrassing moment that he had just witnessed; he also didn't mention it, to my relief.

Lisa continued to study. She had passed lots of her exams and the next stage was a practical exam; I couldn't believe she was asking me to be her 'client'.

"I'm not fit, Lisa, George is only a baby and I still have to lose weight," I said, panicking.

"Mum, it's fine, it's just an induction for my exam," she replied.

"Ok but I might be rubbish, just preparing you, Lisa."

I was put through my paces by her. It was hard work, especially since I hadn't seen the inside of a gym for many years. I kept myself together without embarrassing her, and when we were finally finished, Lisa was called into a large hall with all the other students and was told that she had passed the practical exam with flying colours, even though I was her 'client'. She was ecstatic, as I was – this was great news for her, as she would soon become a qualified physical/personal trainer which was her dream.

Chapter 9

September 2003 we decided to go on holiday to Euro Disney – Graham, me, Jack, Lee and George. We had a fantastic time, the weather was red hot. For the first few nights we stayed in one of the gorgeous Disney hotels, then decided to go to a nearby campsite. As I was driving towards the site, we saw a stream running alongside the road. Graham wanted to stop, so I pulled in and Graham and the boys ran into the stream to cool down. George was strapped in his car seat laughing uncontrollably, it was such a lovely moment, the holiday was really lovely, the weather was hot, the parks were amazing, there were Disney characters to George's amusement, theme parks, and a brilliant carnival on an evening. The holiday went far too quickly, and we soon returned to reality!

Jack left school with good GCSE results and soon started working full time in the business, whilst also attending college to do his bricklaying exams, in which he gained his qualifications. He was very competent at fitting windows as he had been working on site with Graham since he was 11 years old on a weekend, which held him in good stead for his future.

Lisa was working at a local squash club in Harrogate as well as running her own business as a personal trainer; she was working so many hours and doing really well in her life. She also partied hard with her close friends and was enjoying life to the full.

I discussed the idea of having one more baby as George would be like an only child growing up. We thought it was a good idea, and I soon became pregnant, but unfortunately I had another miscarriage. Maybe I was too old – I was 41 by now. Graham said that we would try one last time, and I conceived quickly in May 2004 and was willing this pregnancy to be successful, which thankfully it was.

We planned to go camping August bank holiday weekend for our wedding anniversary. George had loved his first camping trip in France so I was excited for him. We had a lovely summer, spending time in the garden having BBQs, spending time with my brother, who I was very close to, and his family, we had days out at theme parks, trips to local beauty spots, picnics and just the simple things. We lived near an open area where there is a nature reserve, river and beautiful walks, so we spent time around there, it was idyllic.

August bank holiday would soon be here, so I packed a few clothes for me and George. The boys would pack their own cases. We arranged to leave on the Friday to come back on the Sunday – many of our plans seemed to be set in sand and always on Graham's terms. Graham didn't arrive home as planned, so we waited and waited. He finally arrived three hours after the time we had planned to leave – this was quite a typical thing he would do to further enforce his control. He would then cancel our plans on the spot, so as predicted HE decided that we weren't going camping after all. We were all disappointed and asked why. At this he immediately became angry and defensive, shouting that we were pressuring him. Within a few minutes he lost total control and threw the large TV set at me. I had George in my arms and I was three months pregnant. The TV narrowly missed George's head!! We were all disgusted and terrified at this behaviour. Graham then stormed out while asking Jack to go with him, leaving me with Lee and George. I was shaking on the spot after enduring this violent, uncontrollable outburst. This was it, I now had to leave this abusive situation, I couldn't live like this anymore, not knowing what mood he would be in; he was so unpredictable and would get into the most horrendous, violent rages.

I pleaded with Lee to come with me, but he was too scared to leave, so he stayed while I packed the car with mine, George and the unborn baby's belongings and left the house, explaining to Lee that I would be in contact with him and that I would be fine away from this abuse.

I strapped George into his car seat and drove and drove. I had no clue where I was driving to and suddenly ended up in York. All the guest houses and B&Bs I drove past all displayed the "NO VACANCIES" and "FULL" signs in the windows – it was bank holiday after all. I kept driving and driving and eventually ended up at an Indian restaurant with accommodation above. To my delight they had a room to let, so I took George, who was fast asleep, from his car seat and made our way to the room upstairs. I dragged some of the furniture to place behind the door to feel more secure. I lay George in the bed and I climbed in next to him. I lay awake all night feeling lonely, scared, trapped and desperate. A little arm would occasionally slide onto me as if he knew; I just cradled him in my arms, tears rolling down my face, wondering what I could have done to deserve to be treated so badly by the person I loved. My mind was racing.

"What shall I do? Where shall I go? I have NO money so how can I leave? Who can I tell? What will they think? Would they help? I'm pregnant and have a 16 month old baby? I have no money to pay for rent! How can anyone help me, they all have their own lives and families, why should anyone help me?" I thought.

The sun began to rise and I still felt in a hopeless mess. I had racked my brain all night and couldn't see a way out other than going back home and trying to make things work, but when it's a one way effort, it's almost impossible.

So I went back home and was given the silent treatment for days on end. I later found out, to my disbelief, that Graham and Jack had been test driving supercars at showrooms in the area, while I was in turmoil, not knowing which way to turn. But eventually things got better, our differences seemed to have settled down and we had made up and discussed future plans – we had put our bungalow on the market and were looking at properties.

Graham and the boys were enjoying karate and the boys competed in many competitions; the pigeons were also high on the agenda leaving precious little time for us as a couple. The pigeons took priority over everything (he missed most of my brother's wedding to race pigeons)!

At home our life was becoming strained, Graham seemed to have become more anxious and aggressive. One winter evening he had taken Jack and Lee to karate and on the way back, approximately nine miles from home, in the dark, he pulled up and ordered Jack to get out of his car for dropping litter on the floor.

"Don't you dare disrespect my car, boy, get out and walk home!!" he shouted.

Jack was 16 and ran the whole nine miles home next to the main road. When Graham and Lee arrived back, I questioned where Jack was and couldn't believe that any father would throw their own son from his car and expect his 16-year-old son to make his own way home, nine miles. This was appalling and I was very alarmed. I had started to realise that this was a serious problem that Graham WAS (at the time I hadn't heard of narcissism, only now, 40 years on, I recognise that this was what he was) an extreme NARCISSIST, which explained the lack of empathy and ability to love anyone but himself, the selfishness, the greed...but there was much worse to come...

Thursday morning 9.30am February 17th 2005 our 5th baby was born into this world weighing 8lb 8oz – it was a perfect little GIRL. I was overjoyed; she may be 20 years younger than her sister, but Lisa had always wanted a sister albeit a little late. By this time we had not had much communication with Lisa; she seemed busier than ever with multiple jobs. I bumped into her one day in Harrogate while she was with her friend Danni, and she was really pleased to see her baby sister

Marie. "Awwww she's so cute, and tiny," Lisa said adoringly.

"You always wanted a sister, Lisa, now you have one," I replied.

"She's gorgeous, but I have to run, I'm late for work. Bye Mum," she said then rushed off.

This would be the last time Lisa would ever see her sister again.

Lee sailed through his years at the Grammar school, achieving nearly identical results to Lisa. He left school and felt obliged to work in the family business, as any other chosen career mentioned by him to his dad would be ridiculed. He joined the business and took joinery exams at York College. It was here he met Tony, soon to become his close friend; he gained his qualifications, then worked in the factory manufacturing uPVC windows as well as site work fitting.

Chapter 10

A year later, September 2006, I was in the Doctors' Surgery and a close friend of my mum came up to me and told me that my mum was extremely ill. I had seen my dad on occasions and spoke to my mum on the telephone, but in general had been distant with them due to the coercive control at home. I immediately went to see her to find that she wasn't in, I looked through the windows to see oxygen bottles, medication and a bed in the lounge. Suddenly an ambulance arrived – my dad was helping my mum out of the ambulance; she looked pale and had tubes in her nose. I broke down and wanted to help her, but she was so hurt dealing with my absence in recent years, she put up her hand and said with a heavy heart, "I can't deal with this now, Alisha." I could only respect her words, which broke my heart. She went in to her house while I spoke to my dad who told me that she had lung cancer and had only four weeks left to live!

I was distraught. I asked her to see me, but she could hardly speak. I looked at her through the window as I left devastated, our eyes locked, mother and first born child, in a deep, long stare; we both had tears rolling down our faces. This would be the last time we ever looked into each other's eyes.

I sent her emails and phoned her constantly, telling her to be strong, telling her to fight and never give up. At this moment I was just so relieved that we had had that telephone conversation several weeks ago and I now knew what her words to me really meant, I know

now that she already knew she was dying of cancer when she said to me in a broken, soft voice, trying not to sound emotional...

"Alisha, no matter what happens, I will always love you, my first born child, I have always loved you and always will."

"Mum, why are you saying this, I know you love me and I love you too and always will. Are you okay?" I said with a lump in my throat.

"I just wanted you to know, and it broke my heart when we lost contact, you always defended Graham, he could never do any wrong in your eyes, but I could see your pain, Alisha, and I knew he had full control over you; but it was heart-breaking to see my daughter suffering, but I backed off when you told us not to visit you again," she said, holding back her tears.

"Mum, I'm really sorry, HE made me choose between you, or him and the kids – what choice did I have?" By now I was sobbing – in my head, I thought we had more time to make up. I didn't realise she would be gone so soon; she was only 62 and her time had run out. The realisation of losing my mum hit me like a brick, I had always clung on to the thought that we would be close again like we once were, but Graham was the cause of our fallout and I could never forgive him.

The next day I visited her when she was in a coma, I told her how much I loved her and apologised for my absence. Lisa also came to see her nana, whom she was extremely close to; my brother embraced me and we cried together. My dad was obviously distraught and sat with Mum until she eventually passed away that evening at 11pm. I had left around 6pm. Lisa texted me, she was so distressed; she had become very distant with me because of Graham, but she would often ask my friends how I was.

She threw herself back into her work. By now she was working as a pole dancer in gentlemen's clubs in Leeds, Manchester, Birmingham and London, which we were totally unaware of at the time. She had a small rented flat, in London and Harrogate where she worked at the squash club and still had her business 'Bodysense'. The death of my mother deeply affected Lisa, just as it did me; losing my mum broke my heart, the realisation that we couldn't ever be reunited and reconciled was unbearable. When I broke the news to Graham, he just said coldly:

"Oh, when did she die?"

"Last night at 11pm," I said desperate for some affection and support, but he just said "Oh" and carried on with his normal pastime, pigeons, while I lay on my bed, alone, unable to comprehend the pain of losing my mum.

The funeral would be in a couple of weeks' time. I went to see my dad, who was obviously devastated after a 46-year-long happy marriage, to discuss the funeral arrangements etc. He broke down and said that Graham wasn't invited to the funeral as my mum hated him so much, but he knew that it would put me in a horrible position, although that was trivial in the whole scheme of things.

"When's the funeral?" asked Graham on my return.

"A couple of weeks I think."

"Don't know If I want to go," he said.

This was music to my ears, but I quickly realised that this wasn't a statement he was making, this was actually a question, directed at me to get a reaction; this was a typical game he would play, so that he could blame the outcome entirely on me.

"What do you think?" he said, probing me to give an answer, but only the answer HE wanted to hear.

"Think about what?" I replied nervously, knowing what was coming.

"Do you think *we* should go to the funeral?"

"I thought you said you probably won't go" was the only reply that popped into my head. I didn't want to tell him that he wasn't invited, but it's how to tell a narcissist that He CANNOT do something without him creating a major scene. The only option was to just blurt it out and suffer the consequences.

"Well actually, my dad said to me that my mum didn't want you to come to her funeral, so I thought me, Jack and Lee could go and you look after George and Marie, if that's okay, because they are so young and we can't really take them to a funeral," I said in a soft, calming voice as to lessen the blow. The truth is Graham didn't even like her and probably wouldn't have gone anyway, but this was like a red rag to a bull now!

"Your f***ing mother, even in her death she is trying to divide us by making me look the bad one; well she is NOT going to make me look bad, so none of us will go to her funeral. It's either All of us or NONE of us; this is her way of still causing trouble between us, and it's NOT happening. I wouldn't do that to you, I thought we were united!" he screamed at me in a frenzy.

"It's my mum, Graham, and I have to go to her funeral, I couldn't live with myself if I didn't go, I would regret it in later years. It's only one day." I tried to reason with him, then I thought to myself, why am I trying to get permission off him to go to my own mother's funeral – we are only 'united' when it suits him. He had made it clear many times that our marriage wasn't as equals, he still had an arcadian view that women were far beneath men and that MEN should make the rules and women should abide by them; he has NO respect and never has had any respect for women whatsoever, even ridiculing successful women in power, hence why he didn't like my mum – she was far too intelligent for him to try and argue with her, but he would try and ridicule her opinions if they differed from his.

"Bloody women getting top jobs when men should be getting them, women are getting above themselves, they think they are above men nowadays, and that Loose Women programme, a bunch of stupid women talking loads of shit, I can't stand listening to them," he ridiculed.

What planet was *he* on? I would like to see him in a debate with Janet Street-Porter, Jane Moore, Carol McGiffin or any of the women, they would wipe the floor with someone who uses violence, aggression and abuse to get their point across, not having the intellect to have a healthy debate and accept that people have different opinions.

"Right, I've been thinking, why don't we all go on a train journey for the day of your mum's funeral, we could have a really nice day out, me, you, Jack, Lee, George and Marie, we could stop off in Leyburn and get some hot chocolate, then have a look around and make the day about *us,*" Graham suggested a couple of days after his tantrum.

"Well I have already been looking for suits for Jack and Lee for the funeral, I really think me and the boys should go, it was their nanna after all, I couldn't just go out for the day on my mum's funeral," I said.

"F***ing typical, it's as if you want to make *me* look bad just like your mother does. Well I'm sick of being the one who always looks bad! You should respect how *I* feel and how it makes *ME* look, you should be united and stand by ME!" he shouted.

"Since when has this been about YOU? Why have you made my mum's death all about YOU? I have just lost my mum, I'm grieving and it's YOU who is not being supportive or understanding towards *ME,* your WIFE. All you are doing is making it harder and more upsetting for me; you shouldn't be making me choose yet again, it's not fair to do this to me, when I need support," I dared to scream at him.

He immediately punched me in the head. I ran outside but the large wooden gates were closed. He was running behind me and I had nowhere to run, so I fell to my knees, put my arms around my head for protection and endured his beating. It has since come to light that a neighbour had seen it from her bedroom window and she was horrified, but didn't tell me until recently.

Battered and bruised, I went back inside the house. Strangely there were no tears – had I used them all up, or had I become numb? I just went to bed and lay awake all night thinking about what my life had become. We had had some amazing times in between all this carnage and that was what I was trying to focus on to get me through this. I mistook his abuse, control, jealousy, anger, isolation and paranoia as overprotective, insecure love. I believed that it was because he loved me so much that he wanted me in his bubble with NO-ONE allowed in. I love all my children deeply and wanted to keep my family together – my youngest was only 18 months old and I couldn't destroy her little world or George's who was three and a half, and I was sure after the funeral everything would be good.

The next morning came.

"If you want to go to your mother's funeral so badly, you can go, but you can go ALONE. Jack and Lee are NOT going with you; we will all go on the train journey that I suggested, and you go by yourself!"

Jack and Lee really wanted to go to their nanna's funeral and I felt gutted for them.

"The boys want to come to the funeral, it was their nanna." The boys nodded in agreement with me.

"Tough, like I said I'm not going to look the bad one, so you go alone, that way it's not just ME that's not going to the funeral," he replied.

I could see the disappointed look on the boys' faces and my heart ached for them, but like me, they had succumbed to the control of their father, so didn't challenge him!

The funeral day had arrived. Graham and the kids all got ready for their day out, I got my outfit on, and drove myself to the crematorium. I was immediately greeted by my dad. I walked alone into the church and sat down in a dazed state of mind. It was a humanist service. I remember Lisa standing up at the front, she looked stunning with her long dark hair, slim body, deep large brown eyes glistening with tears, large hooped earrings and a beautiful elegant outfit on, completed with high heeled stilettos. She had a piece of paper in her hand. She began to read from it, her voice shaking and her tears escaping her eyes, her words full of love and pain at losing her nanna whom she adored. My heart was breaking listening to her heartfelt speech. The next thing I remember was Jennifer Rush singing 'The power of love' which was so apt, the tears were streaming down my face. I looked at my beautiful daughter and wanted her back in my life but there had been so much destruction between all our relationships and it all boiled down to ONE person!

If only I knew that this would be the very last time I would ever see my beautiful daughter again, I would never hear her voice in person or her infectious laugh ever again. If only I knew then things would have been so different...

I left without attending the after service venue, I couldn't face it, I was too 'estranged' from my own family, I felt unfairly judged due to my controlled, abusive marriage and none of them would understand the trap I was in – only people that have experienced what I have, could possibly understand.

"I am really proud of you, Mum, for coming to Nanna's funeral on your own," Lisa texted me that evening, but unfortunately, Graham saw the message and was fuming, seeing it as a betrayal towards him! Yet again, he made it about HIMSELF, he texted Lisa back from my phone saying that he was annoyed with her text and felt betrayed by her and wanted nothing to do with her again...his OWN Daughter! All because she said she was proud of me for going to the funeral ALONE!

This just added more fuel to the fire which was completely unnecessary and resulted in Lisa feeling more isolated and alone from *us,* her family.

The next six months went by quickly, we had a family holiday in Tenerife just before Christmas, came back and immersed myself in work in the new year, this and looking after two small children, my older boys 17 & 18 and Graham. I was exhausted but I loved being with my children. It was a real family affair at work as we all worked in the business together, I loved being surrounded by my kids but I was still coming to terms with losing my mum.

Chapter 11

2007, Spring was around the corner and the sun had started to shine. Lisa seemed really busy with her working life, so contact was very limited by way of the odd phone call here and there.

May bank holiday weekend, it was lovely hot sunny Sunday, me, Graham, George and Marie went up to the market square where there was a continental market on with stalls from all over Europe selling all kinds of wares, which was lovely. We tasted some of the different foods, found a table and chairs in the sun and sat and had a cold drink while the kids had an ice cream. I remember feeling contented watching ice cream dripping all over the kids' faces. After a lovely day we went home and hired out a DVD, when rental DVD shops were in existence; it was a James Bond film, Casino Royale. We opened a bottle of wine and just relaxed, watching the movie. I went to bed around 10pm, I was so tired, I was about dozing off to sleep when I thought I heard a knock at the door. Surely it couldn't be someone knocking at the front door so late at night? I heard faint voices, then Jack came into my room,

"MUM, MUM, you need to get up, the police are at the door, they want to talk to you." What could the police possibly want at this time of night, it must have been 11pm. I climbed out of bed and quickly put on my dressing gown, shut my bedroom door behind me so as not to disturb Marie sleeping. At the door was a woman PC and a male PC. Lee was asleep upstairs. Graham, Jack and I just looked at each other without speaking. "What is it?" I asked them. They looked very serious.

I didn't know if I wanted their answer with that look on their faces.

"Can we come in?" they said.

"Why, what's this about, what's happened? Has something happened?" I snapped.

We ushered them into the lounge, and they immediately looked up at the large canvas I had hung on the wall of Lisa, Jack, Lee and George.

The WPC put a handful of jewellery onto the coffee table and said, "Do you recognise any of this jewellery?" She was looking directly at me.

Why was she asking this question to me? I was confused. "Why, why would I recognise this jewellery?" I said, impatiently looking through the pieces.

"NO, I don't recognise any of this jewellery, why?" Then I spotted a ring that I recognised; my heart was pounding but I still didn't know the reason they were here, maybe I was in denial, maybe I didn't want to hear why these police officers were sat in my living room at 11pm on bank holiday Sunday, maybe Lisa had lost her jewellery, maybe she had been arrested for something, maybe she had been in an accident and was in hospital...but it couldn't be anything worse than that, could it?

"Is she okay? Where is she? What's happened?" I was frantic by now. Jack and Graham were sat waiting for their reply...

"A young girl, who we believe to be Lisa, your daughter, was found at Knaresborough Viaduct, after falling from a parapet onto the ground below...

I didn't hear anything else. I ran into my room, quickly got dressed, ran to the bathroom and just threw up and threw up. I was sure I was having a heart attack, the pain in my chest was horrendous, I couldn't breathe, I was in a real state of panic. Jack and Graham broke the news to Lee; they were devastated, their big sister was dead! How would they cope with that? My baby was dead! How could I survive this?

Ahh, maybe not, maybe it's not her, I was willing it not to be her, it could be the same ring another person had, there was still a glimmer of hope.

"We need you to come down to the hospital and identify her body," the police said. We have had wine, so we can't drive," Graham said."

"Okay then, we will leave you on your own for now so you can be together and we will pick you up in a couple of hours and take you to the hospital," they calmly said. There was no emotion, no words of kindness from them, it was quite cold how they delivered such devastating news. I hugged the boys; they were distraught. The four of us sat in the lounge, I was in so much shock I couldn't speak, I couldn't cry; my body was sat on the sofa, but I was looking down at myself; it was the weirdest experience, I wasn't in my body, I was looking down on a family ripped apart – was that me, it didn't look like me, I looked old and pale, my eyes looked dead, the pain was unbearable, a pain I have never experienced before in my whole life, and one I never want to feel again. I thought my mother's death was heart-breaking, but this is on a completely different level, this was pain that no human being could endure, surely. I felt that my life had ended on that day, 6th May 2007. It sounds selfish, I had Jack 18, Lee 17, George 4 and Marie 2yrs, but how could I function? How could I care for my family? I just wanted to die, all I could think about was how I could die and end this unbearable pain. I was riddled with guilt, I was her mother, I should have known... Deep down I DID know, in my heart I knew the root cause of the reason she chose to end her life. I could hardly look at Graham – he had disowned her, refused to support her in any way whatsoever after she left home; our daughter couldn't cope with the control and abuse she witnessed and experienced while living at home up to the age of nearly 16 years old, her words were ringing loud in my ears...

"I hate him, Mum, I hate him, he doesn't love me, I want to kill him."

"Why don't you leave him?" she pleaded...

"Mum, don't ever, ever lose your friends, you will need them one day," she said to me. How perceptive she was, she knew that his intention was to drive everyone away so that he had COMPLETE control of us all.

There was a loud bang on the door – where had the two hours gone? I couldn't remember anything about the two hours that the four of us had sat in total shock.

"Jack, will you and Lee stay here and look after the kids while we go to the hospital?" I asked.

The boys were both distraught but we had to go and identify a body...BODY they call it, NOT a woman or person, no, a BODY. We travelled in complete silence the 20 minutes to the hospital. I was praying in my head so hard that it wasn't Lisa... 'Please, please don't let it be her, she has everything to live for, she is beautiful, fun, intelligent, so young, please don't let her short life be over, please.' Maybe this is a nightmare, I thought, and I will wake up soon and it won't be real...

We arrived at the hospital, and I remember walking really, really slowly, Graham took my hand and we walked towards the room that my first born baby was laid in, I thought the slower I walked, the longer she could be alive in my head. We walked into the cold room, the police were already seated in the corner, we looked over at a beautiful, young girl, laid on a bed/table – I have no idea what she was laid on but she looked 10 years old to me, she looked tiny, her long dark hair had been placed over her slim shoulders, she was pale, her arm was bandaged up, she had broken it on impact; there were still traces of blood in her hair, she was covered with a white sheet. I slowly walked to be by her side and heard a scream. LISA, LISA, it came from a deep place inside me, it was a raw animal like scream... This CANNOT be real, I could NOT accept that my baby girl was lying motionless, cold, I wanted to warm her up, I wanted to cuddle her and make it all better, I would have done absolutely anything to bring her back.

Graham lifted up the sheet to expose a long cut down her middle, with untidy, ugly stitches all the way along...they had done a post mortem on her, they had cut open my baby girl then stitched her back up. All I could think was, why did they have to hurt her like that, cut her open, she wouldn't like that. I held her cold, tiny hand. Why did she look so young and tiny? Graham looked at me and said, " She looks happy and contented."

How on earth could my gorgeous baby look happy when her life had gone? She lay motionless, alone; she must be scared, I thought, cold and scared. How could we leave her in this place all alone? The police were ready to leave once we had identified her as our daughter. I don't know how long we stayed, but I didn't want to leave her all alone.

I actually don't remember anything else that night.

The following morning, Graham and myself were advised by the policeman in charge of this investigation, to meet him outside her address, which was a room in a house share in Harrogate. It's all a blur, I remember us stood outside her address waiting for the police; they arrived shortly after us and went into her room first to look around before we were permitted to enter. When we entered her room, all I could see was the massive teddy bear on her bed which I bought her when she was 13 – it was nearly as big as her – and her pink blanket which she had since birth from my mother-in-law. All I could think was that my poor baby was clinging to her childhood every night when she went to sleep. I got a little comfort thinking that she had her teddy to cuddle and maybe didn't feel so alone.

There was a half-eaten sandwich on her bedside table, her computer was on a desk, her wardrobe had very few clothes in; there were a pair of very high shoes which were completely transparent and a long, red skimpy dress. Suddenly there was a knock on her door. I opened the door to find a man in his mid-twenties stood looking visibly upset; he was shaking and asked me, "Is it true?, Is Lisa dead?" I didn't have the strength to speak, I just nodded my head with tears streaming down my face. He broke down and said he felt guilty – she had rang him on the morning of her death and he hadn't answered her.

"If only I had answered her call, maybe this wouldn't have happened, maybe she needed to talk to me and I wasn't there for her. I went to bed really late, she rang me about 6am, I was asleep. We were really close, I can't believe she isn't here, what happened?... She wrote a poem and shoved it under my door, I will get it for you," he said in a daze. "This is what she wrote about a couple of weeks ago, I didn't really think much about it until now and I feel so bad that I didn't see how she was feeling," he said through his devastation.

I waited for his return and he handed me an A4 piece of paper with the following poem written by Lisa. I quickly skimmed the poem before handing it over to the police for the investigation. I couldn't quite comprehend the meaning of it at the time, all I knew is that I wanted my little girl back.

Look at you
Your beauty prevails
Your riches, your wealth
Your confidence shines
Strong you stand, solid and bold
They love you, they love you
For granted you take
Your arrogance, your ignorance
Untouchable you stand, out of reach, unapproachable
For granted you take, for never you shall understand the other side,
Ungrateful and shallow
The grass is greener on your side,
The sun always shines
Look at you
Your imperfections surface
All the jewels, all the riches
You are strong, but oh you are weak
Lonely you stand

Sensitivity scars
The edge is near
You're shy, your strain
Your fear, your pain, for no longer will you have
Dulled your senses
Take the "Beauty"
Take the "riches"
Take the "confidence"
and have too the envy
Have the scars
Have the pain
The void is yours
The grass is dying on my side
the sun rarely shines.

I went back into the room where my baby had been living and my heart broke. She was living a parallel life, by day she was a personal trainer, by night she was a pole dancer working the clubs all over the country. I suddenly saw a young, vulnerable girl, MY DAUGHTER – what had tipped her over the edge? Was someone to blame? Did someone hurt my baby? So many unanswered questions; would they ever be answered, would we ever have closure? Would we ever find out the truth?

All I knew is MY BABY, MY FIRST BORN CHILD, WAS DEAD AT 22 YEARS OLD! WHY?

Her phone had more than 20 outgoing calls from 5am-8am the morning of her death, but no-one answered her calls so early. It looked to me that she was desperate to talk to someone that morning. She had been dancing, then partying the previous night, she arrived by train from Leeds to Harrogate, then got a taxi to Knaresborough. It seemed that she was meeting someone in Knaresborough. She ended up at the train station and we were told by a platform shop owner, that she appeared to be running from someone. She was distraught and asked him when the next train would be arriving, but she has missed it by five minutes. She was crying uncontrollably; he tried to calm her down, he gave her a bottle of water, and she eventually calmed down but on two more occasions she asked about the train times and missed them by minutes. If only she had caught a train, she might still be here today.

We re-traced her steps at Knaresborough viaduct with the help of witnesses. She was seen sat on a bench overlooking the viaduct after returning from eating a sandwich in a cafe in the town centre, she had been into a department store and ordered a block of knives for her new flat that she was buying in Harrogate. None of it made any sense – in two days' time, she would be getting her keys to her very own new home which she had already paid a deposit for. She was meeting someone at Knaresborough, someone who was threatening her, someone who she was scared of, who was chasing her. She had £10 notes in her jeans pocket which looked to have been snatched from her hand as there were tears that corresponded with this, she obviously kept hold of them tightly to still retain them in her possession. It appeared that she had sat with a male on a bench overlooking the viaduct. I believe that this male had goaded her to do what she finally did, knowing the vulnerability and delicate frame of mind she was in. After working the previous night in the clubs, then partying with her friends in Leeds, then arriving at Knaresborough early morning, she had made more than 20 phone calls to friends, but no-one had answered her calls. It was bank holiday Sunday and 6am. She had been described as "running away from her demons" by the shop assistant who had to calm her down; she was sobbing uncontrollably. It was after she calmed down that she eventually went to sit on the bench. By now it was 1.00 pm when she suddenly shot up and ran towards the train station and stopped to ask directions to the viaduct. This was an off-duty policeman who described her as a beautiful young girl who stood extremely close to him while getting directions. When she got the relevant information, she then ran off towards the viaduct. There was a couple visiting from Scotland who saw her running towards them; the lady described her as a stunning young girl who had a beaming smile on her face, her long dark hair, dazzling white teeth and her beautiful eyes had this witness mesmerised, she said she looked almost angel-like as she watched her running through the gates of the station. Lisa had made eye contact with this lady and kept smiling at her, as she approached the railway tracks, she removed her shoes and ducked under the signal box so as not to been seen by the signal man, she looked both ways to check there were no trains approaching, then, as described by this witness, she tiptoed across the track, almost like a dancing angel. The signal man had spotted Lisa and came running out, shouting for her to get down as she lifted herself on top of the second parapet, she swung her legs around, turned to the lady who was still watching her, gave her a "mischievous" look, described by her as if to say, I'm doing something I shouldn't be doing, with a smile on her mischievous face, she put her arms behind her back as if to sit on them, but she pushed her body forwards and she was gone. Thirty metres later, to the sea of screams from the horrified signal man, visiting tourists and locals, she landed on the concrete ground below next to a trauma surgeon who at the time thought Lisa had just fallen down the nearby steps; she attended to her injuries and stayed with her, trying to comfort her. She was suddenly surrounded by crowds of shocked onlookers, ambulance and police sirens were screaming in the background, racing to the scene, there were now three doctors at Lisa's side attending to her, comforting her; they described her as looking happy in the last moments of her life. The ambulance arrived and paramedics proceeded with CPR but she was pronounced dead at the scene, 1.30pm Sunday 6th May 2007.

The nearby cafe owner witnessed this horrific incident and was traumatised by what he saw, the signal man was so shaken and shocked that he couldn't return to work for months. Suddenly on this glorious bank holiday where people were enjoying themselves, the scenery, boating on the lake, eating ice creams, drinking coffees, there was an eerie silence of disbelief, people in shock, upset, dazed and traumatised by what they had witnessed or heard.

After going to her property, we then went to the viaduct where Lisa had died. There was dried blood where she had landed on the ground. It was unbearable to imagine that she had fallen/jumped from the ridiculously high viaduct. We went to the spot where she was sat before she fell, looked down and it was terrifyingly high. I was physically sick thinking of her falling to her death from here, I couldn't bear the thought of the impact to her head... Graham didn't shed a tear, he was just quiet and said very little. Jack and Lee were in total shock and my heart bled for them.

I was completely broken, lost, shocked, panicking, my heart had been ripped from inside me and all I could think was that ultimately it stemmed from Graham, her father who was supposed to protect, nurture, love her unconditionally, be her hero and always be there for her – but NOT Graham, he lacks all the qualities that a father should possess, actually he lacks the basic qualities that a decent human being should possess, his strange, cold, confusing behaviour confirmed to me that he had a serious narcissistic personality disorder (NPD), he blames *everyone* but himself, has absolutely NO empathy, consideration or compassion towards anyone, is self-absorbed, arrogant, cocky, selfish and greedy; he isolates, controls, abuses both verbally and physically anyone who has a different opinion or view from him, usually calling them derogatory names and demeaning them as people. He did this regularly to Lisa, as she was a very determined, strong, independent, motivated, talented girl and her intelligence far outweighed the little intelligence he had; he would challenge her opinions, belittle her if she knew more than him and in general brought her down purely to enforce his control and power.

The one thing that people cannot comprehend is the power that a narcissist has, they spend their whole life convincing you that it's actually

YOU that has the problem, YOU that needs to stop trying to control situations, YOU need to see a doctor, YOU who's paranoid, mental, selfish, greedy and controlling, the brainwashing and demeaning abuse leaves you drained, confused, ashamed and worthless. Trauma bonding, Stockholm syndrome are what I was suffering during this very abusive almost-40-year marriage, I learnt to live in this trap and tried to manage it by imagining a new life, dreaming that I would be free from him one day; the good times now started to become fewer, my self-esteem was at rock bottom and I felt so lonely inside.

There were NO discussions, it was only ever commands and orders; every time I tried to resolve situations, I was met with resistance, aggression, horrendous verbal abuse, so in the end I decided not to justify, argue, defend or explain myself anymore...what was the point? He would ALWAYS blame ME on EVERY single occasion; the scary thing is, this TOXIC relationship becomes normal, you lose all touch with a healthy, loving, normal relationship with mutual respect, loyalty, honesty, trust and love, living in this isolated, controlling situation is exhausting.

They take everything from you, nothing you do is ever good enough, you end up depleted, emotionally, mentally, financially; they are self-absorbed and love ONLY themselves, they don't have the capacity to empathise, they are like parasites, living off you, sucking the life from you, then when you are on your knees they will laugh at you and walk away.

Trying to function was virtually impossible. I had two teenagers and two babies, and a demanding husband. Nothing but my four kids seemed important to me now, my world had been shattered beyond words. With a broken heart, I couldn't face the most menial of tasks, I wanted to hide away forever. Luckily there was so much support from the community, Lisa was well known here and her death was the talk of the town. Everyone was in shock; I remember the first time I went to the shops, I had people coming over crying and hugging me. I couldn't deal with that level of sympathy, it just made it worse for me, so I stopped going into Ripon for a while.

A few days had passed in a blur. Graham and the boys planned most of her funeral as I could barely speak. I remember going into the funeral directors' one day; I was so distraught, the secretary sat me down and said to me...

"It's so terrible for you, but at least you know where she is, poor Maddie McCann's parents don't know where their baby is."

Did I just hear her right? I was well aware of Maddie's disappearance, I had followed the news, it was only three days before Lisa's death and I was heartbroken for them. The comment from her completely destroyed me, I could not comprehend how anyone can compare the level of bereavement suffered by any parents who have lost a child. I was in disbelief to the extent I just walked out and walked until I dropped to my knees feeling utterly helpless and wondered what the point of life was.

I had heard that some people had said that Lisa had chosen to die! This was NOT a CHOICE, this was as a result of an illness!

How could they possibly know, NO-ONE will ever know what really happened; but in the main, most people were supportive and sympathetic.

I had slept on the living room floor with Jack and Lee, the last couple of nights but we didn't sleep, we just talked and cried all night. Morning came and I remember running down the fields to the rear of our house, screaming her name over and over again until I finally lost my voice and couldn't scream any more. I never knew that you could cry all your tears away, but that's exactly what happened to me, no voice and no tears left to cry. I sat by the river not quite remembering how I got there, staring at the river and looking at the wild flowers dancing in the breeze. All I could think is how could I possibly carrying on living when my baby is dead, how is it possible? I just wanted to swap places with her so badly. "Why her? Why not me?" I thought. She had her whole life to live, but mine had ended on that very day. Her funeral would be in a few days' time, but it still didn't seem real. "Maybe after the funeral, I could join Lisa," I thought, and this was the only thought that made me happy. I felt guilty for living when she had died, I felt that Graham was the root cause of her death so how could I carry on with all these feelings inside me? This sounds so selfish and I suddenly felt ashamed of myself and disgusted that I could actually, seriously leave my other four babies without a mother, how could a mother possibly do that to her children? I was so confused and torn, I knew I didn't love Graham anymore, but I was trapped. I didn't even have the strength to think about leaving, I had to face my baby's funeral.

A couple of days later, the funeral director brought Lisa home as previously discussed. She looked so tiny in that coffin, I just wanted to cuddle her. I covered her up with her pink blanket and put her huge teddy bear with her, she was given a silver cross and chain by a friend, I couldn't stop staring at her. "She shouldn't be lying in that box," I sobbed to myself. I lowered my head into the coffin and whispered in her ear, "Lisa, I love you, always have and always will forever. I'm proud of you, my first-born baby, you were so full of life, I'm so sorry, I failed you as a mum. Fly high and be happy, baby, we will meet again soon, I promise you." Then I wiped the tears that had spilled onto her face, stroked her hair and gave her a kiss for the last time ever.

Graham rang his sister, Sheryl, in Scotland to inform her of Lisa's funeral date. She was shocked and upset at the devastating news but explained that she couldn't make the funeral; however, her father-in-law would go in their place. Graham became extremely aggressive to his sister, shouting down the telephone how selfish and disgusting she was for not putting herself out. I couldn't bear listening to yet ANOTHER argument that HE had instigated – not only had he fallen out with my family, Lisa, his own mother, now his sister... "where will it all end," I thought to myself, so I approached the subject of reconciling with his mum and sister when he had calmed down. "OVER MY DEAD

BODY, THEY CAN ALL FUCK OFF!!" he shouted at me... There was absolutely NO reasoning with him, he was becoming more and more impossible by the day. I was just consumed with grief. I had no time for trivial arguments or Graham's games!

Chapter 12

Monday 14th May, it was Lee's 18th birthday. Luckily we had got his present early, but he wasn't really interested in his new laptop. I felt so sorry for him not celebrating his significant birthday, but in two days' time we would be burying his big sister and none of us were functioning normally...

Wednesday May 16th 2007 11.30am in the church connected to the junior school she attended, her funeral was about to start. This would be the last goodbye to our baby. The church was packed, people even standing at the doors and outside, Graham, Jack, Lee, my brother Anthony, my dad and Graham's cousin were the coffin bearers. It was heart-breaking to watch my boys carry their sister, they looked so smart in their suits, and so grown up, I was so proud of them. They came and took their seats, Graham sat next to me and held my hand tight. For the first time I had seen him shed a tear. The funeral was lovely, we celebrated her life, we played her favourite songs and some very emotional songs: "I'll be missing you" Puff Daddy, "Nothing compares to you" Sinéad O'Connor, "Beautiful" Christina Aguilera.

Jack and Lee both gave a lovely speech in front of the whole congregation. Jack was first up and he did so well, it was very emotional, and also humorous. Lisa would have been so proud – I certainly was. It was Lee next to give his heartfelt speech, again he made us proud, he stood tall, held his head high and delivered his heart-breaking speech of losing his big sister, then his lip started to quiver, and my heart broke for him. Both my boys did amazingly well. I love them so much, they were so strong and brave. A couple more speeches were given. The policeman who was supporting us gave a lovely speech and I remember him saying:

"It's better to have lived one day as a tiger than a thousand years as a sheep."

I could hear Lisa's voice echoing exactly the same.

Lisa's ex boyfriend's dad also gave a lovely speech of the times they spent together, all his memories of her were so lovely.

Graham and his cousin had compiled a DVD, footage taken from home videos and from the BBC film crew which was a lovely tribute to her. It ended with her riding her new bike on her 5th birthday, waving while saying "Byeee".

Family and close friends came to the cemetery. It was unbelievable watching my baby being lowered into the ground, I panicked, I felt that she would be alone, scared and freezing cold – how could I leave her here? We threw roses and trinkets onto her coffin, it was the worst feeling in the world, this is it, we would never see her, or hear her ever again.

The wake after the service was full. I was only interested in trying to find out about and make sense of Lisa's death, there were people here who I had never seen before, lots of very attractive young girls, not dissimilar to Lisa.

"Alisha, do you want a drink?" I heard my brother shout to me.

"Yes please, could I have a gin and tonic?"

"Of course you can, I will make it a double," he replied.

Anthony was very supportive and was a huge comfort to us during this horrendous time.

While I mingled with the young girls to get some information, I discovered that Lisa had worked in the gentlemen's clubs in London, Manchester, Leeds and Birmingham as a pole dancer, they said that in recent weeks she had been really generous, giving her possessions away, maybe because she knew she wouldn't need them anymore? The most heart-breaking thing of all is that her death remains unanswered and it always will be, the question WHY? is constantly in my head. One day I think I know the answer then another question will pop in my head, then I have to rethink it through yet again, my head just spins around in circles.

Anthony and his partner came back to our house the same evening. We just had drinks and talked about Lisa, we were all in shock, it still hadn't sunk in yet. The days passed by, we were inundated with cards, flowers, gifts and messages of support from the whole community. I found it difficult being around Graham, I couldn't help but blame him, he said he needed physical comfort from me but that was furthest from my mind – how could anything be important anymore?

A few days later, Graham, myself and the kids visited Knaresborough viaduct to lay large photos of her, bouquets of flowers and gifts at the spot where she lost her life. We were greeted by disgruntled nearby residents, QUAKERS, Christians who are simplistic peace lovers.

"You can't put these photos or flowers here, it will put the tourists off!" said the middle aged woman who appeared from a nearby house.

"I beg your pardon? This was the place where our daughter lost her life after falling from the viaduct above, how can you be so cruel and insensitive?" I said, holding back my tears.

"I'm really sorry for your loss, my son knew your daughter, she was beautiful; but we have to live here and there have been so many people coming here and laying flowers and cards and it doesn't look good for the tourists visiting."

Have I just heard a human being, a Christian, religious, peace loving woman say these words to us? I was mortified.

I didn't even have the strength to respond to her, I just sat on the grass and cried. She then invited us in for a cup of tea as a peace offering, which we politely declined. Her animosity towards my grieving family did not stop us from taking flowers regularly – this was where my baby took her last breath and I wanted to spend time there.

Jack and Lee were still suffering but they were being really strong and helping with the care of George and baby Marie. We closed the business for a few weeks while we were all grieving. I was struggling and not coping with life, I couldn't think straight, let alone look after my babies. I clung to my boys, they were my rock. My neighbour suggested to me that I should make a doctor's appointment to get some antidepressants. "NO, NO, I'm NOT taking any pills," I said, with tears streaming down my face.

When I awoke from a very short sleep the following morning, just for a split second, I forgot Lisa was dead, then suddenly when I remembered, it was like someone had ripped my heart out again and I began to shake uncontrollably. The panic was indescribable. How could I carry on with life, when Lisa's life had so tragically ended?

I decided to go to the doctor's. When I entered her surgery she was visibly shocked and upset. "I cannot believe it was your Lisa when I heard the news. Tom (her son who was in Lisa's class at the grammar school, a good friend) was devastated. Everyone is in shock," she said, clearly upset. "It was such a violent death, most couples don't stay together after such a tragedy."

"Just help me cope, I am struggling," I said to her, sobbing.

"I will prescribe citalopram, an antidepressant, and organise some counselling for you," she said in an *apologetic* voice.

"No, I'm not having any counselling, there is no-one who will understand, they don't know me and didn't know Lisa, so how can they possibly help me?" I said very dismissively. "But I am willing to take the tablets if they will help."

I had started to take my tablets but I was in a very dark place. It felt like there was a massive black cloud above my head, following me everywhere, it drained my energy, it robbed me of my first-born child, my head was spinning. I kept hearing Lisa's laugh and seeing her presence.

I didn't even know what day it was after a few weeks of taking the tablets, all I had were suicidal thoughts. I spent my time planning how to join Lisa, then suddenly it was all clear to me, so I planned my departure from this life: off I went without so much as a thought for my family; I just had this unbearable longing to be with Lisa. I arrived at my chosen place by the river armed with a shed load of tablets and two bottles of red wine at 7pm one Sunday evening. I sat drinking my wine from the bottle neck, it was like being in a dream-like trance, I couldn't quite work out what reality was any more, all my senses were numb so what was the point of living? I was consumed with being dead and being with Lisa. I had drunk half the bottle of wine already and started to feel dizzy, now it was time to pop them pills. I washed several pills down with the wine, I remember crying and talking to Lisa hoping she could hear me, when a passer-by stopped and asked me if I was okay. I was mortified, I had learnt to live a life of suppressing my feelings, my agony, my lack of self-worth, to the point that I would tell myself over and over that no-one must find out that I was living in such a toxic, abusive marriage, I was somehow putting on a brave face, pretending to the outside world that everything was OK, I didn't want to admit that I had failed. I was conditioned, groomed, coerced and brainwashed into believing I was to blame for everything and constantly being told that I was worth nothing.

"I'm fine," I said, "I'm fine."

"You don't look fine, why are you so upset? You don't look well – should I call someone?" said the concerned woman.

"Oh NO, honestly I'm fine, I'm really okay, I know you are trying to help, but trust me, NO-ONE can possibly help so please just leave me alone," I said with tears spilling all over my face, my lips; my nose was running, I just wanted to be alone. She sat down beside me. I couldn't bear to talk to anyone so I just sat in silence watching the swollen river in full flow. She had now realised that I wasn't okay, so she tried to comfort me. I was so desperate for her to leave that I reassured her that I just needed some time alone to think about my life, and she left wishing me good luck.

"I need more than luck, love," I thought to myself; anyway now I could complete my mission. I stood up and immediately fell to my knees, my head spinning. I swallowed my remaining tablets and the rest of the wine. I had no idea how long I was there, I just remember waking up in the darkness trying to make sense of why I was there. I felt so ill, I started vomiting profusely, my stomach kept going into a spasm, coughing and vomiting I was totally exhausted, my head was spinning. I looked up at the stars and saw a big bright shooting star – was that Lisa, I thought to myself. I tried to stand up for a better view but fell straight down again. The next thing I remember was waking up in the pitch black, owls tweeting in the background. I was wet through. I assumed I had slipped to the edge of the river bed and blacked out. I was covered in mud and bruises, I felt cold and scared but managed to stagger home. It took me days to recover, then all I felt was guilt – what about my other babies, I thought, how could I even think of leaving them? This guilt still lives with me today.

I spent a lot of time at the cemetery. One day I even took my duvet and pillow and lay on her grave, totally distraught.

Chapter 13

It was now July and the weather was gorgeous. My brother and his partner, Amy, were taking his two kids, Laura and Tom, to northern France camping and suggested that, me, Graham, Jack, Lee, George and Marie meet them there and join them on holiday. Anthony thought the break would be good for us, so a few days later we met them in France but the weather had turned and it was raining constantly, so we decided between us all that we should pack up and travel down to the South of France – we had been many times before and had always had great weather. We travelled in convoy, stopping off numerous times. We eventually found our perfect campsite in Sète, minutes from the beach, a short walk to the buzzing town, fairground in full swing and a short drive to the supermarket – this was the ideal location. We had no idea how long we would be staying, but I didn't care, I had lost all concept of time.

We had a good holiday and it was a welcome relief for us just to be away. My brother was just the tonic I needed, he has a great sense of humour and I just laugh so much when I'm with him, he sees the funny side of everything and that's exactly what I needed right now.

We ended up staying more than two weeks. The campsite was quiet and relaxing, we played rounders, walked to the beach with our picnic. I just wanted to keep busy but my head was still going round in circles with lots of unanswered questions that still remain unanswered today. It was my 45th birthday while we were there, my brother bought me gifts and a bottle of champagne to celebrate, more than Graham got me, but by this stage my feelings for him were only of contempt. I wanted to leave him but it's not that easy when you are married to a narcissistic, violent, abusive, possessive, jealous control freak who keeps you in this invisible prison with invisible chains on. I had NO access to any money, I had a two year old, a four year old, to consider, also my two eldest sons 18 years and 19 years old, where would I go? How could I afford to leave? I had all these questions in my head, but the bottom line is that it would be just easier to carry on and stay until I had the strength to leave him. I was grieving deeply for Lisa and I needed things to be as 'stable' as possible for now. Jack and Lee, although grieving for their sister, were my support network for which I was so grateful. If my two amazing sons hadn't been there to support me then I really don't think I would have survived this horrendous tragedy.

Travelling back home was a blur, the citalopram was just making me a zombie, I couldn't keep taking these tablets. The journey home was long and uneventful, and we finally arrived home. End of August 2007 it was our 25th wedding anniversary. It meant absolutely NOTHING to me now, but the boys had surprised us with a champagne hot air balloon ride as a gift. I was so overwhelmed by them thinking about getting such a lovely gift, that I embraced the experience to show my appreciation, even though I could hardly face going out.

The next couple of months are missing from my memory completely.

I remember Graham was desperate to get back to "normality" as he called it.

"NORMALITY? NORMALITY? WHAT DO YOU MEAN, WHAT THE F**K IS NORMALITY!!!!!!?" I dared to shout at him, but I was now in a place where I couldn't care less about my life, so the silent treatment, or the verbal abuse, even physical abuse didn't scare me anymore. I had now suffered the worst pain in the world, so there was NOTHING he could do to hurt me anymore.

Chapter 14

Lisa's best friend Danni asked me if she could set up a memorial page on Facebook for Lisa. I was glad that she thought of such a special thing to do which would keep her memory alive. This became a great comfort to me in the years to come, it gave her family and friends a chance to share their special memories on this private group.

I would like to share some of these tributes from people who loved her.

From me, her heartbroken mum

6th May 2007 was the day my life changed forever. Lisa, you chose a different path for whatever reason I will never know, the void you left behind gets bigger with time, the sadness of you gone will never go away, I miss you more than words could ever say, My heart is shattered into a million pieces But I will carry you around in my heart until the day we are together again. ♥♥

*I often think of you
When you were very small.
You left your fingerprints
On almost every wall.*

Back when you were growing up
They were such happy years.
How you would laugh and make up games
I remember through my tears

Some day we will be together
In heaven up above.
But for now my little girl
I send you all my love.
All my love Mum xxxxxx

<u>Jack her brother</u>

Thinking of you as always big sis, still can't believe you aren't
here to share good times with us all, love u loads xxx

Five years have passed and still as painful. Still can't quite believe
you're not here. Miss you more than words could ever describe,
think of you every day. love you loads sis.xxxxxxxxxxx

21111

<u>Lee her brother</u>

happy birthday sis. It's a shame u aren't here to celebrate your
birthday. You are special to me and I will never forget the smiles
you put on people's faces. I will never forget the memories you
have given me. I will never forget you. I love you. Xxxx

*Love u sis, 5 years today u were taken from us. I will
never forget it, the worst feeling ever. I will always
remember you laughing and smiling xxx*

*6 years today you have sadly passed. I miss you every day. This
year will hurt loads as you would have been at my wedding, you
would have looked stunning as a bridesmaid & it would have been
special. I will have a brilliant wedding but there will be a hole in my
heart where you should be. Love you forever & always Lee xxxx*

Lisa's best friend Danni

My special friend xxx

*Well my little chicken licking, my manic little bumble bee, another
year has passed sooo quickly, I still think of you every single day
which passes and the emotions can still be so raw. I miss you
terribly words could never begin to explain how much. some
days when something has happened in my life I think oh I must
tell Lisa and then I remember you're not here any more... and
realisation dawns again. I'll never understand exactly why you
left us, I can go over things time and time again in my mind,
until I can't make any sense of what I'm thinking. we'll never
know, Lisa, you always liked to remain a mystery and keep people
guessing and I suppose in true Lisa style you did it one last time.*

*I know you've gone to a better place and I hope you're at rest and
happy, and I hope you're looking down on us all and we're making
you proud. as you know sweetheart I'm so very proud of you and
all you achieved. we came so far together and grew up in so many
different ways, and I'm so proud to be able to say that we did*

that together. I spent the best years of my life with you and you helped make every day special. I don't think I've ever laughed so hard as I did when I was with you! laughing till we we're on the floor holding our stomachs, tears streaming down our face!!!

I've got lots of wonderful memories of you and the time we spent together, and I will cherish them always.

I'm so proud to have known you and even prouder to have called you my friend, you were always there for me and always pulled me back up when I was down. I just wish you'd given me a chance to have been able to do the same for you, but you were such a proud person and hated to show weakness another thing which I always admired about you.

so Lisa... rest in peace sweetheart, you may be gone but certainly never forgotten... Always in our hearts and in our thoughts. xxxxxxxxxxxxxxxxxxxxxxx

Her Friend Anton

My first encounter with Lisa xxx

Hey Lisa. While I was out today walking on the sands at St Annes I was thinking about you and when we first met. It's a bit blurry [we were all very drunk that night] but what I do remember is that it was Ripon, I'm fairly sure you were staying at your Grandparents then and we'd picked you up. Carrie was there and I think her mate was driving and I'm sure there was someone else too. On our way back to Harrogate we stopped off at a garage to get booze and fags and you and Carrie were pretending to flash *either a customer or the guys who were working there LOL. It was so funny. I couldn't believe how gorgeous, funny, in your face and sexy you were. I remember thinking 'who the heck is this'.*

When we got to Harrogate we went to a bar near Chico's Pizza shop, I think it's still there. You were sitting on a low sofa opposite me flashing your knickers to the world [you didn't know you were lol and I had to tell Carrie who told you to cover yourself up. It was so funny. Right there and then I knew I wanted to get to know you and be mates, I did and we were, I think because in many ways we were very alike.

I know we fell out sometimes, we were both hot heads but we always made up and I'm so glad we were cool with each other when you left us.

I have never really been the same since, inside I mean, you left such a huge hole in my life. You'll never know how much I miss you. For me the sun rose and set with you Lisa and it's very hard knowing I'll never see you again. I love you, Anton xxx

Hey Lisa. You'll be glad to hear I'll be getting back into my running and training next week. I've let it slip since the hotel fire. The first month I got shipped off to Stirling in Scotland and I spent the next 2 months working 13-15 hr shifts at Hotel Du Vin so training wasn't top of my list lol. However, now I'm back at the Majestic and things are starting to get back to normal so I've time to get my training back on track.

Do you remember when we went down to the studio to do some boxing? I was winding you up about how good I was and you were telling me you were going to kick my ass lol. You beat the crap out of me and got me with an awesome right hook in my eye, it watered for ages and I couldn't see properly, you thought it was hilarious, I didn't lol. I couldn't believe how good you were or how hard you could punch but I did after that! You loved your boxing didn't you mate, I'd love one more round with you.

Miss you xxx

Shared memories xxx

Hey Lisa. I don't want to embarrass you but do you remember that night you and I went out into town? We were getting ready in my room [you were wearing the most amazing little black number, it really showed off your figure] and you were kicking off because you didn't have any eye liner. I said you didn't need it, I thought your eyes were beautiful enough but you wouldn't have it and you made me go knocking on doors all over 5th floor trying to find a girl who had some you could use. I got some in the end and you put it on and you were right, it set your eyes ablaze, I couldn't stop staring at them, I just got lost in how dark and beautiful they were, that's when you said 'stop staring at me dick head' lol, a typical response from you lol, you never knew just how beautiful you are. It wasn't long after that that I told you how I felt about you. That I'd fallen for you big time. As soon as I said it I wish I hadn't. I remember you saying to me 'Do you think I'm stupid? I know, I can tell by the way you look at me'. But you told me that all we would ever be is mates and you didn't look at me that way. It hurt but I knew that having you as a mate was a lot better than not having you in my life at all so I agreed never to bring it up again and I didn't which allowed us to stay friends. Now, I'm glad I told you, I'm glad you went away knowing how I felt about you.

In town that night I felt like the luckiest man in the world.
Every bar we walked into the guys heads all turned to look at
you, you had such a presence, a night I will never forget xxx

<u>Her Friend Kelly</u>

2yrs.... still feels like 2 mins. Lisa was just one of the people
who never let anything stand in her way. She knew what
she wanted and would do almost anything to get there. We
were practically born together, shared birthdays, lived a
few mins from each other, schools... very similar lives.

We had our ups and downs in life but still had shared many laughs
and tears. She was always there for other people, but for some reason
she decided to bottle things up and visit the angels in the sky.

When Lisa was around everyone knew she had arrived, life n soul
of any party. I'm sure everyone is asking the same thing 'why' we
will never know till we meet her again, but I'm also sure people
who are thinking about her today will not just be feeling sad for
the loss, but have smiles on their faces thinking about the good
times and memories we all love and remember about Lisa.

R.I.P Hun.... gone but never forgotten

Kelly xxxx (or as Lisa called me 'criterial JAFFA'

Her Friend Katy

That is one thing I loved about Lisa, bless her. If there was a problem it usually got sorted! Many a time have fond memories of us eating out and if Lisa wasn't satisfied then she had no problem in voicing her opinion, many a free meal was had ha ha.

I used to Love the spontaneous side to her, the amount of times I'd get a call at silly o'clock after going to bed on a weekend at some ungodly hour from her wanting to go out. So the PJ's were off and we hit the town.

She never seemed to care what people thought of her like the time she dragged me to the car boot, decided to buy a duvet then get in it in the middle of the race course and wondered why people were giving us strange looks.

I first met Lisa when she started at Aidan's 6th form and we had our ups and downs but always remained friends in the end.

There will never ever be another Lisa and she will be hard to be matched with because she was a wicked friend, so much fun and I miss her dearly. Ktxx

A friend of mine who had a son the same age as Lisa

Happy Birthday Lisa 27 oh how time flies. Doesn't seem that long ago you and Craig were babies. My thoughts are with your family and how they will be wishing you were there with them. I know you will be there in spirit a very special girl. Luv Lorraine and family in OZ

Chapter 15

Autumn 2007, Jack and Lee announced that they wanted to leave home and get a place together. This was devastating news to me. Selfishly, I pleaded with them to reconsider – the thought of them 'leaving me with HIM' terrified me... "Just stay at least until after Christmas?" I asked them and they agreed. This was such a huge relief to me, for now at least. I wanted to make this Christmas as special as I could knowing that Jack and Lee would probably be in their own home next year.

Christmas would soon be here but I couldn't get excited. It was Lisa's favourite time of the year and it would be so painful her not being here. I started to get myself together though, as I didn't want to spoil the kids' Christmas, so as always, I did ALL the Christmas shopping, ALL the Christmas wrapping, ALL the Christmas food shopping, decorating the tree, ALL the Christmas cooking, ALL the Christmas cleaning up etc. etc. but I just wanted to see my kids excited. George and Marie were only four and two, Jack and Lee were 19 and 18. Graham never took any interest in Christmas, he said it was MY job, he never ever lifted a finger in the house, I did absolutely EVERYTHING as well as work full time.

Christmas Eve afternoon came. Graham and I were outside pointing a wall, Jack and Lee came out of the house to go and finish their Christmas shopping. As they walked past us Graham shouted abuse at them. "Where are you two going?" he asked aggressively. "Just up town to finish our Christmas shopping," they explained,

"Are you telling me that you are going swanning up town while me and your mother are working outside? Your mother is mixing concrete and you two are just going into town, you are both disgusting, you two should be doing this NOT your mother, go on then F**K off up town!!" he screamed at them for the whole street to hear, but Graham was by far the most tactless, inconsiderate and shameless person I knew, he was an embarrassment to us all. This was not Graham being considerate to me, it was about him using me as an excuse to abuse Jack and Lee born out of sheer jealousy of them being so supportive of me. I was so tired and worn down with Graham being constantly confrontational and so unnecessarily abusive and nasty, it was draining and so depressing, was this really my life? How long could I live like this? Who is this monster I married? He is NOT normal! What am I to do?

Jack and Lee came back home and asked if they could go out with friends. Graham gave them a 10pm curfew – 18 and 19 yr old boys on Christmas Eve!

"They can stay out later than that, it's Christmas Eve after all," I pleaded.

"They're not coming in at all hours in the morning, waking me up," he retaliated.

"It's okay, Mum, we will be back in time," they both said disappointedly.

The boys went out, and after I cooked dinner, I put George and Marie to bed. It was just me and Graham sat eating our steaks, not saying much to each other, when Graham suddenly brought up the subject of Lisa.

"I don't want to talk about it," I said with tears rolling down my cheeks. Why would I want to talk about my beautiful daughter's death, knowing that he had disowned her, ostracized her and seemed to lack any empathy or feeling towards her? Graham was trying to look like he cared about me and felt sad for me, I knew him better by now, it was just another 'act' .

It was getting late, but the lads had arrived home on time and gone straight to bed, so I proceeded to bring all the presents down and place them in four piles, while Graham typically lay snoring on the sofa. I went to bed totally exhausted.

Early hours of the morning, I heard shouting and banging from the lads' room. I went in to see what was going on. Graham had taken a suitcase into their room and told them to leave.

"It's the middle of the night, what are you talking about?" I said half asleep.

"They climbed out of their Velux roof light, went out, then brought some girls back home through the roof lights. I'm sick to death of them, they cause me nothing but hassle," he explained.

I was lost for words...HE did NOT deserve such lovely, hardworking, handsome, smart, intelligent sons, but that was the problem: he was jealous of his own sons.

I was super proud of all five of my kids. The boys didn't leave, where would they go for God's sake? On Christmas Eve/Day? How unbelievably cruel. Is this really a 'father'? A human being? I think NOT, he's the Devil in disguise! My heart bled for my lovely boys, and I refused to let them leave.

Christmas Day was bittersweet – Lisa's favourite time of the year, and it was heartbreaking, but as always I made Christmas Day as special as I could for my four kids, Jack, Lee, George and Marie. The youngest two were still only four and two years old, they were oblivious to anything other than opening their presents from Santa Claus, their innocence, their little faces alight with joy and their screams of excitement was what Christmas was about. Jack and Lee were a little more reserved than usual, not only had they just lost their big sister, but they were suffering unforgivable abuse from Graham.

The boys talked to me about leaving home, but selfishly again I pleaded with them to stay. I couldn't bear not having them there, they were my biggest support, the thought of my boys leaving broke my heart... They just wanted to get away from Graham. It was bad enough for them having to work with him never mind living with him, I completely understood, but they were brilliant and stayed for me and their little brother and sister, which I was extremely grateful for.

Lee had met a girl called Louise on Christmas Eve and soon brought her round to introduce us. She was very shy, she was only 16 and very quiet, she was beautiful with long dark hair, she had a long fringe which nearly covered her big brown eyes. We ordered a takeaway and sat chatting. Lee asked if she could stay but we were reluctant. She said she had asked her mum and it was okay with her. The next morning, Graham stormed upstairs up to where Lee and Louise were lying together. "GET THE FUCK OUT OF HERE!" he screamed at Louise, pulling off the duvet violently from them both – luckily they were both decent, but this was extremely frightening and disturbing for Louise, she was visibly scared. I apologised on his behalf as she was leaving, upset; this, unfortunately, would be her first experience of Graham's abuse.

Lee decided that he wanted to leave home. Jack was ready to leave too, so it was agreed that they would buy a caravan to live in and Graham said that it could stand behind the factory of our family business on some scrap land and he would hook it up to the electric from the factory. I was concerned about them living in a caravan but they seemed excited about it. This was their first taste of freedom and they loved it – they could literally roll out of bed and into work for 8am on a morning. They enjoyed socialising regularly and Louise would stay with them the majority of the time, they all three had a very close bond which I was really pleased about.

One morning at 7.59 the electric was turned off in their caravan. The boys went to work as normal and asked Graham why the electric had gone off. "I turned it off," he said with a smirk on his face. "Why did you do that?" they responded, confused.

"Don't take the piss out of me by being late for work – you live on MY property and if you are late, I will do it again!"

He was by now successfully turning his owns sons against him, they felt that they were still under his control, he would blackmail them into doing what *HE* expected of them. Jack and Lee decided to move out of their caravan into a place of their own.

Soon after this, Jack and Lee had found a rental property they wanted to move into together; they felt like there was NO escape from Graham, it was too claustrophobic for them.

"RENT? Why rent, you would be better getting a mortgage and BUY a property," he said. I did agree with Graham – it made more sense to buy a property than rent (after all, Graham was taking half their wages as rent to live at home!). The boys agreed and soon found a renovation project not far away from us to buy, they organised a mortgage and a few months later my boys left home and moved into their bungalow. I missed them at home but saw them every day at work, which was lovely. I brought both George and Marie to work with me, so they saw their brothers most of the time. George loved his big brothers and they adored both George and Marie...

While I was adjusting at home, missing Jack and Lee, work was going really well. Jack was predominately on site, fitting windows, doors and conservatories, while Lee was more factory-bound and involved with the manufacturing side of the business. I was office/reception/ manufacturing and did whatever was necessary and it worked well.

Jack had met Steph, a very pretty girl with sparkling blue eyes and long blonde hair, she was very petite, and Jack was really happy.

Louise and Steph were regular visitors at their bungalow, although the boys were working full time in our business, they were renovating their property while trying to spend time with their girlfriends, so they were pulled in all directions.

My relationship with Louise had become very close, she loved George and Marie and would spend hours playing with them. I started to look at her as a daughter.

Graham tried to have his input into their lives, he felt like he was still in control of 'their' decision making, but this was causing unrest between them. He would criticise Lee to Jack then Jack to Lee, it was like a deliberate act to divide two brothers, his own sons. I now know that he was jealous of their close relationship, which I find very disturbing.

Graham's interference in the boys' lives started to take its toll on their relationship, arguments started between them. Jack and Louise had a massive row one evening. Jack came to see us, I opened a bottle of wine and got some beers out for Graham and Jack, we had a few drinks and he told us about the incident. There were scratches on his back. I was sympathetic towards him, but I really didn't want to get involved, I loved both my boys, they were old enough to deal with this. Graham, however, ironically said that Louise was completely out of order, he didn't like her at all, so had a field day with this news – this was his chance to really stick the knife in.

"Tell Lee that Louise is NOT to come round to the bungalow EVER again, Lee should have stuck up for YOU, NOT her! He's got no backbone, he's too soft." He went on and on and on.

"I'm sorry, Jack, I don't want to get involved, only you three knows what happened so I can't comment, nor can anyone else comment, I'm sure you will resolve your differences but I don't want to come in between you two."

"HOW CAN YOU TAKE SIDES WITH LEE?" Graham shouted at me.

"I'm NOT taking any sides, if you listened to me, I said that I don't want to get involved, I cannot take sides, they are both my sons," I said defensively.

"You should stick up for Jack, Lee is the one in the wrong!" he argued.

"I don't want to talk about this anymore, I'm tired; have we not had enough upset losing Lisa?" I retaliated.

The subject was dropped and we just made idle chit chat until late. Jack said he needed to leave, he was tired and had work in the morning. I got up to see him to the door, I hugged him and smiled. "Night, Jack," I said as he left.

I locked up and went back into the house.

"WHAT THE FUCK WERE YOU GIVING ME A DIRTY LOOK FOR WHEN JACK WAS HERE?" he shouted.

I was so sick of his aggressive behaviour, his false accusations and I had some Dutch courage and felt brave for once.

"YOU ARE BEING RIDICULOUS, I HAVEN'T GIVEN YOU A DIRTY LOOK, WHY ARE YOU BEING LIKE THIS? I'M SICK OF LIVING LIKE THIS!" I dared to respond in a raised voice.

"WELL FUCK OFF AND LEAVE THEN, WE (referring to him, George 4yrs and Marie 2yrs old) DON'T WANT YOU HERE ANYWAY!"

This should have been a massive warning sign to me, that he was using 'gang' culture, using my own babies against me – this would prove to be devastating as George and Marie got older.

He then angrily got a suitcase out and started grabbing my clothes from my wardrobe and stuffing them in, he was raging by now. I was begging him to stop but he opened the door and threw them outside.

"Come on, this is ridiculous, please let's stop this, Graham. It's wearing me down, I can't cope with this anymore, please let's try and work things out," I pleaded.

"YOU'RE THE ONE WHO DOESN'T WANT TO LIVE LIKE THIS ANYMORE, Alisha, LIVE LIKE WHAT? LIVE LIKE WHAT?" he shouted so close to my face I could smell his beer breath.

"I just want things to be normal and happy, that's all."

"It doesn't look like that to me when you and Jack gave me dirty looks!" He raised his fist and lifted it above the left side of my head, his eyes bulging and teeth gritted.

"Please, please Graham, please don't hit me, I'm begging you, please don't do this," I begged him, tears streaming down my face. The next thing I remembered I was lying on the floor with blurred vision.

"Go back to bed, George, everything is okay, go back to bed like a good boy, I'll come in a minute to see you," Graham said in a calm, quiet voice to George who had obviously heard everything and had come to investigate.

I managed to stumble to my feet. Graham was still shouting at me, but I couldn't make sense of what he was saying, I looked down and saw a clump of my hair on the carpet, I felt the back of my head and touched a bald patch the size of a 50p coin and a massive lump on the side of my head. Graham had left the room. I heard him go upstairs to see George – this was my chance to get out. I grabbed my phone, quietly opened the front door, ran to safety and rang Jack. "Please come and get me, Jack, Dad has just punched me."

Within minutes Jack was outside our house. He got out of his van, got hold of me, put me inside the vehicle and locked the door with me inside.

Graham came running out. "Jack, it was her, she started on me, *she* hit me, you have no idea what it's like living with her. Get her out of the van, Jack, I will deal with her," he tried to convince Jack.

"Oh NO WAY am I letting her come near you, Mum is nursing a massive lump the size of a golf ball on her head. I'm taking her to mine!"

Jack drove me to his bungalow. I was shaking and crying. I walked in and Lee was there; they made up the spare bed for me and comforted me, I felt really embarrassed that my sons had to see this, but I had nowhere else to turn. Jack went back to check that George and Marie were okay. He saw Graham, who tried yet again to blame me, but Jack was only interested in his siblings. Graham was lying with them both, and after Jack was satisfied that they were both safe, he returned to me and Lee.

"Mum, you have to leave him, one day he might actually kill you," both my concerned boys said to me.

"It's not that simple – he has made sure that I have NO money, NO family or friends to turn to and nowhere to go, and I can't rip George and Marie's little world apart, can I?" I said, only divulging the minimum to them. This was all true but there were more worrying reasons that I had to stay with this mentally unstable, abusive narcissist... "IF YOU EVER LEAVE ME, I WILL HUNT YOU DOWN AND KILL YOU, ANYWAY YOU HAVE NOWHERE TO GO BECAUSE EVERYONE HATES YOU SO YOU COULDN'T LEAVE ME," he would say to me with a smirk on his face which made me go cold.

The reality was that it was easier and safer to stay. I knew my life was in danger whether I stayed or left, and I had two small children to look after – how could I possibly care for them on the run with absolutely nothing? I had been in this relationship with him for 27 years, I was trauma-bonded.

Not long after Jack and Lee left home, Graham would come into my room in the middle of the night (we had separate bedrooms) and he would start off by saying he needed to talk to me and it would be a nice conversation initially, then he would become angry, and start punching me in the body, spit in my face, shout horrific abuse at me, even shouting "I'VE SHIT ON YOU BIG TIME!" then went to his bed. I would lie awake, shaking and crying, trying to make sense of this nightmare. I already had my suspicions that he had cheated – he would shamelessly flirt with women even when I was with him, I would cringe at the way he clearly fancied himself and thought he was God's gift to all women. The next morning, I asked him what he meant by the comment from the previous night, and he said it was nothing and that he was just angry. Only a week later during yet another row, he said again, "I HAVE SHIT ON YOU BIG TIME, I'VE BEEN SHAGGING TEENA." This was no surprise to me, Teena was a rep and very promiscuous, she would shamelessly flirt round Graham and all other men; she worked for a local newspaper and would get him cheap advertising; she spent *a lot* of time "selling him advertising space". Only now am I aware of the full facts that Graham was actually shagging most of his female reps and some of his female customers, even once bragging that some of the customers were "gagging for it".

I now knew that this vile monster was a cheat – even though he later retracted his admission of cheating – but this was just the beginning of a web of deceit on the most horrendous scale, as I was to find out a few years later.

"Alisha babe, I didn't mean what I said last night, please believe me, I only said that to hurt you. It's not true, why would I want to go with anyone else when I have you, especially Teena, she's a dirty little slapper. Come on, babe, it doesn't make sense, look at you, you are gorgeous – why would I have beef burger when I have steak at home? It was just to hurt you, honestly," he said convincingly, while hugging me tightly. He was an expert liar, but he had had all his life to perfect his skills. He was so good, that he believed his own lies. It was just easy for me to go along with this, which I did.

Chapter 16

Life was just passing by, peppered with good and bad times. I tried to make life as normal as I could for my kids – my life was all about them. I took George and Marie to swimming lessons, after school clubs, ski lessons (at the age of 5 & 3 they were in the Slalom race team winning medals and trophies), they were excellent skiers which enhanced our skiing holidays no end. Jack and Lee were already excellent skiers – they had always been very sporty, playing cricket for many years and both held the British Karate titles in their late teens. I was so happy that Jack and Lee had many things to focus on to divert their thoughts from their home life growing up with an abusive father.

Spring 2009, while we were all working, Lee received a phone call from Louise. She was really upset – after taking the dogs for a walk, one of them had run off. She had tried looking for him but couldn't find him anywhere so she asked Lee if he could come and help her find Jez their dog. Graham snatched the phone from Lee as he had heard the conversation. "NO, LEE IS WORKING, STOP FUCKING RINGING HIM, LOUISE, YOU SHOULDN'T HAVE LET JEZ OFF THE LEAD." Then he hung up. This obviously left Lee feeling anxious. "RIGHT, LEE, I'M TAKING YOUR FUCKING PHONE OFF YOU AND WILL LOCK IT AWAY WHILE YOU ARE WORKING, I'M FUCKING SICK OF LOUISE CONSTANTLY RINGING YOU!"

Lee didn't respond; he felt humiliated in front of the lads working in the factory. He just carried on working, worrying about his missing dog. I had heard all this from my office, but that was normal. Louise had managed to find Jez and text Lee to put his mind at rest, but Graham had taken his phone, so Lee spent the day worrying. So I decided to go and see Lee and Louise that evening.

"I heard what happened today, is everything okay?"

"He's an absolute bastard, I hate him, I think I will leave and get another job, I can't work with him any longer."

I didn't blame him; I felt the same most of the time. Graham made Lee's life difficult at work – he would give him the worst jobs, constantly criticise and penalise him relentlessly, so consequently after a barrage of vile abuse from Graham, Lee left the family business. Graham was infuriated with this news and used this to fall out with him. This was unbearable for me because I knew that if Graham fell out with anyone, then we all had to "support" him, meaning that if I, Jack or the kids were to still have a relationship with Lee, then we were being 'disloyal' and betraying Graham. Since Jack and Lee lived together, this proved very difficult for Jack. Graham was determined to isolate Lee from us all; he didn't do anything alone, he always had to have a 'gang' with him; my mum had always said, "I don't like the way he operates". This is how his twisted mind worked and my heart broke for Lee. I was just thankful that he had Louise by his side for support. Jack and Lee's relationship became strained and Graham took great pleasure at this; he felt empowered knowing that he had destroyed his son's close bond.

Today I now know that Graham's narcissistic personality disorder caused him to be jealous, insecure, paranoid, greedy and selfish; he had absolutely no empathy or consideration for anyone's feelings but his own; he was an ugly person and I despised his traits.

The next 24 months passed without contact with Lee. I knew he was working with Louise at a local dentistry company and that he was happy with her, but Jack and Lee's relationship had become impossible. Graham had made it his mission to stir things up between them; he would constantly bitch Lee off to Jack, he was determined to cause as much pain to Lee as possible, through Jack, until Lee felt he needed to leave and move in with Louise. He didn't inform his brother so as to avoid any confrontation; he also stopped paying his share of the mortgage, requesting to Jack that he wanted to sell his share of the bungalow – either Jack buy him out, or they sell the property and equally split the proceeds. This was just the news that Graham revelled in. "Take him to court, why should he decide to sell the bungalow, you have done more renovations than him, he's left you in the lurch; you need to fight him in court and push for a 60/40 split, don't take any less, drag him through the courts, Jack."

"I'm sure that they can sort it out between themselves without spending money on solicitors and court costs."

"FUCKING TYPICAL, YOU WOULD SIDE WITH LEE, THAT'S YOU ALL OVER!" he screamed in front of Jack and his girlfriend Steph.

"Don't be so ridiculous, I'm not taking sides, how immature..."

"EXCUSES, EXCUSES, I DON'T WANT TO HEAR IT!" he shouted over me. His behaviour was of someone who had 'lost the plot'; he had always been unable to have a reasonable discussion or debate without resorting to violence. I believe this was due to his low intelligence – he would have tantrums like a child, but he was a man in his 50s, making a tantrum very dangerous.

Jack and Lee did end up going to court, the bungalow was sold and they both got an equal share, but the boys continued to be distant with each other, which was immensely sad. There was only 15 months between them and growing up they were very close – most people mistook them for twins, they even shared the same friends; they had already lost their sister and now each other, when they probably needed each other more than ever, but whenever Graham was involved, all our relationships would be destroyed. George and Marie would soon become his little puppets, his little gang whom he could abuse and control.

Chapter 17

24th February 2011 was my best friend Sheila's 50th birthday party. Her partner Dave had organised a surprise party in a very popular hotel in Harrogate where they lived. I had met Sheila many years before when our children were babies, almost 30 years ago. We were invited to attend; although Graham was not keen on going, as predicted, it was unthinkable that I could go alone –, he would NEVER *allow* such a thing – so we attended together. The evening started off really well, the drinks were flowing the food was amazing and Sheila's gorgeous kids, Hannah, Rachael and Marc, had compiled a beautiful book of memories and photos of all her friends with space for everyone at the party to sign their names. The book was passed around all the guests to write their birthday greetings and signatures next to their photo. The book was passed to me, I wrote my message and signed next to my photo, then Graham proceeded to look through the book and came across a photo of my sister. He vehemently despised her for reasons unknown to me (he had by this time successfully alienated me from all my family except my brother – maybe he knew that she was deceptive enough to see that he was a nasty, evil scumbag. The sad thing about living with a narcissist is that they isolate you from all family and friends so that they remain in complete control of you and they know that you have no-one to go to in case you escape the prison they have created). He took the pen from me and started to draw a moustache and glasses on her face, just like a five year old would do. He found it highly amusing and didn't understand why everyone was disgusted at such disrespectful, immature and extremely disgraceful behaviour. I was mortified for Sheila, I felt completely embarrassed and ashamed of being with this complete moron. We left the party soon after. I couldn't bring myself to even look at him on the way home, all I felt was sorrow for Sheila having her party ruined.

The next day I phoned her to apologise but she didn't answer, so I texted her with my heartfelt apology on his behalf. We had been friends for so long, I couldn't bear losing her friendship – she was the one person who had always been there for me and vice versa. She didn't reply to my text. I sent more texts with my deep apologies again, but no reply. A couple of days went by and I rang her again. Finally she took my call, and it was a very distressing, emotional conversation; she was understandably devastated that her daughters and son had spent so much time, thought and effort making her this beautiful, momentous special gift which gave her so much pride – this would be a keepsake of her 50th birthday, now tarnished and ruined by Graham's utter disrespectful behaviour, which could've easily resulted in me losing my best friend, which would have devastated me. Luckily, Sheila didn't blame me – she knew what Graham was like, she had experienced his disgraceful behaviour first-hand when he had subjected her ex-husband to an unprovoked attack many years earlier. Her partner Dave wasn't so forgiving, he was very angry and couldn't understand why Sheila would still be my friend. I totally understood his feelings and was just grateful that Sheila valued our long friendship enough to continue it. I wouldn't speak about this to Graham at all, I just wanted to try and forget about it, which was inevitably difficult. Graham seemed to be really happy and I couldn't help feeling it was because he thought that he had successfully severed my friendship with Sheila. A couple of days later, after both of us had been at work, Graham came home all happy again. "Do you fancy fish and chips for tea, babe?"

"Yes that sounds good," I replied.

"OK, I just need to go to the factory to lock up, won't be long."

"Oh, while you are there could you bring my phone back? I left it in the office," I requested. "OK, will do, babe."

He returned home 15 minutes later. I saw the most angry look on his face as he walked down the drive. My heart sank – why was he looking so annoyed? He came through the back door shouting, "YOU FUCKING BITCH, I CANNOT BELIEVE YOU WOULD BETRAY ME LIKE THAT!" as he stormed over to me, screaming in my face. I had no idea why he was raging so much so in a state of fear I managed to ask him what he was talking about. When he finally allowed me to get a word in edgeways, he threw my phone in my face and shouted, "YOU TEXTING SHEILA APOLOGISING ON MY BEHALF, HOW FUCKING DARE YOU... AGAIN MAKING ME LOOK THE BAD ONE AND BEING DISLOYAL TO ME."

"So you looked on my phone," I dared to reply, which just added fuel to the fire. He picked up the nearest object closest to him, which was a TV remote control device and threw it straight in my face causing a burst lip. Blood was streaming down my face along with my tears. This was yet another blow to me, I was already emotionally on my knees; I felt so helpless, drained, anxious, and low, how much more could I actually take, I thought to myself, how long could I live like this with such an evil monster? My heart was already ripped into a million pieces after losing my beautiful daughter Lisa, it was also aching for Jack and Lee, being witnesses and victims of abuse at the hands of their father, and for George and Marie witnessing their mummy being assaulted and abused by their "daddy".

I was riddled with guilt that all my beautiful children had all been brought up with an abusive father. I felt like a failed mother – wasn't I supposed to protect them from such things? I struggled on a daily basis with this guilt and it was destroying me from within.

June 2011, my dad came to see me one day while I was at work. "There is something I need to tell you," he said, looking really worried.

"Right, I will make us a cup of tea and you can tell me what's bothering you." I knew he was struggling after losing my mum.

"Alisha, I have to tell you that I have been diagnosed with Alzheimer's," he said, with tears rolling down his cheeks. "But don't worry, it's not hereditary." His voice was shaking.

"Oh Dad, listen, don't worry about anyone else. We are all here for you, we will get you all the help and support you need, the best medication, whatever you need, Dad, you will be okay," I said to him, my tears falling into my tea. He stayed a while then left feeling more reassured. "Bye, Dad, I will come round soon." His partner was with him most of the time, so I knew he had her by his side.

I broke down after he left. Graham hugged me – he seemed very sympathetic; I was devastated. The following weekend my dad's partner called me, Anthony and Jane to ask if we could all meet up and discuss the plans to put in place to care for my dad. I was willing to do all I could to help, the meeting was arranged, but by now me and my sister could hardly bear to be in the same room as each other after many arguments throughout the years (mainly instigated by Graham to cause a rift between us, which still really hurts me to this day); but we managed, for my dad's sake, to put our differences aside just for this meeting.

I offered to clean my dad's house and cook him meals in between working and looking after the kids, so I was busy, but enjoyed it.

Graham, on the other hand, became more angry as the next couple of weeks passed. Life was very tense both at home and at work with his constant, unpredictable tantrums; he would regularly take the car keys off me as a punishment if he was in that mood, so I would have to walk to the school, even in the rain, to pick up George and Marie from school – so he was actually punishing them too, it was like walking on broken glass.

He said I was spending too much time with my dad. This was so typical of him, his craving for constant excessive attention and admiration was to him the most important thing in the world, so how could I even think of spending time, with anyone other than him? I resented his selfishness and this only angered him more.

Tuesday July 5th 2011 was a day I wouldn't forget in a hurry. I dropped George and Marie off at school as normal, then went to work (in our family business). Graham was already there as normal, but was particularly angry this day. Jack was out on site fitting uPVC windows for a customer, so it was me and Graham in the office and three members of staff down in the factory. On a "normal day" we'd both sit and have a cup of tea before starting on the paperwork, but this day, I was greeted by "right get some work done, you lazy cow"! Lazy I was NOT, from the day I left school, I had worked full time, run a home, raised five kids practically on my own as racing pigeons were Graham's priority (or so I thought at the time). I would even drive down the motorway at 6am dicing with death most mornings to train his pigeons before I took the kids to school; most mornings this would mean I didn't have time for breakfast, so lazy is definitely not a description of me, but this was a typical thing he would say to bring me down and make me feel completely worthless. So I went into my office to start work; we barely spoke – this was another of his traits, to give me the silent treatment. It was about 11.00am and a rep from a uPVC profile company was due. Graham greeted him and directed him into his office, I heard Graham offer the rep a cup of tea, but completely ignored me, so I went to make my own and took it into my office. I had my head down immersed in the accounts, when Graham came into my office and demanded that I take out the purchase ledger file from the cabinet ready for the rep to look at, then went back into his office. Only a couple of minutes later, before I had time to even get to the cabinet, he stormed in shouting "for fuck's sake, how long does it take to get the fucking ledger out". Before I had chance to say anything, he grabbed me by the throat, slammed me up against the metal cabinet, grabbed my arm and dragged me across the office, then threw my red hot tea at me. The rep and the staff must have heard my screams, but no-one came to my aid. I stood there frozen to the spot for a few seconds in shock before I ran down to my car and drove to the nearby leisure centre car park. My neck hurt and my arm was throbbing, but luckily I didn't suffer any burns – my clothes had protected me from that. I was shaking, then I vomited in the car park terrified that he would find me and inflict another attack on me.

My first thought was to ring the police, but Graham was an expert liar and manipulator, so I was worried that the police would listen to his lies. I rang Jack and told him what had happened. He was obviously disgusted and told me to ring the police and he would support me. This was extremely hard for Jack, as Graham would sack him if he supported me, so I did feel guilty for that.

"This is it now, there were witnesses, I have massive bruising to my arm and neck, surely this was the time to finally report his abuse to the police," I thought to myself, so I drove home, parked outside our house with my doors locked and rang 999. "Police please," I heard this shaky, little woman's voice say. I couldn't believe that was me calling the police. The woman on the other end of the phone asked why I needed the police. "My husband has just attacked me," I said, sobbing.

"OK, you stay on the line while I get the police dispatched to you. Are you in a safe place now?" she asked.

"Yes I'm in my car." I gave her my address whilst she was trying to calm me down.

"OK, listen, the police are on their way, but stay on the line to me until they arrive," she said.

Then suddenly I saw Graham speeding around the corner. "Oh my God, he's here, he's in his car coming towards me." By this time I was hysterical.

"Don't panic, the police will be there soon, I'm here until they arrive," she reassured me, then I heard sirens and saw lots of blue lights flashing towards me…I couldn't believe that there were two police vans.

"They are here now," I said.

"Right, I will hang up now that the police have arrived, take care," she said. I just thanked her for getting the police to me so quickly and being so nice.

All I could think is that Graham will be livid that I called the police. I got out of the car and the police came over to me. As we walked towards the house to the front door, one of the officers said, "Are you prepared to go to court?" I immediately said yes, then they knocked on the door. Graham answered and they began to read out his rights, then Graham shouted, "She attacked me, I have scratches on my arm to prove it." The police then turned to me and arrested me too.

"I need to ring my son to ask him to pick George and Marie up from school," I said, panicking and shocked that I was being arrested. "Jack, could you pick the kids up from school please, I will leave a key under the plant pot, Dad has accused me of assaulting him so they are arresting both of us."

"He is fucking unbelievable, what a complete bastard he is. Of course I will pick the kids up, Mum."

"Thank you, I will see you later, Jack."

We were both taken in separate police vans to Harrogate police station to be interviewed. Upon arrival, I was taken into a room where I was fingerprinted and had my DNA taken whilst telling this man (with tears streaming down my face) who was conducting this procedure, that I had done nothing wrong and I was the one who had been attacked. He was really sympathetic towards me, he took photos of all my bruises as evidence and reassured me that the truth would prevail.

I was taken into a small room and interviewed at length. Meanwhile Graham was in another room spinning all his lies, but the rep who was present in the next office was giving a statement to the police about what he had heard during my attack. He didn't actually see the attack, but he heard everything; this was exactly what I needed – a witness who could verify the attack. The police later told me that after Graham had assaulted me, he then went back into the office laughing and said to the rep, "That's how you deal with them…"

Graham was arrested for battery and issued with a restraining order preventing him having any contact with me at all. He was detained at the police station while I was taken back home by the police who suggested that I needed security measures in place in the form of panic alarms fitted in the house and to notify the neighbours that he wasn't to attend the house. I agreed to the panic alarms and had them fitted, but I didn't want all the neighbours knowing; I felt embarrassed and ashamed.

Jack had agreed to stay with me initially and he was a great support. He went into work the following day before Graham was released from the police station. I was in regular contact with the police as they were going to let me know when Graham was to be released. Later that day while Jack was home with the kids, he heard the van which he used for work start up – Graham had instructed Shaun, a member of staff, to go and take the van from Jack, knowing it was parked at our house. Jack rushed out when he heard the engine running to see Shaun in the driver's seat. Jack told him that he couldn't take the van because it was the vehicle that Jack needed for work, so Shaun left the van and the house.

I had an appointment at the solicitor's the same evening in Harrogate. Jack looked after George and Marie while I attended my appointment. I drove to the solicitor's and talked through my options, divorce being the most favourable one. I felt more positive after our meeting and arranged to be in contact within the next few days. As I left the solicitor's, I saw that my car wasn't there, I went into panic mode and rushed back into the solicitor's to tell her my car had been stolen. She made me a cup of tea. Could things get any worse? I thought to myself. I rang the police to report my stolen car, and during the phone call, they told me that they had released Graham.

"Why didn't you tell me, Jack is at home with the kids, he will go there, he has stolen my car. I can't believe you didn't tell me that he was out of custody – how am I supposed to get home?" I cried.

"We will take you home, and also check the CCTV footage from Harrogate to Ripon to see of the car is travelling that way." They picked me up almost immediately, and told me that they had seen the car travelling to Ripon. I was seriously concerned that Graham would ignore the restraining order and go straight to the house. I rang Jack and told him to lock all the doors and keep himself and the kids safe. When I arrived home I was in total shock, I could hardly believe the last two days' events. Jack was brilliant, he calmed me down and helped me so much. Graham didn't show his face that evening, but I couldn't settle. I stayed up all night looking out of the windows, I saw the police drive by twice, which made me feel slightly better. I also had the panic alarms fitted, yet I still felt extremely anxious. Jack stayed overnight and went to work the next day only to be greeted by Graham with his P45 and no wages for the work he had done. There was no real explanation, but we knew the reason. He was angry that Jack was supporting me. Jack was now unemployed. I was so upset and felt so angry at myself for allowing Graham to destroy all our lives by his abuse and control.

I walked the kids to school which took about an hour there and back and on my return I noticed a few things missing from the house – Graham's clothes, duvet, some personal items and household items including a TV. I felt sick thinking of him being in the house while I took the kids to school. I stood and cried. I had no money at all and needed to do a food shop. I called my brother who came to my aid with bags of food. After he left I just broke down, then my mind was working overtime – how did Graham know where my car was? I started to think about all the times he knew where I was, it felt like he was watching me, invading my privacy, but how could that be possible?

The police had advised me to go to the benefits office as I was now unemployed, like Jack.

I had two small children to care for, no income, no car. I felt helpless. Then to further twist the knife, the call to the benefits office was to be the last call I made before Graham ended my phone contract which was through the business. This nutter was out to destroy me and his kids in the process.

My friend Shelle was a life saver. I had been to see her and told her about what had happened. She was so supportive, she helped me so much. Her daughter Annie and my Marie were best friends.

"I will take the kids to school, Alisha, get them ready for 8.30am and I will pick them up, then drop them off after school," she said.

"Shelle, I can't thank you enough, this will really help me as I need time to sort out what I need to do."

"Listen, I will help you all I can, just let me know."

"Thanks, Shelle, I will."

A couple of days later, my father's partner lent me this tiny little car which was a Godsend to be back mobile again.

"Shelle, I have been lent a car so I can pick the kids up after school."

"OK, I will see you outside school," she said.

I pulled up outside the school gates, got out, and walked over to Shelle. We stood chatting for a while, then took the kids to the park over the road for an hour. On returning to our cars, Shelle said, "Is that little red flintstone car the one you have been lent?"

Well, we both just stood and laughed hysterically until we cried; it was such a bizarre moment, it was like all the adrenaline had come rushing in; we were laughing uncontrollably. This was just the medicine I needed right now, I will never forget that moment. Shelle became my right-hand woman, she supported me and helped me out so much, I would have been totally lost without her support. We laughed until we cried and we cried tears of sorrow together. I will always treasure our times together forever, and we still laugh about that today.

It was time I pulled myself together for the sake of my kids. I had to be strong and start thinking rationally. Jack was doing his own work now, which was a relief, so I had to get things sorted and stop moping around.

I was now able to get the kids to school and back in good time. I went to the benefits office and started applying for jobs. I was quickly in receipt of benefits which eased my dire financial situation almost immediately. I bought myself a cheap pay-as-you-go-phone and started to feel much better about my situation. It was not at all easy, as my life had completely changed. I had a lot of support from my Jack, which made my life bearable.

As the days went by I was coping quite well, then one night out of the blue I received an email from Graham saying that he loved me and couldn't live without me, he was so distraught being away from me and the kids; he said he was desperate to see me, he pleaded and begged me to take him back and promised to change, saying he would do anything to be back with me, I was the love of his life and without me there was no point to his life. The email was lengthy and made personal references regarding how he was immensely physically attracted to me. I was so shocked to receive the email after what had happened that I didn't respond.

More and more emails came. He bombarded me with the most loving emails, he told me that he was living at the factory and had bought George and Marie presents. He asked if we could meet, he desperately wanted to see me, he missed me and the kids beyond belief. He begged to come round, saying he could just drive round and give George and Marie their gifts, and see me. I was starting to cave in, unbelievably, and to this day, I cannot understand why, after all the abuse, him stealing my car, cheating and lying and everything else he had put me through, I actually started to feel sorry for him; it was like he had changed into the person that I dreamed he would be. I agreed to meet him outside the house. When he arrived he looked unkempt, he had clearly been crying and when he saw me and the kids he broke down.

"You are my world, I live for you and the kids, my heart is broken, I miss you so much. Can I come back please, babe, I love you so, so much," he said, utterly distraught.

"There is a restraining order against you coming here," I said, feeling sorry for him.

"Well if you drop the charges against me, we could move forward. I am so sorry for what I did and I promise, I have realised what I have done, and I will change. I love you so much, babe."

After he left, I started to envisage a life without abuse, with a changed man who'd had a short, sharp shock looking at a prosecution; I saw a family life filled with happiness and love, which is all I ever wanted.

I lay awake that night imagining only a new happy future. Looking back, I can only think that I was desperate and scared, the 'love bombing' was working, he was an expert liar, manipulative cheating abuser, and I was falling into his trap yet again.

The emails were coming thick and fast; he was completely ignoring the restraining order in place.

"I will pick you and the kids up and take you on a lovely picnic. I have a customer who said we can use his house as a little getaway, we could go for weekends just for a little break, the kids would love it. I know your birthday isn't until August, but I have been looking at hotels for me and you, babe, so we can have time together. I just want to be with you so much. What do you think, could you get a babysitter and I will book it for a night next week?"

"I'm not sure it's a good idea, let me think." I was now nearly under his spell again and I was desperate to live a life like I imagined. I had been through the most traumatic times, surely life will be better now? I could give him the benefit of the doubt and I believed his lies; I failed to see that this was just a desperate attempt by him to persuade me to drop the charges. I had decided, the messages he was sending me were all I ever wanted, he might've changed but if I didn't give him the chance to prove it, then I would never know and could potentially deny my kids a happy family life, with their mum and dad. We all deserved to be happy.

After a lot of thought, I made my decision and agreed to his proposals. I emailed him back, explaining that I was willing to spend time together and as a family to rebuild our relationship. Graham was ecstatic and couldn't wait to organise our picnic day, and it came round quickly. He arrived to pick us up, got out of the car, came to me and hugged me tightly, whispering in my ear "You are the love of my life, always have been and always will be, you are beautiful, Alisha and I love you with all my heart. Let's make this a new beginning." Just the right words to reel me in hook, line and sinker...if only I hadn't been so blinded by his words, I could have saved myself from much further heartache to come.

I had spent the time while alone in the house, decorating all the bedrooms. I bought brand new bedding for us all, decorated George and Marie's rooms – we all went shopping together so the kids could choose what they wanted. I could afford it now I had benefits coming in.

The picnic was lovely. Graham had bought all the food and wine and I brought a tablecloth and games for the kids. We went to a secluded little place near Brimham Rocks, the sun was shining, the kids were happy and I was revelling in my little new world with this changed man, telling me I was his whole world...while all the time he was sleeping around with multiple women, lying and living a double life I was to discover later on. How could I have been so blind? I realise now that it was sheer desperation to keep my family together; after all I had parents who were amazing role models, having a long, loving marriage, and devoted to us three kids, while Graham had only known abuse, a broken family and rejection from his mother. After the lovely day we had, Graham dropped us back home saying he would check out the best hotels in Harrogate to book. I keenly agreed.

I felt amazing, elated and thought that this was the beginning of a new happy chapter. How very wrong could I be?

The next six weeks were like a dream: he would pick me up from home, take me to fancy restaurants, we stayed overnight in the Majestic hotel in Harrogate, he had bought masses of flowers, rose petals on the bed, champagne on ice, he ran me a bubble bath in the jacuzzi before whisking me out to a gorgeous restaurant then to the bars around Harrogate on this beautiful summer evening. I was on cloud nine, he treated me like I always dreamed of being treated, he couldn't do or say enough to show me he was a changed man. I now know this to be 'love bombing'.

In the meantime, Graham had gone round to see Lee and Louise. He was desperate to have some support, he would be extremely distressed, he would cry and tell them how he was desperate to get his family back, he was so desperate to have someone whom he could talk to, so who better than his son? He would also try and entice Lee back to work by offering him more money, profit sharing and other perks. Lee was apprehensive after what had previously happened. He did agree to think about it, but Graham wouldn't let it drop. He would persist and make it look very attractive to him – "You could be office bound, it would be more money, you would be a manager, Lee, and at the end of the tax year, you will get profit sharing," he said in a desperate attempt to entice him back. But the reality was that Graham selfishly just wanted someone there whom he could trust, while he went off to live his double life...

A few weeks later Lee decided to take up Graham's offer. He wanted to save up and put down a deposit on a house for him and Louise. Graham had done it, all he needed to do now was to get me to drop the charges then he could start weaving his next web.

He would get emotional and plead with me to drop the charges of BATTERY saying he could go to prison and that he wouldn't be able to see his kids again.

"Please Graham, don't pressure me, let's just spend and enjoy the time together." I still failed to recognise that his only aim was to coerce me into dropping the charges against him!

I had a conversation with Jack and a few friends, telling them that Graham had changed, things were going to be great, he had realised what me and the kids meant to him...

"DON'T take him back, he's a horrible, nasty bastard, a leopard never changes its spots, how can you trust him? How can you believe he's suddenly changed into prince charming?" Jack said. "Mum, he *will* change, he will change tack, he won't use violence now, but he will mentally and emotionally abuse you," he said, frustrated with me.

How perceptive he was. If only I had listened to him – he did, after all, only want to protect his mum.

I decided to drop the charges if he agreed to do an anger management course and both of us to go to Relate.

"Babe, I will do anything you want, I just want you back. I will arrange appointments with Relate and anger management courses, just leave it with me, I promise, this is a new start for us now..." His eyes filled with tears. I looked at George and Marie's little faces, and felt that it was the right thing to do. He grabbed me and hugged me so hard. "You won't regret it, I promise you, babe, we will have the best times, you will see. Let's drive to Harrogate police station now," he said, hardly drawing breath; he couldn't drive there quick enough; "then after we will go on a shopping spree and take the kids out somewhere nice. I love you so much, babe." We soon arrived at the police station. "Just tell them you want to drop the charges, babe, then I can move back in and we can all be a family again."

This was yet more LIES after LIES after LIES; all he was interested in was that I dropped the BATTERY charges against him, then he could come home and play his nasty little mental games; this nutter was out for revenge big time...how dare I call the police and press charges against this person who thought he was God Almighty, better than anyone else, more successful than anyone else in Ripon, wealthier, more attractive, the Georgie Best of Kirkby Malzeard, the list goes on and on and on. His inflated sense of his own importance and his huge ego was an embarrassment to me and our kids, we would cringe when he would repeatedly tell us all how good he was at absolutely everything.

Taking him back was to be the biggest mistake I could ever make, but, naively, I walked into the police station and told the policeman who was dealing with the case, "I want to drop the charges against Graham please."

"Why? It's been eight weeks, has something happened, has he forced you to do this? We get this a lot, where witnesses have been threatened to drop the charges."

"No," I said, "I believe he's really changed and want to try again." He just looked at me in disbelief and said, "Alisha, they DON'T change. We see this all the time; and you cannot drop the charges because it's in the hands of the CPS now and they are pursuing it, it's not up to you now."

"Well I won't be a witness," I said, "they can pursue it all they like but I won't attend court."

"Well I will have to look into this, I will be in touch with you soon," he said disappointedly. He had been so good during this and I felt like I had let him down, but this was about my new, happy life and the future... Why, why, why didn't I listen to people who could see more clearly than me?

My 49th birthday had arrived. There was a knock at the door – Graham was stood there with the most beautiful bouquets of flowers, his car boot open to reveal a boot full of presents, jewellery, perfume, leather jacket, more flowers and lots more presents. "Happy birthday, babe," he said as he hugged and kissed me. I was walking on air, the weather was gorgeous, and I was very happy right now. "Can I come home, babe, I miss you so much."

"OK, come home then, let's make this work, you can come home, and we will…"

"You won't regret this, I love you so much, can I come in then?"

As he walked down the hallway, I was excited to show him my decorating. We had two bedrooms on the ground floor and two on the first floor, so I started off in "our" room. He loved it: "Wow, this is great, I love it, you have made it all romantic, I'm well impressed, babe." Then he spotted the panic alarm and all the internal door locks which Jack had fitted for my security. "What's this? And why are all these locks on all the doors?" he said in a disappointed tone.

"That's a panic alarm that the police fitted and Jack fitted the locks for my piece of mind," I said, almost apologetic.

"I can't live like this, knowing there is a panic alarm in the house. You don't need it now, babe, will you get it taken out and I will remove all the door locks?"

"I will ring the police and ask them to remove it then." I did ring the police who suggested that I keep it in place for a while just to make sure I had protection. I agreed as it did make me feel more secure. I told Graham that the police would come and move it when they had the chance, in an attempt to pacify him. A couple of days later, he arrived home with a car for me – he had hid the other car at his cousin's in Durham – it was an old Citroen Picasso, but I was just over the moon to have my own vehicle. I didn't expect a brand new Audi A5 like Graham's; my expectations were very low by now anyway.

We spent lots of family time together, we would go on lovely family walks every Sunday, I would bake cakes to take with us and have a meal ready to come home to in the slow cooker. Graham would pick me flowers and was being very romantic. We would have picnics, breaks at Centre Parcs, days out at theme parks and zoos, which the kids loved, stayed at his friend's bungalow in a nearby village, we would feed the horses in the fields, take bike rides together; it was quality time that we all needed together. We camped a lot at our favourite campsite in the Lake District. This was all I ever wanted, a happy family, and this was just perfect.

Graham said that he didn't have a problem with Jack supporting me, which was another lie. I suggested he made amends with both the boys, and he agreed, but yet again, had no intentions of doing this – he was much happier destroying people's lives than making things amicable. Not long after we bumped into Jack in the supermarket, he made all the right noises, said all the right things. "Jack, I love Mum and the kids, I regret what happened, let's start afresh and put it behind us. I don't have any hard feelings about you supporting Mum, I just want things to be good between us all." Graham went to hug Jack and all was okay...NOT...Jack, didn't buy into his lies, he knew him too well, but for my sake he would try.

I told Graham that I had decided not to work in the family business anymore; I needed my own space, I would find myself a job. Graham wasn't very happy but agreed that it was probably for the best

It was the best period of time that we had together in years, it was so refreshing that I was able to speak without being shouted over, for him to actually listen to me. Sadly it had become almost normal life to live with no voice, so to have this placid person who actually seemed to appreciate me, show me respect and love, to be kind and gentle, he really had changed so I thought.

Graham came home one evening. "Let's book a holiday." (We usually had a ski holiday every year and winter sun holiday in Tenerife.) We decided to book somewhere we had never been before – we usually went to France and Austria. "What about Bulgaria, we have never been there before, it will be different?" he said suspiciously.

"I didn't think you wanted to go to Bulgaria, you always said it was a beginners resort?" But I agreed. I was happy with wherever we went.

"Well let's have a change and try it. Do you want to look for one, babe, and pay it on your credit card and I will give you the cash at the end of the month?"

This became a nasty little game of financial and emotional abuse; it was a way he could control me, but I didn't give it much thought. I looked and looked, there were so many to choose from. A couple of days passed.

"Babe, look for the Rila Hotel in Bulgaria for this particular week in February, it looks really nice."

Well I just assumed he had been looking for a holiday too, but no, this was not the case. Lee had mentioned to him that he would like a week off to go skiing with Louise. Graham had repeatedly asked where they planned to go but Lee didn't want to disclose it; however, Graham would persist, manipulate and try his utmost to get the information from Lee. Eventually he caught Lee off guard and the details of his holiday spilled out.

"We can't book the same holiday as Lee and Louise, they want to be on their own. How would we feel if someone did that to us? It will spoil their holiday," I reasoned with him.

"No, it won't, we wouldn't be with them through the day much, but if we met up on an evening for some drinks, then that would be nice. We could even invite your brother and Emma. It will be really good, I'm sure Lee and Louise won't mind."

This didn't feel right, we were invading Lee's holiday,

"What about Jack?" I said. "Shouldn't we invite him?" Jack was the one that had been my saviour.

"I don't think Lee would be happy, since they have fallen out," he said.

I could see his point, as this was really Lee and Louise's holiday after all. But I felt guilty and bad for Jack, I thought that maybe this could be an opportunity for us all to get back on track... I was reluctant to go, but Graham spent time selling it to me over the next few days, he texted my brother who agreed to come and we booked it, the same holiday as Lee and Louise. I felt uncomfortable about it, but tried to be positive. We Booked and paid for on it on MY credit card.

Graham was eager to tell Lee about *our* holiday... Lee was understandably annoyed and knew that Louise would feel the same... The holiday arrived. We met Anthony and Emma at the airport and I was now looking forward to the holiday, though my heart was aching that Jack wasn't with us; I felt torn.

Lee and Louise arrived, and we soon got to our hotel, the weather was lovely, the hotel was 'ski to door' and close to the lifts, our room was great and Graham was still being very affectionate and attentive to me. I was determined to enjoy this much needed break, the holiday went well, lots of skiing, sun, pony treks for George and Marie, hot wine in our favourite bar on the way down from the last run of the day, skied back to the hotel for dinner ...yes this was a good holiday so far.

A couple of days into the holiday, we had all spent the day together skiing. Graham, Anthony, Emma, the kids and me were sat having a cold beer (lemonade for George and Marie) waiting for Lee and Louise, and they soon followed us down, sat and had a cold beer; they looked so happy. Louise put her hand in front of my eyes, dazzling in the sun, a beautiful diamond ring placed on her ring finger... "Lee proposed to me on one knee at the top of the mountain," she said excitedly.

This was lovely news, we were all so happy for them. Lee had asked her dad for his approval a few weeks previous – he had a really good relationship with him, looking up to him as a father figure. Louise's dad was over the moon for them both. We celebrated that evening with champagne and continued the holiday on a high... Lee and Louise had decided summer 2014 would be when they would be married; this was something to look forward to.

The evening before the last day, Lee had suggested that himself, Graham, Anthony and George ski the last day together and us *girls* ski the last day together and we all meet up for lunch on the mountain. This suggestion was enough to cause Graham to have a tantrum.

"No, I want to spend the last day skiing with mum and the kids!" he yelled at Lee – totally unnecessary, he made such a huge issue about it, he always had to spoil things; but I now know that he was using me and the kids as an excuse to have a go at Lee for reasons only known to himself...he gave Lee the silent treatment, which was his usual tactic; this was getting far too familiar. The last day proved to be bitter-sweet between us all, yet again because of this one, self-centred, nasty, immature idiot who knows nothing else but to cause trouble. On the other hand he was desperate to keep me happy so he could continue to keep me in his trap.

"Babe, I just want to be with you and the kids, this is our last day, I just want to spend it with you and have a lovely last day together on holiday. I'm annoyed that Lee even suggested that," he tried to convince me, and I didn't want this to spoil what I thought was a new start with us.

On our return home I decided I wanted to have my own little business sewing. I could make curtains, blinds, home furnishings; it made perfect sense. I had already made blinds for home and made most of Marie's clothes. I loved sewing, so this could be perfect. I excitedly discussed this with Graham.

"Yes, babe, that's a great idea, if you're happy then I'm happy," he lied.

"Yes, I could also make jewellery, do craft fairs and hire a stall in the local indoor market."

"Go for it, babe."

I was tiring of the *babe*, it almost seemed patronising and certainly not genuine, but I didn't complain. It was better than the "You are a fat, ugly minger and everyone hates you", which was his usual saying.

I was at Jack's just after the skiing holiday and the holiday was mentioned. I knew he wouldn't be happy about it. He did feel betrayed by me, and I did feel like I had let him down. This really upset me knowing how hurt Jack was – understandably, he felt like he was the one being left out after he was my saviour, and I completely understood how he felt. That guilt has never left me, especially knowing that Graham had orchestrated this deliberately to not only spoil Lee's holiday, and put me in an extremely difficult position but also to ostracise Jack – triple whammy in his eyes.

I was the only one in the family who was in contact with Jack, so I would go and see him regularly with George and Marie (which angered Graham – he accused me of being disloyal again because I was close to *Our* son). Jack and I would take the kids to the park, play football and take them to McDonald's. Sometimes we would just go and chill with Jack at home in his garden.

Chapter 18

I had minor surgery pending and my appointment finally arrived, March 2012, only a few weeks away. This was the ideal time, then after I could recover at home whilst planning my new business.

"Yes, babe, that makes sense, and I will do the school run while you recover," Graham agreed. I had put off this surgery for ages as Graham was opposed to me having the recovery time off work.

The morning of my surgery had arrived. Graham came with me. While I was in the ward getting prepared, Graham hugged me tight. "Remember, babe, I love you with all my heart, I always have and always will, you and the kids are my world, you are my life," he said, voice quivering.

As I looked at him, tears were running down his cheeks. "Don't get upset, I'm not going to die," I joked. "I love you too, we will be okay now, don't worry, Graham."

They wheeled me into theatre, and a couple of hours later after recovery I was taken to the ward where Graham was stood waiting with a bouquet of flowers, looking like the cat that got the cream. "I was worrying about you so much, I'm so relieved you're here," he said with tears in his eyes.

Was this really the same person? I thought to myself. I spent the next eight weeks recovering at home.

"Take as much time as you need to recover, babe, don't worry about money, I will support you until you start working again."

Oh that's very kind of you to say that, I'm your wife of 30 years, and have worked my whole life, I thought angrily to myself, but didn't rise to it. I was reluctant to cause any unrest, especially while recuperating. He couldn't do enough for me, so I just enjoyed it while it lasted. Was this the person who, only eight months ago, attacked me? Who was an abusive, vile, evil, cheating liar? The answer was NO, he was a million times worse, he was extremely angry and revengeful; his plan was to completely destroy me.

It was summer 2012 and I had started my own little business and loved it. I spent my days sewing and making jewellery, hired a stall in the market and booked lots of craft fairs. I was earning my own money and loving selling things that I had made. I was taking lots of orders for home furnishings, wedding outfits and jewellery, I was so busy, and loved it; this was very fulfilling, I was really happy. Home life seemed to be perfect, I even had time to meet my best friend, Sheila for coffees on her day off work. I felt normal sat in a bar drinking coffee with my bestie, this was predominately in secret ...or so I thought. I just wanted to save arguments with Graham. I look back now and cannot believe what life with him was like – it's only looking from the outside that it's actually shocking, but in that situation, it's hard to see.

Graham came home after my meeting with Sheila. "Let me smell your breath!" he demanded, "You have been on a pub crawl with Sheila, haven't you?"

"What are you talking about?" I breathed heavily into his face – if coffee smelt like alcohol then I was screwed.

"I saw you and Sheila coming out of Wetherspoons today," he said angrily.

"Yes, I met Sheila for a coffee in Wetherspoons, there is no crime in that, I'm an adult, I can do what I like," I dared reply.

"Oh right, well I'm an adult too, so I will do what I like," he smirked. Even though he had cheated and lied our whole marriage, he would now take it to an extreme level.

"I'm not supporting you while you swan off with your dad, and Sheila and piss about with your sewing – you need to claim for benefits," he said.

"Are you for real," I said. "You were all in favour of me having my own little business? What's changed?"

"We can't afford for you to sit on your arse sewing and seeing your dad all the time. Either you get a full-time job or you get benefits; and while we are on, I don't want you to ever come down to the factory ever again."

Well, that little 'honeymoon period' didn't last long, I thought to myself. The actual reality of him banning me from entering the factory, which I was later to find out, is that he had a bed in his office, his motorbike and accessories, which he had bought without my knowledge, and many other items, documents etc. which would eventually reveal his double life.

This was all because of HIS insecurity, HIS jealousy. He couldn't bear not to have the control over me.

I worked all hours, sewing until the early hours, doing car boot sales on a Sunday morning, seeing my dad… I was exhausted. Jack even offered to pay me to clean for him while he was working which I was extremely grateful for. I also claimed carers allowance. I was scraping by with the money I was earning and using my credit card. Graham was delighted that I was working so much – he was in control again!

Chapter 19

Lee and Louise had brought their wedding forward and decided on the date 14th June 2013, which was my dad's birthday. I was really looking forward to it. We had looked around numerous venues together and they eventually chose a beautiful hall in Northallerton, so the next few months were spent organising the wedding. They had asked Marie to be a flower girl, and she was so excited. Louise had bought the flower girl dresses but later decided that the deep pleated waistband and bow at the back was to be changed to a gorgeous peachy coral colour, so she asked me to do the alterations. I was so pleased to 'remake' these lovely dresses.

I had a conversation with Lee about inviting Jack to the wedding. Their communication had become non-existent by now, but I was desperate for my boys, who were once so close, to become close brothers again. However, this was virtually impossible whilst Graham was around – his deep-seated jealousy of his two sons being so close, ate him up inside, as all relationships that didn't revolve around him did. It would please Graham to think that he could be responsible for Jack missing Lee's wedding, but this sickened me to the core.

This was a very hard situation to deal with, my heart was ripped in two – one of my sons getting married and the other one not invited was heart-breaking for me. Lee and Louise didn't want Jack at the wedding since they had fallen out previously. I went to see Jack and discussed the situation about him not being invited to his brother's wedding.

Obviously Jack was very hurt by this, but even more so by me wanting to attend the wedding. "Are you going to the wedding, Mum?" he asked.

"Jack, this is tearing me up inside, I know how painful this is for you, when not so long ago, you would have been his best man. My heart breaks for you and you will feel betrayed by me, but I can't miss my son's wedding; it's not betrayal or disloyal, Jack. I really feel like I'm being pulled in two directions. I hope you will understand that I have to go to Lee's wedding, I'm not the one who's had any fallouts with him or you," I said, choked up.

"Yes, I understand, it's hard for you, it's okay, me and Matty are booking a holiday for that week, so I will be away," he said quietly.

"That will be nice for you to have a relaxing time in the sun with your friend," I replied. This was a good solution for Jack and just the diversion he needed.

The wedding day arrived. Graham travelled 11 miles, to Harrogate to collect his elderly aunt. I was surprised as she had expressed to Graham that she didn't feel very well, only days before, and that she certainly wasn't well enough to attend a wedding all day, but he was adamant that she should attend. Only now do I know why. So Graham, his aunt, George, Marie and I all travelled to Northallerton where we would also meet my dad and his partner. The sun was shining. Lee looked so smart in his top hat and tails, his sparkly blue eyes, blonde hair and super white teeth dazzling in the sunlight, he was walking on air marrying the love of his life.

George looked so cute in his tails. He was 10 now, he was a little mini-mixture of Jack and Lee, all having gorgeous good looks, Jack and Lee with their blue eyes and blonde hair, George having lovely green eyes, the exact same colour as mine, and blond hair, all three brothers were very much alike. George looked up to his big brothers and Jack and Lee adored him.

Marie looked beautiful in her flower girl dress, her long fair hair tucked back with flowers. She was eight now and was looking more like Lisa every day, apart from their eye colour – Marie has the same eye colour as her big brothers, Lisa had the most beautiful, big, deep, dark brown eyes. Marie was so excited, she felt like a little princess and looked adorable.

We were all seated. Lee stood waiting at the altar for his bride. The music started to play and Louise walked towards him. She looked absolutely stunning wearing the most beautiful wedding dress, off the shoulder with a silk bodice to the waistline, then so beautifully delicate almost like white feathers to the floor, complete with a diamanté tiara and a veil, her long, almost jet black glossy hair was pinned up on the top of her head with long ringlets spilling out. They were a gorgeous couple and both looked so very happy together. After the wedding breakfast and the speeches were done, "*happy birthday*" started to play, and a birthday cake was brought over to my dad, which was so lovely. He was very confused, but blew out his candles to a loud applause and lapped up the attention.

It was time for the photos to be taken, so the photographers selected certain groups of guests etc. Some were taken outside and some inside, our very small party(in comparison to Louise's, who has a very large family) sat in the beautiful garden room overlooking the stunning rolling gardens drinking our champagne. We wandered around the grounds in the glorious sunshine, but I did notice that Graham was anxious and distracted, frequently looking at his phone.

"Do you have an appointment, Graham?" I said sarcastically.

"What do you mean?" he snapped.

"Well you really seem like you don't want to be here, as if this is in the way of something much more important, but I can't possibly think what could be more important than your son's wedding."

"I'm just keeping an eye on the time, my aunt will want to be getting home soon, so I will take her back; in fact we will go now." He beckoned to his aunt who reluctantly agreed as she was having a lovely time, but Graham insisted anxiously, "Right, babe, here's some money for drinks–" (putting a couple of £20 notes in my hand hoping that this would satisfy my curiosity)– "I won't be long," he said as he rushed out of the venue with his aunt slowly following behind.

George and Marie went to play with the other kids at the wedding while I sat and talked to my dad. We talked and walked around the gardens; my dad was loving the sun so we decided to sit outside. The kids were happy and all the guests were mingling, a few more drinks and three hours later my thoughts jumped back to Graham.

It's only a 50-minute round trip to Harrogate, even less when he's driving, so even if it was a 90-minute trip, there are 90 minutes unaccounted for, another disappearing act. Then my thoughts were consumed by his previous nights away, his confessions of cheating, even though he retracted that later; his distraction and distance from me; his extremely close relationship with his phone, which he treated like the crown jewels, locking and hiding it away when it wasn't on his person; his extreme, abnormal obsession with himself, always in the mirror, convincing us all how good looking he was, and that his female 'customers' would constantly tell him how young he looked for his age; his preoccupation with things that he didn't ever divulge to me, then when I would ask a question it would be the same scenario over and over again:

"FOR FUCK'S SAKE, why can't you just leave people alone, let me live my life, you are fucking paranoid, what's your problem, you have a huge big problem, you are so jealous and greedy, why can't you just be happy instead of trying to interfere with what I'm doing, I'm doing NOTHING WRONG, you are so fucking selfish, it's all about YOU, YOU, YOU!!!! POOR LITTLE ALISHA, DOESN'T GET TO KNOW EVERYTHING, POOR YOU... YOUR'E JUST A FUCKING MARTYR, AREN'T YOU!"

When I analysed all what he had said to me, I realised that this was projection, he was actually talking about himself.

He was the one who was SELFISH, living his secret, double life with no regard or consideration for anyone but himself, building a shanty town of disgusting pigeon sheds in *OUR* garden, without so much as a discussion with me, he was SELF-OBSESSED with his appearance. HE was GREEDY, keeping all *our* income from me, depriving me of any money, so as to financially control me. He was the one that our life revolved around, certainly not me. He was the paranoid one, following and stalking me, which I would discover to my absolute horror in the next few years.

This became more and more frequent as time went by, the sense of helplessness was unbearable, only a couple of years had passed since he was arrested for battery, and this was to be my punishment for reporting him to the police.

He arrived back at the wedding venue, nearly four hours later. I didn't even ask where he had been. It was Lee and Louise's day and nothing was going to spoil it, especially Graham – he had caused enough destruction in his path.

I now know that he had arranged to go and see one of his little whores in his wedding attire. He obviously thought that he was so irresistible all dressed up, that one of his little whores would drop their knickers for him, maybe he even went to see more than one of them. I'm not exactly sure whether these whores actually thought they were Graham's ONLY 'bit on the side' but I can assure them all, Marie, Teena, Kate, Sarah, Gill, Jill, Debbie and the rest, that they were far from special, they were sharing him with anyone and everyone with a pulse. Graham would brag to them all that *He* was a very wealthy, businessman and property owner, so the truth is more likely that they only dropped their knickers because they had ££££ signs in their eyes and thought they would financially benefit from him. Well, that would come as a massive disappointment to them, apart from Gill, his little old whore who was his favourite, whom he treated to a little cream MINI (which is probably why he later tried to persuade me to get one) as Graham was the tightest, greediest man I had ever come across in my life.

We stayed at the evening do which Graham made uncomfortable as usual, he was eager to leave; we left just before midnight, said our goodbyes to the bride and groom, then headed home with very little to say to each other, while George and Marie fell fast asleep in the car.

Chapter 20

The next three months passed quickly. I spent most of the time in the garden entertaining the kids, and spent endless hours with George preparing him for the 11+ exam in September. I helped him with the non-verbal, verbal reasoning, maths and English books. Graham on the other hand was his usual absent self, other than when he was training and racing his pigeons. This also involved George, so on a Friday and Saturday evening during the racing season, me and Marie would enjoy mummy and daughter time which usually involved nail varnish and hair products. I adored my gorgeous little girl and treasure these memories always.

I had decided that it would be easier if I got a job. The sewing was becoming so time-consuming and my dad was deteriorating, so I applied for part-time jobs and in October 2013, I got a job at the local hardware store; it was only for Christmas cover, but it was regular work and I was happy to have the company of the staff and also customers. I needed this job for my own sanity, it wasn't a job I particularity liked but I made the most of it. Graham seemed pleased and the next few months were lovely at home, Graham seemed really happy and I was just enjoying my life right now. We had booked a family ski holiday to Austria – again on MY credit card, which seemed to be the 'norm' now, then Graham would pay me the cash before the end of the month, which gave him four weeks to threaten, control and blackmail me!

We were all really looking forward to the holiday in March and life seemed good. Jack had met a girl called Rose. She was lovely, and Jack seemed really happy.

Lee and Louise announced that they were expecting their first baby, due in July 2014 so everything was looking really positive and we were ecstatic about the baby news. I couldn't wait to meet our new grandchild.

There was less physical contact between me and Graham; he withheld any form of affection as a punishment to me, like he would use the silent treatment, he would insult and criticise me daily. "You should think yourself lucky, no-one else would put up with you, you're crazy, insecure, jealous, selfish, paranoid and greedy, you are always mad and angry, you will never get anyone better than me, me and the kids put up with you, but Alisha, it's so hard to live with you like this, you need to go to the doctors and get some help, you need serious help, babe." His voice softened, "Look, Alisha, I will help you all I can, but you are getting worse in your old age, you should be more mellow, more laid back, go and see a doctor, please, babe, take on board what I am saying, for all our sakes."

Tears streaming down my face, I was helpless and alone, I was drowning inside and had no-one to save me, and he was now using my own kids against me. Panic alarms were ringing in my head, oh no not the kids, please do not turn the kids against me, I couldn't bear that; they were only 11 and nine. My heart was pounding, my mouth was dry, I felt physically sick at the thought of my kids being brainwashed, groomed, blackmailed, manipulated and used for Graham to punish me. I was pleading in my head. I had already noticed that George hung on every word Graham said, he was terrified of him. George had been roped in by Graham at the age of six to help with the racing pigeons, he didn't have any choice, he was only young.

Graham would again use the word *WE* to further ostracize me and to gain favour with George and Marie. This was the start, or so

I believed at the time, that the gang culture started. Graham was a coward, he would prey on the weak and vulnerable; he felt powerful when he had his gang and was in control. Little did I know then, that since Graham came back in August 2011, he had been saying, mainly to George, "I'm going to buy a house for me, you and Marie and we will all leave Mum; it will have a lovely garden, but we can't tell her; it's our secret and one day, we will just go and she won't know where we are." He would say this to George in an excitable way. I can't imagine what damage that must do to a child, it is the worst form of CHILD ABUSE ever. These were two innocent children who were being groomed by their own father to hate their mother; this was inconceivable to me. I was completely unaware of this at the time. I would find this out much later when the damage had already been done and it was too late.

Graham was even more obsessed with himself, more than usual. He was always immensely vain and had an inflated sense of self-importance, he had always dyed his hair, gone on the sunbed and even got me to shave his hairy back. He had started to lose weight and buy clothes that only a 20 year old toned man would look good in, he would accuse me of trying to get him fat when he came in to a home-made meal that I had cooked for us all. He was coming home from work later and later, it was so obvious that he was cheating but I had my head in the sand, my only interests were my kids. I hadn't loved him for a while.

January 13th, 2014, I was picking George up from his after-school cricket club, it was approx 6pm, and my phone rang. "Hi Graham."

"Hi babe, I'm stuck on a job up north and need to come back first thing in the morning, so I thought it made sense to find a B&B and stay overnight," he lied.

"Oh I didn't know you were on site, I thought you was working on a machine at the factory today?" – which is what he had told me this morning...

"Why do I have to answer to you? It's like you don't trust me, what the fuck is wrong with you nowadays, you question everything I do, I'm

NOT filling a fucking time sheet for you, I'm an adult and can do what I like, remember? I'm not answerable to you or anyone!" he screamed down the phone before hanging up.

Do I continue to live with this horrible, abusive monster? Well what choice did I have, he would hunt me down if I left him, it was too dangerous to stay in the house if I kicked him out, how would I pay the bills anyway, where could I go? How could I support me and an 11 and a nine year old? My head was spinning. I knew there was no future like this but I always arrived at the same answer: it is easier to stay for the kids. I didn't have the energy or mental strength to change anything right now.

I had a conversation with Lee about the "job up North"; he would know. But he seemed confused when I asked him about it, which confirmed to me that Graham was lying AGAIN, he was a habitual liar.

"He has a motorbike, you know, Mum, he probably went out on that."

"Lee, are you sure? I didn't know he had a motorbike, in fact I didn't know he had even taken a bike test. Why would he lie to me about that, where does he keep it, how could he have a motorbike behind my back?"

But I knew my son wasn't lying – why would he lie to me about that! When Graham came home, I immediately questioned him about it.

"Fucking hell, here we go again, I'm sick of you questioning me all the time...No, I don't have a motorbike, I sometimes go to see Dave (an ex-employee) at Thirsk and ride his, and sometimes I just test ride them from the bike garage at Thirsk. Do you have a problem with that? Lee is a fucking LIAR, shit stirring!" he shouted.

OK, I thought, everything that comes out of his mouth is a complete LIE.

At work, he made Lee's life a misery, penalising him for 'shit stirring'.

February 11th, 2014, Jack's birthday, Graham used the excuse that he was working away AGAIN so stayed out all night. The next day I dared to question him again. He was raging that I had the audacity to ask where he had been.

"I've been out shagging, OK, now you know, I've been out shagging," he repeated. "Well look at you, I've had the best of you when you were slim and gorgeous, now you are a fat, ugly minger who doesn't let people live their lives, always questioning me. Well remember, I'm an adult too and I won't be questioned by you" was his vulgar response. Then he stormed out of the house, slamming the door behind him. I later found out that he had stayed in a hotel with one of his slags.

I was emotionally drained, I had such low self-esteem, I was a mess. I would physically shake, my heart would pound out from my chest. I had always taken care of my appearance, I was 5'6, size 8/10, I always made an effort to wear make-up, and I had given birth to five children. I hardly even had the energy to cry at this point, not that that would help anyway.

Valentine's Day 2014, it was a Friday, my day off. I had been to see my dad, took him a cappuccino and cooked his evening meal for him to heat up in the microwave later, went home, did the usual cleaning, then I opened the mail – one letter was from my employer terminating my employment; it was only Christmas cover, and they had kept me on longer than they anticipated, so it was no surprise really, but I felt anxious about telling Graham. I needn't have been: he came home with a beautiful bouquet of roses, bottle of champagne and a valentine's card. I had cooked a lovely 3-course meal.

"Before we eat, I just want to tell you something, I got this letter today from work, terminating my employment," I explained.

"Don't worry, babe, it will be fine, you can always get another job. Let's just enjoy this lovely meal that you have cooked, everything is good, babe," he said reassuringly. Only now I know why he seemed so happy, almost smug...

As I was later to find out, he had embarked on not one, but two affairs – one was with a woman from Barclays Bank, and the other a woman from Knaresborough!

We had our holiday, but Graham seemed a bit distant. He spent a lot of time on his phone when we weren't skiing, he seemed distracted and very abrupt with me. I was starting to feel that it was a huge mistake giving him a second chance.

As the weeks went by, Graham became worse. He didn't physically harm me for fear of repeated arrest... No, this was far, far worse, this was horrendous mental abuse, by a narcissist who was hellbent on causing me as much pain and heartache as possible... What would my life be like now?

Wednesday 12th March 2014, I received a phone call from Graham saying that he was staying out again overnight.

"What AGAIN, this is becoming a regular thing. Where are you?" I said suspiciously.

"I'm not answerable to you, it's none of your business, I'm away tonight, that's all you need to know," he said in a monotone, almost smug voice.

Again another phone call 7th April. "I won't be home tonight, I have to go to Scotland to survey a big job, so probably won't be back for a few days," he told me matter of factly.

"OK, no worries." Then I hung up. I had decided that I would try not to punish myself, thinking that he was possibly having an affair, which I was now becoming certain of. I also didn't want to give him the pleasure of him knowing I was hurting. I just spent the time enjoying the kids, as this was now a monthly occurrence.

He arrived back on the 10th April, looking like the cat that got the cream; he was trying to be nice. He grabbed me. "I've missed you, babe, what have you been up to?" he said jollily, knowing that I couldn't get up to much.

"Working and looking after the kids – what do you think I've been doing?" I replied.

I had previously applied for a housekeeping job nearby, and was offered it within days of my application. It was for a really lovely family, husband, wife and three kids. I was so excited. They lived in a large, beautiful barn conversion and I immediately liked Ellen, she was bubbly and always smiling; she was naturally stunning, really tall and slim with amazing long shiny dark hair, beautiful white teeth; she looked like a supermodel. The kids were lovely, too, it was such a lovely atmosphere to work in. I did all the required housekeeping and really enjoyed it. I could lose myself while getting job satisfaction. I really enjoyed the relationship I had struck up with Ellen, she was literally the loveliest person anyone could meet. I would work three mornings a week and looked forward to every day working there. I worked there for approx 12 months, during which time, Ellen and I became good friends and still remain so today.

Spring 2014 I had an interview at the local comprehensive school. I didn't get the job I wanted, but was offered a job as an examination invigilator which I accepted. I really enjoyed working there and made friends with the staff there. They were all so lovely, especially Tracey, the exams officer. I also became friends with Jean. We had common ground in the fact that we had both lost a child – she had lost her son before I lost Lisa; we really hit it off., I loved my job. I could work around my housekeeping job which was perfect for me.

On the face of it home life was improving, Graham was more pleasant, although very preoccupied, and it was a nice easy-going next few months. We planned a holiday to Tenerife in November, which we were all looking forward to, and the summer was lovely. I just focused on the positives and concentrated on my jobs and the kids.

11th July 2014 Lee and Louise had a beautiful, perfect little baby boy, they were thrilled to bits. I for one couldn't wait to see him, I went into town and bought mountains of baby boy clothes. George and Marie were an excited uncle and aunty, there was only Graham, yes typically HE, who couldn't bear the lack of attention, wasn't really that excited! I couldn't believe I was a grandma, I was so happy for them, they were over the moon. He was named Ryan and just adorable, born just a year after their wedding he was the icing on the cake.

Chapter 21

Me and my sister never really saw eye to eye, but on September 6th, 2014, for reasons that escape my mind now, we became embroiled in a text argument. The messages became more and more aggressive as they went on, and near the end of our argument, Jane typed:

"Well did you know that Graham is having an affair with a friend of mine?"

"If this is true, you would name her, so I don't believe a word you say," I retaliated, but I didn't doubt her word at all; I knew in my heart she was telling the truth as this tied into everything he was doing and it was obvious he was cheating, but I knew she was lashing out to hurt me. I felt physically sick and immediately confronted Graham when he arrived home from work.

"Me and Jane have had a texting argument and she accused you of having an affair with a friend of hers," I said, visibly upset.

He burst out laughing loudly. "Oh, Alisha babe, that is hilarious, you two hate each other, she's only saying it to hurt you and cause trouble between us. Come on, you have to admit that it's laughable coming from her– if someone else had said that to you, then I would understand it if you believed them, but it's obvious she's lying. Anyway, who's this 'friend' of hers who I'm supposed to be having an affair with?" he said, still ridiculing the very idea that he was being accused of such a thing.

"I don't know, she didn't say."

"EXACTLY, that proves she is a lying bitch!" He hugged me and said convincingly, "Things are going along nicely, babe, don't let a thing like that spoil it."

My job at the school would finish after the exams so I was keeping my feelers out for a part-time job to fit around my job at Ellen's. While in the local jewellers having a battery fitted to my watch, the manager, Sue, and myself struck up a conversation, she asked where I worked, and mentioned that they were looking for part-time staff.

"Get your CV in, you will be perfect for this job, I will put in a good word for you," she said.

I loved jewellery and liked the idea of working in a jeweller's. This shop was one of two owned by the same company. "Oh, I'm not sure, I don't have any experience at all," I replied, but I did decide that there was no harm in taking my CV into the other jeweller's. I went into the shop with my CV in hand to see the then manager, Roger, a man in his 50s, big in stature, with dark hair and a gentle voice – he's worked there for years so I knew him slightly. "I was told by Sue, that you are looking for part-time staff, and I have brought my CV in for you to look at," I said while looking around at the bling thinking, yes I could see myself working here selling diamonds.

"Sorry, we are looking for full-time staff," he replied.

"Could I still leave my CV with you in case you're looking for part-time staff in the future?" I said, feeling disappointed. I immediately went over to Sue. "Thank you, Sue, for letting me know there is a job going, but Roger said it was only full-time, and I have other commitments, so couldn't work here full-time."

"I'm going to phone Rachael, the owner, and talk to her about it, I think you would be perfect for the job and I'm sure they would be interested in you even if it is part-time, leave it with me," she said, slightly frustrated.

"OK, thanks, I really appreciate that." And I left it in their hands.

Our holiday soon came round and we were looking forward to our break.

The day before our flight, I was sat in the hairdresser's getting my hair done, when I received a phone call from an unfamiliar number. I hardly got hello from my mouth, when I heard Sue: "Hi hun, just calling to let you know that you have got the job here and the hours you want, I'm so pleased," she said excitedly.

"Oh thank you, that has made my day, I'm so happy, I can't wait to start. I'm going away tomorrow but will be back on 5th November and could start on the following day."

"Great, hun, looking forward to working with you, see you next week."

I was so delighted with this news, after the hairdresser's, I quickly called to the florist and bought Sue a bouquet of flowers as a thank you for the high recommendation she had put forward for me. I called in with the flowers and I just knew that we would enjoy working together and Sue felt exactly the same.

I picked George and Marie up from school and told them on the way home, they were pleased for me, they could see how happy I was. They were already excited about the holiday, and it was a bonus that I had landed this job.

Dinner on the table, Graham arrived home. "Hi, how's you, babe, you look happy?" he said, looking like the cat that got the cream; although he seemed very distracted, he was happy.

"Yes, I'm good, I had a phone call from the jeweller's today offering me a part-time job, so I'm really happy.

"Oh, that's great news, babe, well done," he replied almost disinterested and a little peeved about it, yet trying not to show it. "Anyway, are we all looking forward to our holiday tomorrow?" he diverted the conversation.

"Yeeeeees!" shouted the kids in unison.

I noticed that Graham was glued to his phone most of the evening in between him nipping out in a rush a couple of times. But obviously he had his mistresses to keep sweet. He had also been a busy, busy boy, as I later would discover: he was buying a house, a four-bed detached house on a very desirable estate, literally around the corner from where we lived, he had paid £88,000 deposit and got the remaining funds from a buy to let mortgage lender. He would always plead poverty to me and say we couldn't afford anything – now I know why: he was funding his secret, double life!

Looking back now, I'm surprised that he could fit in a holiday with his family while juggling two affairs and casual sex with prostitutes and wherever else he could find it, riding his motorbike, buying properties, cars, and jet skis, going to the casinos in Leeds, hiding large amounts of money in accounts in George and Marie's name, taking his girlfriends for days out and hotel breaks away, buying one of his whores a Mini, advertising and interviewing tenants for his secret house, appointments with solicitors to make his will out, going around to his hairdresser, cousin, accountant and his manager to ask them to be executors and power of attorneys...

He must have been exhausted.

Jack and Lee are to have ABSOLUTELY NOTHING, they have caused me nothing but grief. Alisha can work in the family business drawing a minimum wage that my accountant and my manager see fit, the profit from the business to be split between Alisha, my manager and George and Marie. All rental income and properties, stock and shares and all investments and everything else to be given to George and Marie.

This was a section in his will, which I would have the pleasure of reading a few years later.

There are no words in the dictionary to describe such a lowlife, evil scumbag, he didn't deserve to have such fantastic kids and a devoted wife, he leaves a mass of destruction behind wherever he goes.

The day of our holiday arrived, the plane landed, the sun was shining, it was 30 degrees, and we soon arrived at our very impressive, gorgeous 5* luxury hotel. The holiday was lovely. We mainly chilled around the pool while George and Marie went to the kids clubs, and one day we did our usual excursion to Siam Water Park. We had gone there many times before, and enjoyed all the rides, but I had never done the Tower of Power before, the 28 metre high water slide which was a vertical drop. It looked terrifying, as the ride comes to an end to pass through a glass tunnel with sharks swimming around. I had intended to do it this time, but couldn't pluck up the courage. George and Marie were keen to go on it but were too small. "Next time we come, when you are tall enough, we will all do the ride," I said to them both. "I bet you don't do it, Mum, you will be too scared," George teased. "Wait and see, I might just shock you," I said, knowing that George was probably right.

We arrived home, back to reality and almost immediately, Graham went to "work" – well he told me he was at work, when the fact was, he was hardly ever there, Wednesday and Saturday were the usual days he spent with one of his 'girlfriends', Gill, and when I eventually knocked on her door, I was shocked to see a woman who looked to be in her late 60s, frail and scruffy with blonde scraped back hair, no make-up on and had a shaky, quiet voice – surely this couldn't be right, and if I didn't have the evidence and voice recordings which I would later gather, then I wouldn't believe this 'old' woman and Graham were having an affair; this would be where Graham kept not one, but two of his motorbikes in her garage, verified by her then neighbour.

On 6th November 2014 I started my new job at the jeweller's. I already knew Chloe, who had a daughter in the same class as Marie, so we had chatted before at the school gates, she was so lovely and friendly and I was looking forward to working with her and Sue in both of the jewellers'. Chloe had lovely long hair which was caramel blonde at the time, and I nicknamed her Rapunzel – it was a term of endearment as we became really close friends.

I loved my job, and made many friends through it, working between the two jewellers' and one of our other shops in Thirsk, which I covered, gave me the variety that I liked.

Sue and I had a great working relationship and had many laughs together.

This job has really helped me build my confidence.

It was an escape for me. I was still spending lots of time with my dad when the carers weren't there and even when they *were* there sometimes; they were all really nice and loved my dad because he was always happy and laughing.

Graham didn't like him coming to our house, for fear Alzheimer's might be contagious!

I just put all my efforts into the kids, my new job and my dad, which took up most of my time. This must have been ideal for Graham – he was coming home to a cooked meal, clean house, food in the cupboard, laundry done, lawn cut, wow he must have been laughing his head off while he was swanning around in his brand new Audi A5, living his double life, having the best of both worlds. This explains why we never went out to local bars and restaurants, for fear I would be told or find out about what he was doing behind my back – if we ever went out it would always be at least 25 miles away, into York, or Leeds, and that was a rarity; it all made perfect sense now.

Chapter 22

Within a few weeks, we had booked our ski holiday to Sol in Austria, for February 2016, and Graham announced one night that he had acquired VIP tickets to see Beyoncé in London on 2nd July 2016. We had lots to look forward to and, as always, I hoped that things would improve between us, we were all so excited to see Beyoncé.

My dad was deteriorating but had lots of support around him. However, in early February, a few days before our holiday, I got a phone call at work – my dad had had a stroke and was taken to Harrogate hospital. Roger the manager was very understanding and gave me the day off to go and see him, so I immediately collected his essential belongings from his house and went to the hospital to see him. When I arrived I was taken into a room to discuss my dad.

"He's had a massive bleed on his brain and coupled with his advanced Alzheimer's, it doesn't look good. He's coming in and out of consciousness and it's likely that he will not regain full consciousness, and if he does, his quality of life will be extremely poor," the doctor explained.

I was devastated. I went to sit with my dad and held his hand. "Don't worry, Dad, it will be okay, I love you," I said, tears streaming down my face. He squeezed my hand tightly and put his other hand up to his head; it was heart-breaking to see him like this. I visited him every day but there was no change in him. I had explained to the doctor that we had a holiday due within days and that I would cancel it. He said that there was no point in doing that and I should go, that there was nothing I could do whether I was here or not. I discussed with Graham that I felt guilty going away while my dad lay ill in hospital and maybe we should cancel. This went down like a lead balloon.

"Anthony and Jane could always visit him, and he is in the right place. What could you do if you were there anyway?" he said.

"Well I would be with him if he dies."

"He won't even know you are there, babe, he's unconscious," Graham responded convincingly so I decided to go on the holiday and it was bitter-sweet. I felt guilty but didn't want to spoil it for the kids either. The holiday was lovely, apart from a tantrum from Graham over something so trivial, I can't even remember what it was about. I had rang the hospital daily for any updates, but there was no change until the day before we were due to fly home, I received the dreaded phone call from the hospital informing me that my dad had passed away in the night. I was absolutely devastated.

After returning home, I was busy dealing with the formalities of my dad's death. I took a few weeks off work until I felt strong enough to return. During the next few weeks there was so much to do. I had asked Graham if he would help me clear my dad's house out – "yes, I will get a couple of the lads to help out, why don't you call Jack and ask if he could help us too". This was music to my ears, as Graham and Jack hadn't really spoken much since our split in 2011. "It might help get me and Jack's relationship back on track," he continued.

I was just happy that Jack was to be part of our family again and hopefully Graham wouldn't mess it all up again. Jack was happy to help and brought his friend Matt to help also. When Jack arrived we were already at the bungalow. Graham came over to him and hugged him. They seemed happy to be amicable with each other. I was hopeful that this would be a way forward as a family again, and this did improve relations between us all; in fact, Graham had invited Jack out for meals with us as a family, and this is when Jack introduced us to his girlfriend

Rose. Everything was going along well.

Although I was grieving for my dad, I was happy at work and that Jack was back in our lives. Home life was good for the next few weeks at least until one Friday night in March, Graham had phoned me and asked if I could run him a bath for his return home from work. I ran him a hot bubble bath, lit all the candles around the bathroom, opened a nice bottle of rioja and poured out a large glass each. I had cooked a chicken and chorizo paella topped with mussels and king prawns, with a fresh warm French baguette – one of our favourite meals. I took his glass of wine and put it by his bath. He arrived home shortly in a very good mood. As he was getting into his lovely bath, which he thanked me for, I noticed he had been on the sunbed and looked like he had just come from the gym (which he vehemently denies to this day,) and that there were scratches on his back. I didn't acknowledge my observation to him.

"Bring your glass in here, babe, sit and have chat with me," he said lovingly. Our bathroom had two steps up to a sunken bath, so I would usually sit on them. Graham would always want me to sit and chat over a bottle of wine while he was bathing. This was purely for his own selfish reasons, but I humoured him. We just chatted about trivia, usually work and pigeons, but tonight he was talking about future plans, which very rarely materialised. He talked about progressing with our half renovated house, having a resin drive put down, completing the balconies from the rear bedrooms when they were ever going to be finished, buying a ski chalet in France where we would retire to... all lies just to keep me there for his own purpose because, without me, how could he live his double life? I had already been accustomed to the realisation that Graham had no intention of ever carrying out these flimsy, non-existent 'plans'; it was all just another sick game he played just to mess with my head. He would try and entice me into being all excited and fall for this farcical rubbish, but because there were never such plans, he would then say when we were arguing, "RIGHT, YOU

CAN FORGET ABOUT GETTING THE DRIVE BEING DONE" etc, knowing full well that it was never to be done anyway. I had been wise to this for a long time, but was now bored of living this pretence... so I would just agree in a monotone voice which irritated Graham immensely.

"Why are you being like that?" he asked.

Playing dumb, I responded, "Like what?"

"Like you are not interested."

Not wanting him to know that I had sussed out his mental abusive games, I just said that I was tired and that it was hard going through my dad's possessions which immediately prompted him to ask me for payment for helping me clear my dad's house out... Did I really hear this right? I might be deaf in one ear, but I could have sworn that I heard my *husband* ask me to pay him for helping me to clear out my, just deceased, dad's house.

"What, what did you say? I have to pay you to help me clear my dad's house out, is that right, is that what you are saying?" I asked in disbelief.

"YES, that's exactly what I'm saying. I brought two members of staff to help for half a day, I have to pay them for that, and my time is valuable, so I think it's only fair that you pay me. Stop being so fucking tight, Alisha, you will be getting some inheritance from your dad's will, so you can at least pay me for my time!"

I looked him straight in the eye and saw that this absolute nut job was deadly serious. It was the sheer fact that he couldn't bear the thought that I was to inherit a substantial amount of money from my dad, this made him feel more insecure, this could potentially mean that I could be in such a good financial position, that I might leave him. Well he couldn't have that so he would invent any excuse for me to spend my inheritance so that I would be once again financially dependent on him, and this was before I had even received my inheritance.

"I don't have any money to pay you with," I replied in shock. "I can't believe you are asking me for money, my dad has just died and all you can think about is money; this is unbelievable!" I screamed.

"No, Alisha, it's you who's unbelievable, you are GREEDY AND SELFISH, you're so tight just like your dad was – what did they call him 'the tightest Yorkshire man in Yorkshire'?" he sniggered...

"You are fucking vile, you absolutely disgust me!" I shouted as I left the bathroom with tears streaming down my face. I lay on my bed thinking about what had just happened. Graham had started to become more and more evil. I couldn't comprehend his mentality, but I soon started to think that this 'monster' had effectively been stopped from being physically abusive towards me, by the laws in place, so he now was more dangerous, calculated, deceitful, revengeful and secretive; but could my life actually get much worse, I thought. The answer to that was DEFINITELY! This would be the challenge that nearly killed me!

"Anyway, have you got the money you owe me?" Graham said with George at his heels.

"I don't have any money, like I said."

"Well you will have to sell your dad's guitars and musical instruments then, and your mum's dulcimers," he scoffed.

"I wanted to keep them as memorabilia, my dad loved his guitars, he would hate it if I sold them, it would break his heart. He even had one with an autograph on which he acquired in America and my mum loved plaything dulcimer, I can't just sell them," I retaliated.

"Well your dad is dead now, so he won't even know if you sell them or not. I want £500 to cover my costs, so you had better start advertising them or going to more car boot sales," he said with a grin across his face that I wanted to wipe off, preferably with a sledge hammer.

"Yeah, Dad is right, you should sell them instruments, they are no use to you, then at least you could pay Dad back what you owe him, you have more money than Dad, he has massive bills to pay and has no money," George said bravely, gaining lots of brownie points from his dad.

I decided not to reply; my heart broke so badly for George, he was Graham's little number one fan, he had no idea what damage his own 'father' was inflicting upon him, what long term damage he would suffer, and I was helpless. George was too far gone, he didn't know he was being groomed by the one person who was supposed to protect and look after him.

The situation at home became much more intense. Graham was adamant that he would finally alienate George and Marie from me, our 'family' became divided. 'DIVIDE AND CONQUER' was Graham's motto, 'STRENGTH IN NUMBERS' he would constantly say, so this was his mission: to deny me a relationship with my beautiful kids. He had already made George his no. 1, giving him priority over me, even defending him when he was abusing me, calling me a bad mother, a nag. He would say, after I would ask George nicely to tidy his room, "Fucking hell, Alisha, leave the lad alone, you are always nagging him, *you* tidy his room if it bothers you that much!" He would say this in front of George, completely undermining me.

This obviously gave George the green light to verbally abuse me without consequences. "Yeah, Mum, you tidy my fucking room if it bothers you that much," he would repeat.

I was in a hopeless position and didn't even defend my request. Graham looked over at George, and they might as well have given each other a high five, looking at their faces. This was a losing battle against a narcissistic, manipulative, evil control freak. This would be the start of much more horrendous abuse by Graham's little 'gang'.

One night while in Graham's bedroom, he asked me if I could shave his hairy back, which was a regular occurrence. I agreed, as I normally did. There were still obvious scratches on his back, but I ignored this and continued to shave him.

"Oh babe, do it with some tender loving care, put some emotion into it," he said in a pathetic voice.

Why he said such things, when he was clearly being groomed for his whores, leaves me in disbelief. I never ever mentioned the claw marks down his back. We did resume our intimacy for a while, but this would only prove to me that he was definitely a massive cheat, as he would make comparisons about my physical body, albeit flattering …but it was like he was hinting to me that he was cheating!

I managed to sell my dad's guitars and banjos to a private seller and raised the money that Graham had demanded from me, so one day in April a few weeks after my dad's death, I handed Graham a cheque for £500.00, which he cashed on 13th June 2016. Graham was still emotionally abusing me, but in a much more subtle way. He seemed to be a lot happier in himself, he was attending lots of exhibitions for 'work' in London and Birmingham, which would entail him being away for 3-4 days at a time. He would phone me at approx 8pm most evenings he was away. "Hi babe is everything OK?" he would ask.

"Yes fine, how was your day?"

"Oh busy, busy, busy, babe, put the kids on the phone, I haven't eaten yet and need to go. I'm absolutely knackered, I need an early night."

Well it must be hard work entertaining young 'promo' girls every night... He would spend a couple of minutes saying goodnight to George and Marie, then hang up and proceed to indulge in partying, clubbing and having casual sex with whoever he could find (his sense of grandiose and his vanity was so insanely inflated) ... HE would book 'promotional girls' to be on his exhibition stand, then later go clubbing with them. This all came to light when he accidentally sent me a photo of him with a couple of girls sat on his knee in a crowded club. He looked old enough to be their father; it turned my stomach. This was a middle aged, balding married man with kids who were probably older than the girls Graham was shagging, but I did intend to confront him about it when he returned home. Meanwhile it was me and the kids just chilling out at home. It was a nice relief not to have the tense atmosphere in the house and the drama from Graham.

A few days later when Graham arrived home, he looked so tired like he hadn't slept in weeks; he looked old and drained. I decided I wouldn't bring up the photo he sent to me, I couldn't bear the confrontation.

The one good thing was that we had become closer to Jack and Rose, frequently going out with them for meals. They would come and stay with us occasionally, and we talked about booking a cottage in the Lake District for January 2017 for a weekend break, which I was really looking forward to.

The next few months were a confusing and contradictory barrage of 'love bombing' and sick mental torture. His mood swings were up and down by the day – he could switch from being in a demonic rage over the most trivial issue, then turn into Mr Charming the next.

He would hide things from me then say I must have dementia because I couldn't locate them. "What are you looking for, babe?" Graham would say as if he was concerned.

"My phone, I could've sworn it was just here a minute ago," I said, confused. Did I have dementia? After all, my dad had Alzheimer's, so it was possible. I would search and search in places where I would normally leave it, but it was nowhere to be found. When I asked Graham to ring it, he brushed it off saying it would turn up somewhere and went on to 'sympathise' with my 'non-existent' dementia.

"Babe, listen, I really think you need to go to the doctor's, you are always forgetting things and you get confused. I think you are mentally unstable. I've noticed it for a while. You are so paranoid and question me all the time like you don't trust me. I actually think you're fucked up in the head, you definitely need help, babe for all our sakes," he said softly but patronisingly, leaving me doubting my sanity.

Then, as my back was turned, he would suddenly find my phone. "Here's your phone, babe," holding it up with a satisfied grin on his face.

"Where was it? I looked everywhere and couldn't find it."

"It was just here on the window sill, I'm really worried about you, I think you need help?" he coaxed.

I was starting to think that I was cracking up, so I would really try and make an effort to be more methodical and meticulous in future.

January 6th, 2017 we set off to Cockermouth for our weekend away with Jack and Rose. We had booked a beautiful large house with a games room, lovely views and next door to a village pub. We were looking forward to it. Graham had bought himself a new phone and said he would take it along and set it up when we arrived. I had packed food and wine etc. I also bought soft drinks for Rose as she was five months pregnant. It was approx 6pm when we arrived, so immediately we put some pizzas in the oven and the beers in the fridge, and after we explored the house, we all sat in front of the log fire, all very relaxed and civilised. George and Marie went to play snooker in the games room while listening to the entertainment system. Graham sat on a chair while me, Jack and Rose sat on the very large sofa just chatting. Graham was unpacking his new phone and had started to set it up; meanwhile, the beers were flowing. I had noticed that Graham was very detached from us, busy with his phone. I was thinking how rude he was being, hardly joining in with our conversation, so I offered to help him with setting up his phone.

"NO, NO, it's fine, I'm quite capable of setting up my phone, thank you," he snapped. Only a couple of minutes later, George came in to sit with us, and Graham immediately beckoned him to help him set up his phone. It was obvious that he didn't want me to see his phone as he held it away from my view, then the whispering started between them. I chose to ignore them and continued talking to Jack and Rose. She then decided to go up to bed, leaving me, Jack, Graham and the kids.

Graham was being his usual immature self. "I bet Mum wants to know my password," he said sniggering to George while looking at me.

I just carried on talking to Jack, we just chatted, ignoring Graham. He always treated his phone like the crown jewels, so it was no surprise that I would never see it. Me and Jack continued to chat and drink until late while everyone else slept. I really enjoyed Jack's company, it was just lovely to spend the time alone with him.

The next morning we all decided to have a drive into Keswick. It was a cold day but bright and sunny. Jack and Rose decided to follow and meet us there, so we arrived in Keswick, found a lovely lakeside restaurant and while sitting out on the terrace drinking our hot chocolates, Graham was being lovely to me. "Oh, babe, doesn't time fly, we've had our ups and downs but we are still together and you still look amazing, we have had some fantastic times and done really well. I know I get angry at times and lash out, but it's only because of stress at work. I love you and the kids to bits, you know that, don't you? I just feel sad, George and Marie are growing up so fast, it makes me realise that we are getting old, babe," he said, with tears in his eyes... Now I was confused – was I a fat, ugly, lazy minger, or the amazing wife?

We walked alongside the lake; it was lovely walking hand in hand along the pebble lakeside.

"Babe, stand against that tree, I want to take some photos of you, you look so lovely," he said.

I had now just learned to accept things as they were, I enjoyed these moments just as much as I hated the horrific times. He took multiple photos, of just me, then me and Marie, then family selfie ones, and while enjoying our family walk, my mind cast back to Jack and Rose. I mentioned to Graham about catching up with them, but he dismissed it saying let them do their own thing, this is nice just us four, I'm enjoying it. We found a little a lovely little cafe and had lunch, then decided to return to the house and it wasn't long before Jack and Rose turned up. We lit the fire, all played snooker and listened to music in the games room. There were many board games to play, and I spotted Scrabble so suggested that while whoever was waiting their turn to play snooker, we could play. Graham was very illiterate and inarticulate, and we had many arguments at home when he would have a tantrum when I wouldn't allow words which he couldn't spell, so not the ideal game for him.

Jack and George had had a £10 bet on a football match earlier that day, and when the results went in George's favour, he excitedly shouted, "Yes, I won, you owe me £10, Jack."

"OK, OK, I will give you it later," he said.

Graham, as usual, chipped in with "he won't give you the money, George, he's too tight, you shouldn't bet with him". It was so typical of him to stir things up and interfere in things that were really none of his business.

"NO! Give me the fucking tenner now!" George shouted to Jack, knowing that he had Graham's full support...

"I beg your pardon, how dare you speak to me like that! You are so disrespectful and I see you be disregardful to Mum too, it's disgusting, George. I said I would give you the £10 later, but after that outburst, I'm not giving you it now, and I don't agree that you don't get reprimanded for such appalling behaviour, you should not get away with talking to people in that manner," said Jack. He looked at Graham. "You never pull him up on his terrible behaviour, he needs disciplining, if me, Lee or Lisa behaved like that, you would hit us. I'm not condoning that, I'm just saying that George has no boundaries, he's aggressive and rude and you as a parent should tell him that he can't behave like that."

"That's up to me!" Graham replied.

"Well I think that George owes Jack an apology, he was completely out of order reacting like that, and Jack did say he would pay him initially," I said, agreeing with Jack.

"Oh come on, he's just a kid, who was upset because Jack wouldn't give him the £10 that he owed him." As usual Graham had completely turned all this around to blame Jack. George was soon to be 14, he was a teenager, not a young kid.

Jack and Rose retreated to the games room to listen to music. I went in to see them and apologised on George's behalf.

"You shouldn't have to apologise, Mum," Jack said.

Things had calmed down, but I felt embarrassed and disappointed about what had just happened.

"Alisha, me and the kids are going out for a walk, are you coming?" Graham said after everything had calmed down. I needed some air so I agreed to go with them. We called into the pub next door for a drink before our walk, and the conversation soon turned around to the betting incident. Leaving the pub to set off for our walk, I didn't really want to discuss it anymore, so I tried to divert the chat to our lovely day out yesterday, but the conversation started again.

"Jack was out of order, he should have given you the £10 straight away then none of this would have happened," Graham said to George.

"I agree, but George shouldn't've reacted like that, it was bound to get heated when George was so abrupt," I chipped in.

"It's okay because I got my own back on him," George replied, laughing and Graham started to laugh.

"Oh George, what have you done?"

"I poured a jug full of water in their bed."

Graham and George found this highly amusing, sniggering like two little kids.

"I hope this is a joke. Rose is five months pregnant, you better not have done that," I said feeling panicky about what would kick off. This was supposed to be a lovely weekend with no drama!

"Come on, Alisha, it's only a bit of mischief, the lad is upset that Jack didn't give him the money he owed him; that's what kids do. Did you never do anything mischievous when you were younger, Miss goody two shoes? For fuck's sake, it's just a bit of water, it will dry" was Graham's flimsy reply.

When we arrived back at the house, we were understandably greeted by a very angry Jack. "George, why the hell have you poured water all over our bed? Rose is pregnant, I'm fuming!" he said.

"Hey, hey, calm down, it was just a stupid prank and he was upset that you didn't pay him and rightly so," said Graham.

"Oh yes, defend George as always. How would you feel if he poured water in your bed? I bet you wouldn't be so forgiving then. George gets away with everything because you let him, he needs to learn to be respectful. Rose is pregnant!"

He left the room to go and console Rose, and I followed and apologised to them both. Rose was surprisingly forgiving, excusing it as mischief.

Graham was angry that I had apologised to them and decided to sleep with the kids that night and give me the silent treatment – which I was used to by now.

The next morning we left early. Graham ushered George and Marie quickly into the car without letting them say goodbye, Graham completely ignored the others, while I said my goodbyes. This was yet another example of Graham's arrogant, vile behaviour.

Graham and Jack didn't have much contact after that.

Chapter 23

January 21st 2017, it was now time for the Blackpool pigeon show, which Graham would attend annually, and this year George would go with him. It is a two-day show, but Graham was adamant that they would be just going on the Saturday and would be back in the evening.

"Right, me and George are off, we will be back around 7pm. Do you fancy cooking a nice curry tonight and get the kids some treats and us some wine and have a cosy night in, maybe watch a good film on Netflix?" he said to me.

"Sounds good, great, I will have it ready for about 7.30-8.00pm. See you later, have a good day."

Marie and I spent the day just being together doing girlie things. The phone rang at 6pm.

"There are some pigeons I want to buy, but they are not here today. They will be here tomorrow, so we might as well try and book into a bed and breakfast tonight and come back tomorrow night. Did you make that curry? I was really looking forward to it, sorry, babe, we can have it tomorrow night instead," he said.

Well there was no point in questioning a narcissistic pathological LIAR, but I knew he was lying. EVERYTHING that came out of his mouth was a complete lie, so I decided to check his pockets and lo and behold there was an A4 sheet of paper ripped up in his jeans pocket. I pieced it together to reveal that it was a booking.com confirmation letter detailing the 5* hotel in Blackpool which was booked three weeks earlier!

This was becoming normal. It seemed like he was incapable of being honest, though I was confused as to why he had ripped the evidence up, yet left it in his pocket – did he want me to see it? Did he forget that it was in his pocket? Why tear it up? Why did he not put it in the rubbish bin if he really wanted to keep this a secret from me? Answers only that pathetic excuse for a man would know. My mind was working overtime now. I sat thinking about all the other lies he had told me, all the things he had said in one of his rages... My heart began to race, I felt sick. What is this monster capable of? It was so scary living with that unpredictability, no trust and no remorse or empathy, and to question him would send him into the most horrendous rage, his eyes bulging and fists in the air, screaming at the top of his voice, the most disgusting abusive language imaginable, but I couldn't help myself to question him, when I knew he was lying. I wanted him to know that I knew he was lying, even though most of the time it wasn't worth it.

When they finally arrived home, I asked, "Did you get the pigeon that you wanted then?"

"Yes, it was good, wasn't it, George, we got talking to other fanciers and saw lots of people we knew, it was a good crack. Do you fancy putting the kettle on, babe, I'm knackered," he replied.

I duly went to put on the kettle while wondering how to approach this. The tea was made and I took it in to the living room and handed Graham his mug. He looked contented, almost excited while discussing the weekend events with George. Should I approach this, and if so, how?

"Was it busy?" I asked.

"Yes, there were loads of people there, it was good."

"I'm surprised you managed to get a B&B at such short notice, they are usually rammed," I said, looking at his expression intensely.

With a stupid smirk on his face, as if he was being clever, he replied, "Oh yes, they were nearly all full, but we managed to find a little B&B

a bit further out than we wanted, but it was cheap and cheerful, wasn't it, George?"

"Yes, it was alright," he confirmed.

They then both carried on discussing the weekend. I had left the pieced-together booking form on Graham's bed and patiently waited for him to go into his room, which he did after his cuppa. I quickly followed him to show him my find.

"So what's this hotel booking that was booked weeks ago doing torn up in your jeans pocket? Why lie to me, and even worse, make OUR son lie to ME, his mum; and to tell me you were coming home and ask me to cook a curry for tea, knowing you were not coming home, is unbelievable!" I dared to question, but surprisingly to me, he did actually let me finish my question which was a very rare occurrence, especially if I called him out he would shout me down all the time.

"We didn't tell you because you didn't need to know, remember? I'm an adult and can do what I like. So what, we booked a hotel, what's the big issue, there's nothing wrong with that, is there? You don't need to know EVERYTHING. Why do you always have to make a mountain out of a mole hill? It's trivial," he said with a sly grin across his face while trying to justify his lie. "And anyway, what gives you the right to search my pockets? How would you feel if I was to go through all your pockets?"

"Feel free, I don't have anything to hide, I don't have secrets like you!" I retaliated.

Graham wasn't as angry as I thought, and I felt uneasy that he didn't fly off the handle like he usually did, it wasn't *normal* behaviour from him. We did actually have the curry and wine that evening, and I was just grateful that he didn't get extremely angry.

I needed to be more observant and aware of him. All the trust had gone a few years ago when he'd shouted "I'M SHAGGING TEENA, I'VE SHIT ON YOU BIG TIME" – even after he desperately tried to retract it, the words wouldn't leave my head, but I had no strength or energy to do anything about it.

Chapter 24

March 2017 I had received my inheritance from my dad, so I decided to invest it into a property, I bought a nice car first, then went property hunting and found a lovely 3-bed house in Northallerton, which I intended to rent out. I put in an offer far lower than the asking price and on 10th April 2017 the offer was accepted and completed in June. Once I had the keys, I spent a few weeks renovating it ready for the rental market and within a couple of weeks I had tenants in.

This house would become my 'GOLDEN TICKET' to freedom, a new life away from abuse, this house would allow me to divorce Graham – but not yet, I wasn't ready yet, I had to be mentally strong. So for now it would be rented out. My dad effectively helped me get a divorce, which he would have been ecstatic about.

Graham would constantly tell George and Marie, that he had bought a four-bed detached house not far away, and that they would all leave me to go and live there, promising them the world. "But whatever you do, DO NOT tell Mum," he made them promise. I was oblivious to all the lies he was telling them, but "DON'T TELL MUM" was now imprinted on their brains and he had normalised keeping secrets from me. It was his way of controlling and grooming them while punishing me at the same time. This all amounts to child abuse by making me the common enemy, but in a way that it's almost acceptable to them.

May 2017 Jack and Rose announced the safe arrival of their newborn baby boy, Harry. I couldn't wait to visit them in hospital, so went to Harrogate hospital just hours after his birth. He was a beautiful, healthy little boy, I was completely in love with this little boy. I was now the proud grandma of two gorgeous boys, Ryan and Harry, I was so happy. Jack now had his own perfect little family and I couldn't be happier for them.

Graham seemed unconcerned about this new addition, his newborn grandson, and had even convinced George and Marie not to show much excitement towards this amazing news.

After I had arrived home excitedly describing this little nephew to George and Marie, Graham butted in...

"Oh God, I hope you are not going to be one of these sad grandmothers who wants to look after the grandchildren all the time, I see them pushing pushchairs around town, and I just think how sad they are...

Graham has no concept of the important things in life – after all, he spent his life destroying family bonds and relationships and this was yet another one of his cruel, sick games to cause further pain, division and control. I made it clear that I love my grandchildren and would be ecstatic to be pushing them around in their pushchairs, but he was determined to make that almost impossible for me because he would be extremely jealous that they were more important to me than he was, and that is so true: EVERYONE is more important to me than him and that's entirely his own doing.

18th June 2017 Father's Day

The previous day, I had asked Graham if he could help me with a little job at the house in Northallerton. I just needed an internal door easing. "Yes, no problem," he agreed.

"I know it's Father's Day, but it won't take you long at the house, then we can go out afterwards, then a carvery later on," I explained.

"Yes, that sounds fine to me," he agreed.

"Morning Dad, happy Father's Day," George and Marie said excitedly walking precariously into the living room with a tray of breakfast and presents. They were more excited than Graham.

"Open your presents, Dad," they said, handing them over to him.

"Awwwww thanks, kids, this is lovely, thank you." He hugged them both then opened his gifts of smellies and other items which escape my memory...

"Mum has booked a meal for us later at the carvery pub you like, Dad" they said. George and Marie were just such lovely, kind, thoughtful kids, I was just so proud and full of love for my gorgeous kids.

"Shall I make us another cuppa before we head to Northallerton, Graham?" I asked.

"Yes, we will have a cuppa, but I've changed my mind about going to Northallerton, I need to spend the day sorting my pigeons out ready for the racing, I need to get them down the road. I will try and do it next weekend," he said calmly...

Just typical of our whole life, he had absolutely no intentions of helping me, this was just yet another empty promise like everything else he would agree to do then pull the rug from underneath it.

"Oh, I really need this doing before I can let it out. Please can you do it today, it won't take long, Graham, we will be back in a couple of hours then you will have the rest of the day with your pigeons," I pleaded.

"It's Father's Day, Alisha, I want to spend the day with the pigeons, I will do it another day...stop making issues!" he snapped.

I was so disappointed and couldn't hide it.

"RIGHT, let's go then, seeing as you are so insistent."

I was so relieved. We set off in the van soon after, but it was a very uncomfortable, silent 30-minute drive, apart from me thanking him for doing this for us, not ME, but US.

We arrived and as I got out of the van to walk to the house, I heard Graham swearing: "For fuck's sake, I have better things than this to do on Father's Day."

Then he started throwing his tools into a bag like a petulant child, then followed me into the house. I was being as helpful as I could to make this less painful for Graham. He unhinged the door and started to plane it then proceeded to scream demands at me. "GO GET THE JIGSAW FROM THE VAN."

Well, this had been brewing since I dared to ask for his help. I did go into the van but while stood looking around for the jigsaw I started to feel extremely angry at being shouted at for no reason, and at this point refused to allow myself to be treated like this so I retaliated, went back into the house and decided to return the favour and scream back at him: "I CAN'T FIND IT!!!"

Well, this was just enough to send him into the most violent rage. "RIGHT, THAT'S IT, I'M FUCKING SICK OF YOU, I'VE HAD ENOUGH OF THIS SHIT, I'M OFF!" he screamed while throwing his tools into his bag, some of them narrowly missing my head, and with no regard for the neighbours.

"GET IN THE VAN NOW OR YOU CAN WALK HOME!" he shouted for the neighbourhood to hear.

He drove like a total maniac. "Calm down, Graham, you will have a crash! What's your problem?" I said.

"YOU ARE MY FUCKING PROBLEM, ALISHA, YOU!" He carried on shouting obscenities at me and divorce was mentioned, the same old shit came rolling off his tongue, he hates me, the kids hate me, no wonder Lisa killed herself and he went on and on and on.

"Yes, let's get a divorce, I fucking hate you, you are one nasty piece of shit..." I dared to retaliate.

The van came to a sudden stop, forcing my body to shoot forward then back on my seat.

"GET OUT, GET OUT OF THIS VAN NOW!" he screamed, his face bright red, eyes bulging and spraying saliva in my face as he shouted at me.

"No, Graham, NO, please don't do this, I won't be able to get home, please don't leave me here," I said, tears spilling from my eyes. "I won't speak, I promise, I won't say another word."

He seemed to soften then and carried on driving, but he drove the rest of the way home in anger. This person was far from normal, he has huge anger issues, he was incapable of reasoning and being respectful, he didn't have the intelligence to have a disagreement without resorting to violence and was impossible to have a normal conversation with. My thoughts the whole journey home were purely on planning my escape without him guessing.

We were soon home and the minute he saw George and Marie, he typically began to reel off his poor, badly done-to Graham tales: "Mum has caused me so much stress today, she's ruined Father's Day…" Blah blah blah. He was determined to gain sympathy from them while turning them against me at the same time. I was totally helpless. Brainwashing his own children was a skill that he had practised his whole life and he was an expert at it. I could not possibly win against such evil.

It was during this month that Graham had been diagnosed with a leaky heart valve. When he broke the news with tears in his eyes, we were all upset and worried, but I never imagined that he would use this in a cruel and sadistic way to further his power and control.

"George and Marie, I love you so, so much." Tears now streaming down his face – by now we were all crying.

"You're not going to die, are you, Dad?" George asked. He was utterly distraught as was Marie by now. He made them believe that not only was he terminally ill and would possibly die, but that it was MY fault for causing HIM stress. This was perfect for him, getting support and sympathy from his kids, but also making them hate me for him being ill! Double whammy. Little did I know about any heart conditions, but one day not long after, an acquaintance of mine came in with her husband, both in their 70s. As we passed the time of day, it transpired that the husband had been diagnosed with the exact same thing, so I told him about Graham.

"Oh, he will be fine, he might not need surgery, but if he does, tell him from me, an old man, that it's a very common condition and he might just need a stent, which is a simple operation. I'm 75 and still fit as a butcher's dog after my op. Tell him not to worry. If it was a transplant or a bypass, then that's different," he said.

This was interesting and I was keen to research it, and not that I am belittling his diagnosis in any way at all, as any illness is worrying, but Graham was massively over exaggerating it. Any loving, normal, decent father would not inflict this unnecessary pain on their child, they would protect them and reassure them that it is not life threatening and successfully treatable, but NO, why would he when he can use this to his full advantage?

The next five months passed by relatively pleasant. I had become accustomed to living like this and accepted trying to enjoy the good times and trying to suppress the bad. I put my energy into work and tried hard to work out a way to undo the damage that Graham had caused to his own children, but the brainwashing done over many years had, I feared, manifested into Stockholm syndrome. I felt that George was completely lost to Graham's evil web; I was devastated and totally heartbroken seeing George under such an evil influence. Marie hadn't quite got that far yet, but she was scared of upsetting Graham so I had to be aware of how to avoid her being stressed around me while trying to strengthen the relationship between me and my baby girl, my only daughter.

Christmas was coming up, and I always made a big effort to make it special for the kids, but when I asked them what they wanted, George looked at me tearfully. "I don't care about Christmas, I just want Dad to be alright, I don't want him to die." Then Marie started to cry so I reassuringly explained to them that Dad had a minor heart condition which could be treated, and that the likelihood of him dying was virtually zero and not to worry too much and be positive.

"You're just saying that to make yourself feel better, because YOU caused Dad to be ill!" he accused. "Why would Dad tell us that he could die? It's all YOUR fault."

"Listen, George, I am NOT the cause of Dad's illness, lots of people get it, and let's be honest he's the one who causes all the stress anyway, he will be fine, OK?" I softly said to him. My heart was breaking seeing them so upset.

Over the next few days, George and Marie asked for specific presents, not realising how expensive they were, and I panicked as Graham insisted that I pay half of everything. I spoke to Graham about their Christmas lists and the cost.

"Just get them everything they want," he said. "I don't have nearly £1000." But maybe he would now put things in perspective and calm down, if he thinks stress will escalate his condition.

"Oh no, not this again, I'm sick of hearing you bleating on about you having no money. You have loads of money. I worked out exactly how much you are getting a month, so stop being so tight and get your hand in your pocket, and if you don't have it, then put it on your credit card; in fact put all of it on your credit card and I will pay half at the end of the month," he snapped.

There was absolutely no point in arguing as he would just use it against me to make me look bad.

I had already bought presents for Jack, Rose and Harry (that Graham refused to contribute to), and Graham and I had spent a quite a lot of money on him to lift him after his diagnosis – I got him an expensive watch, Doc Martens which he wanted, and men's perfume along with other little bits, so I was really feeling the pinch now and regretted spending so much on Graham.

I would later learn that Graham had received a massive inheritance payout from an old aunt of his, it must've slipped his mind to tell me, his wife of 35 years, that he had hundreds of thousands of pounds in his bank, yet we lived in a half built house with very few luxuries. This should not have been a shock to me as I already knew he was a habitual LIAR, GREEDY AND SELFISH BEYOND BELIEF.

Chapter 25

Christmas morning, the kids came down around 8am excited to open their presents, they were so happy; I just loved seeing them happy. While I was checking the dinner in the kitchen, Marie came running in all excited. "Mum come in the living room and see what Dad has bought you, it's really big," she said hardly containing herself. *Big*, I thought, didn't sound good to me, it was hardly jewellery or perfume. "Come on, Mum," she said. I went into the living room to see a large tall box. As I unwrapped it, I saw the word 'cleaner' on the box – oh that would be right, I thought, a cleaning item. Yes, it was a Dyson vacuum cleaner.

"Oh a household item," I said to Graham disappointedly.

"What's wrong? Don't you like it? I thought you would be dying to use it," he said.

"Yes, I do like it, but it's not exactly personal, is it. This is a household item that we need," I replied.

"Oh, I got you something else."

Marie gave it to me, she was so sweet, her little face beaming. "Dad got you this."

"Thank you, baby." I opened it and was pleased – it was a box of goodies from the body shop. I was easily pleased, but this was better than a bunch of flowers from the supermarket he usually bought me. I then opened my presents from Jack and Rose. They always got us lovely presents. "Are you going to open mine, Graham?" I said.

He began opening his Dr Martens and was over the moon with them. "Awww, babe, these are just what I wanted, thank you, I love these," he said happily. I needn't have bought him anything else. He began opening his other presents, and was really happy with the watch etc. "Babe, you have really spoilt me, thank you, I love them all," he gushed.

New Years Eve 2017

It was especially hard for me, this was Lisa's favourite big night out, she would pull out all the stops, even making her own costumes to wear. One year she made an amazing Christmas bunny outfit to go out in Blackpool, she looked stunning as usual. I had grown to hate new year since she died.

It was about 7pm, Graham and George were sat in their usual place together on the sofa against the wall so no-one could peak at their laptop and phones, it was all 'Top secret'. I was on the sofa opposite Marie. I had been staring into space reminiscing about the good times whilst screaming inside thinking about the bad times. I looked over at Graham and George who were in their secret little world, sniggering and whispering to each other. I looked over at Marie and she looked sad; this was a normal scene in our house. I remembered when George was born, I was so happy, but now he was coming up 15 and I felt like I had lost him to Graham's trap. I was so upset and couldn't hide it from Marie, tears streaming down my face as I sat in absolute silence. My baby girl daren't even speak to me in front of Graham...

I received a text message and looked down at my phone but couldn't read it for the tears in my eyes. I wiped my eyes to see...

"Love u happy new year
xxxxxx?????? be happy!
Shhhhhh??"

Thank you baby love you.
I am happy xxxxxxxx
I got you baby so am well happy
♥

Love U xxxxxxxxxxxx you seam sad
that makes me sad??

I'm not sad baby just tired lol
and dad not spending time with
us, always on his phone lol
xxxxxxxxxxxxx

well focusse on being happy
smile create new meamorys ??

I am happy and will create new
memories baby love you xxxxxxxxxxx

My heart was breaking. Graham and George were still on their devices while me and Marie watched the TV. I was exhausted and drained. It was now 10.30pm and I knew I couldn't stay awake any longer, so I bid them all happy new year and went to bed. Marie came in to see me shortly afterwards. "Are you not going to see the new year in with us?" she pleaded.

"Well how can I refuse you, baby, I love you so much, you know that, don't you?"

"I love you too, Mum" she said as we hugged each other tight; me and Marie were very close, but Graham was determined to break that bond, he needed to turn everyone against me so that I had no support at all.

We all saw the new year in together and it was really nice, but I could feel the resentment, the iciness and distance from Graham. This time it seemed much more sinister than it had been previously. I wondered if it was due to his diagnosis, but I felt now that something was very seriously wrong and felt terrified, my gut feeling was usually right. After a sleepless night, I got up and put the kettle on as normal.

"Make me a cup of tea, babe," Graham shouted from the living room.

I was so confused – was I paranoid, was I going crazy? I took him his cuppa. "Did you sleep okay?" I asked him tentatively.

He hesitated as if thinking about his answer, or distracted by other thoughts. "Mmm yes, did you?" he said with a very vacant look on his face.

It wasn't long before his attention turned back to his phone. I could tell that he was typing but when I asked him he told me that he was deleting old photos – yet more and more LIES. I left it about half an hour, but he was still glued to his phone. I went on my phone and opened up WhatsApp to see that Graham was online. I didn't say anything at first, I just kept checking his WhatsApp – he had already blocked me from his Facebook, the business Facebook, Twitter and LinkedIn so I was surprised to see he was on WhatsApp, and 15 minutes later he was still on WhatsApp.

"It's taking a long time to delete a few photos?" I quizzed him.

"Yes I know, I have loads of photos to sort out," he replied.

"Why don't you do it later, it's New Year's Day, let's have a day off our phones."

"No, I'm in the middle of doing it now, so I might as well carry on." I checked my WhatsApp again and Graham was ONLINE! ... "Can I ask you a question?" This was like a red rag to bull, a very angry bull – how dare ANYONE question the very important, special, almighty Graham who is NEVER wrong, NEVER accountable and NEVER should be questioned!

"What?" he said, already raring to burst into a full blown demonic rage. I knew that his response would be extremely aggressive, but I couldn't help myself. NARCISSISTS do NOT take kindly to be exposed or called out...

"Do you have WhatsApp?" I said.

"NO, I told you I never use it. It might be on my phone but I don't know because I DON'T use it. You know that I'm rubbish with technology. I just use normal text messages or Messenger, anyway why? Why are you asking about that?" he snapped.

"Well I went on my WhatsApp and pressed you and it displayed that you were ONLINE..."

"RIGHT, THAT'S IT, I'M NOT LIVING LIKE THIS ANYMORE WITH A WIFE WHO DOESN'T TRUST ME AND QUESTIONS EVERYTHING I DO, I'M NOT FILLING A TIME SHEET IN. YOU ARE SO PARANOID AND JEALOUS, YOU ARE MENTAL, I'M SICK OF YOU NEVER BELIEVING ME. WELL WE'VE ALL HAD ENOUGH OF YOU, WE ARE SICK TO DEATH OF LIVING WITH SUCH A GREEDY, SELFISH, FAT UGLY MINGER. WE HAVE ALREADY TALKED ABOUT IT, AND WE ARE GOING TO LEAVE YOU!" he screamed at the top of his voice for the whole street to hear while he was exiting the door. "George, Marie, get ready, get your stuff, we are leaving; she's a fucking nutter. No wonder I have a heart condition, it's living with her that's caused it, she's fucking paranoid. Come on, we aren't living like this anymore, she needs to crawl under a stone and DIE. She's making me worse – what sort of wife causes unnecessary stress knowing that it will KILL me?" he shouted to the kids.

"Come on, please don't do this to me, don't take the kids, please Graham," I cried, distraught. "Why are you doing this, PLEASE DON'T do this, I only asked you a question, this is ridiculous," I cried as George and Marie brushed past me. "George, Marie, please don't go with him, I love you both so much," I begged, but they were far too scared to disobey Graham.

I followed them onto the driveway crying and shouting. I had no idea where they were going, I just knew that I couldn't bear the pain of losing my two babies – how can he be so cruel? They were being used purely to empower himself, they didn't decide to leave their mum, he made all the decisions for them. I grabbed the door handle of the car to try and reason with him. Graham quickly slammed his door then locked it from the inside and sped off with my two babies in the car. I fell to the floor in despair, trying to make sense of what had just happened; this was mental torture. I started to scream and cry hysterically on my knees on the drive, and one of the neighbours came out to see if I was okay. I felt so embarrassed, I couldn't tell anyone for fear of Graham finding out. She said she was about to call the police. "NO, NO, don't call the police," I begged. I needed to be alone, I picked my sorry self up and went inside. I curled up on my bed in the foetal position and howled like a wild animal.

This was the start of 2018 and it would only get worse. What's the point of my life? I couldn't cope any longer, the torment, the abuse and Graham's rages had turned me into a complete nervous wreck. Should I just end it all now, this was too much to bear? I had already gone through the most horrific pain losing Lisa, how much more pain could I endure? My thoughts were racing – there are lots of tablets in the house, maybe I could just down them all with a bottle of wine; that would be easy and I would be finally free from pain... while I was contemplating my *escape* thinking of being with my Angel Lisa, then suddenly, I heard Lisa's voice in my head, '*No, you are stronger than that!* You will get through this...' From that day on I felt like she was guiding me and giving me the strength to carry on. It was extremely hard sat in an empty house all alone when it has always been full with my children – it was eerily quiet. I picked myself up, walked around the empty house, 'the house of horrors' – if only the walls could speak. I heard Lisa, Jack, Lee, George and Marie's voices, laughing and playing as children, tears streaming down my face, looking around George and

Marie's bedrooms, looking through at the empty large void in the roof which was to be made into bigger bedrooms etc. I looked at the bare brick in George's bedroom which had been like that since the new roof was built over the existing roof a few years before – another job never finished off. Marie was in a tiny bedroom and was excitedly waiting for her new bedroom to be finished, she had planned how she wanted it decorated, what her colour scheme would be, looking at furniture etc, etc. She was so patient when each time she would ask Graham when the work would be finished, he would always reply... "We can't afford it at moment, darling." If only she knew that Graham was sat on over half a million pounds, while all Marie wanted was a bigger bedroom with a wardrobe; she had by far outgrown her tiny room. It would have only taken a tiny amount of money to complete the work, in comparison to what was sat in Graham's bank... But his GREED was obscene, he had absolutely no intention of sharing this money with us, his family... One day in particular Marie was feeling upset because there was so little space to hang her clothes.

"I will speak to Dad," I said to her. "Graham, is there no way we could do the work upstairs, Marie is upset, there is no space for her to put anything. Surely it wouldn't take much to finish it off, it would be lovely to get it done for us all?" I asked.

"We CANNOT afford it," he LIED. "Why don't you pay for it if you're so bothered. You have no idea of the bills I have to pay, the business is struggling and one of the rental properties is empty and I don't see you putting your hand in your pocket."

"Graham, I'm on minimum wage, I have to contribute 50% towards holidays, Christmas, and any other things we do. I am maxed out on my credit card and all my wages go on food, broadband, school dinners, kids' phone bills, my phone bill, TV licence; I even had to pay for the dishwasher and the fridge freezer, my car tax, insurance and fuel, school uniforms, general clothes, the list goes on and on, and I'm skint," I reasoned.

"Oh no, here we go again, poor little martyr always playing the victim. What about the rental income you get from your house? What do you do with all your money? I'm sick of hearing how skint you are. You need to cut your cloth if you are so skint, or do more car boot sales," he smirked.

"All my wages and the rental income doesn't cover what I pay out."

"Well that's your look out, you should manage your money better then," he said.

"This is ridiculous, we are supposed to be a couple and I'm struggling here."

"Yes well that's what happen when you report your husband to the police!" he quipped…

Well he had said it out loud now and this was nearly seven years on – obviously he has been punishing me for that since 2011.

He's now taken my kids away from me, the ultimate punishment… I went into the kitchen and poured myself a large glass of wine. It might just help me get through today and it was New Year's Day after all… I left a voicemail begging them to come back, sent messages, but no reply from any of them.

I didn't know if they were ever coming back. I couldn't bear it, the house was so quiet it was almost deafening. I looked at myself in the mirror. I saw a woman with so much pain in her eyes, ghostly white. I screamed and shouted to the mirror… "Look at the state of you, how much more pain can you take? You are stupid, you are weak and you have failed as a mother. How can you live with yourself, why do you put up with this? If he doesn't kill you, you might kill yourself! GET A FUCKING GRIP, ALISHA!" I screamed. "What would Lisa think of you?"…

I lay back on my bed, my mind racing. Suddenly it was starting to get dark. I rang Graham again and to my surprise he answered… "Yes, what do you want?" he said.

"Please come back," I sobbed.

"If you behave and stop causing stress all the time then me and the kids will come back, but you have to promise to stop getting mad and angry."

I was just so desperate to get my kids back, which was the only reason I stayed with him anyway. "I won't cause any stress, please come home," I begged.

"Right, we will come back, but any more stress and we will leave and never come back, understand? I have a heart condition and don't need all this stress – it will kill me."

I just agreed to keep the peace. ME causing stress! Oh my God, this lunatic is badly damaged in the head, how am I going to deal with this? I thought to myself, feeling very, very vulnerable.

They soon arrived home. I went to hug George only to be pushed away, then went to Marie who looked too scared to hug me. Graham and I barely spoke apart from him saying: "One day, you will come home and we will have gone, I have a place in France, we will go there." This was something he would often say to me, to keep me 'under control'! Yet another secret, place in France... My marriage was a farce, it was built on sand, full of lies, cheating, deceit and abuse... What a waste of my life, I thought, the only good thing that came out of this marriage was my beautiful five kids, but he has done his best to destroy their lives too.

The next day I went to work with a very heavy heart. Chloe knew there was something wrong. I had a very close relationship with her so we both could confide in each other, not that I could divulge my nightmare of a life fully, but I told her about the previous day.

"I know," she said.

"What, how do you know?" I was completely shocked.

"Graham texted me and said, they had to leave because you were mental and they were scared to go back, that you should be sectioned, you need help and they were looking to book a B&B for the night," she replied.

I could hardly believe my ears – she was concerned about me after reading his text message?!

"Are you okay?" she asked.

I broke down uncontrollably, Graham was now trying to convince everyone that I was the one who was mentally ill. Who else had he said this to? Does everyone think that about me? I felt helpless.

Chloe consoled me and said that she didn't believe Graham, which was some comfort, but all day I felt sick, I couldn't eat or think straight. Yesterday was playing over and over in my head, I was constantly worried about going home to an empty house. It hung over me like a constant dark cloud. As work was nearly finished, I felt terrified to go home.

As we left work, Chloe turned to me and reassured me, "I'm always here for you, you can call me anytime, night or day."

I thanked her then set off home. It was dark and as I approached the house, it was in complete darkness. I opened the door and immediately I thought we had been burgled, the house looked like it had been ransacked. I raced around the house shouting for the kids: no reply. I checked every room, no sign of anyone. Then I heard the dog barking; she was in the conservatory. I was panicking now, so confused I felt dizzy and sick. I noticed that all their ski wear had gone, so I immediately checked for the passports, which were missing. My heart was pounding, this was the day Graham had mentioned many times and it was finally here. I was so distraught, I called Graham, George and Marie, I texted them, I left voice mails but received no reply from any of them. I called his manager from work – he said he didn't know anything.

I rang Jack. "They have gone, Jack, he's taken them to France, their passports have gone and all their ski gear has gone too." I hardly drew breath.

"Right, calm down, Mum, drive to us and we will ring the police. In fact, call the police now then drive over to us," he said.

I immediately called 999... "Police please, my kids are missing, they have been abducted, they have been taken to France," I explained, sobbing.

"I will just put you through. Hello, how can I help you?"

"My kids are missing, they have been kidnapped, I think they have gone to France."

"Okay, what makes you think that?" he said, so I explained that Graham had threatened this many times, and that they weren't answering their phones etc. "OK, let's take some details, I know you are very upset. What's Graham's phone number? When did you last see them? Would there be any reason that they have gone?" I quickly answered all his questions, I was desperate to get them found. "I will contact him and call you straight back."

He hung up and I called Chloe on the way to Jack's. "He's took the kids, the passports have gone, have you heard anything from them at all?"

"No, nothing, listen, calm down and drive carefully..."

"I have a call coming in, I will call you later," I replied.

"Hi, is that Alisha? It's PC.:. here, right I have been in contact with him, they are at Xscape at Castleford, skiing. Graham said that he had told you they were going for a day out before you left for work this morning, and that you must have forgotten; it's just a dad having a day out with his kids and they are both safe and well," he said dismissively.

"Why are they not answering my calls? Why are their passports missing? He NEVER told me they were going out for the day, I would have remembered that, he's LYING," I cried. "Listen, I have spoke to him and he reassured me that they are just having a nice day out. Graham said that you were suffering with depression and anxiety, and you have been stressed lately, but I can assure you that they are all safe."

He's even convinced the police that I'm mad; this was more than I could take. I arrived at Jack's and he was a great support. "Call Dad and the kids again," he said.

I called lots more and sent more texts with NO response. "He answered the phone straight away to the police but is ignoring me."

"I know, send him a text saying that you are going to let all his pigeons out. He will soon respond to that," Jack said, so I sent a text saying that and within seconds he replied: "DON'T YOU DARE go near my pigeons, behave yourself, and why did you ring the police? You knew damn well we were at Castleford, I told you this morning, you just made yourself look stupid to the police, they just think that you are mental like everyone else does. We will be home about 8pm, you better not be funny with us when we get back."

"I'm staying at Jack and Rose's tonight, I've brought the dog, because I didn't know if you were coming back and I couldn't leave her on her own. I will be back tomorrow, but the house is trashed and I refuse to tidy and clean it, I refuse to clean and tidy it up on my day off," I said.

He made a massive drama about me 'stealing' the kid's dog. "The kids hate you for taking the dog, all you are doing is turning them against you even more."

I didn't even have the energy to respond, I was fighting a losing battle.

"I told you he would respond when you mentioned the pigeons," Jack laughed.

The next day I arrived home, surprisingly to a tidy house.

"I HATE you for taking the dog, you are just turning us against you more when you do things like that," George snapped at me, and before I could get a word out, Marie also looked at me in disgust. "I HATE you for doing this!"

I had become numb, there was no point even trying to reason with them. Graham was doing a good job, poisoning my kids against me. I had now started to plan my escape. I refused to live like this any longer, so my thoughts were consumed with planning to leave. I searched rental properties, I tried to cut down on my spending and started to sell household items and old clothes on shopping sites – I needed to save for an escape fund. It might take a few months, but I was determined.

Chapter 26

We had already booked our ski holiday for the beginning of February and I really didn't want to go, but in the lead up to the holiday, Graham had changed into Mr Charming, love bombing me with compliments and flowers. I was very confused. He would still say he was worried about MY mental health.

"I will help you all I can, do you want me to come to the doctor's with you, babe? What about some counselling sessions and stronger anti-depressants? I just want to get you better," he said in a concerned, soft voice.

He could be so convincing. I had even started to think that I was a quivering mess; he would project all that he was, onto me, and he was an expert at it. The next few weeks he continued to be 'caring' and 'loving' but it was only to my face. I had already decided to 'play the game'. He didn't think I could hear him say to George while they were in the garage, and I was listening outside:

"I can't wait until you become of age, George. Remember, I'm going to leave everything to you and Marie, and I will make my will watertight so that *she* doesn't get anything. I have wrote a covering letter to say that JACK AND LEE ARE TO GET ABSOLUTELY NOTHING AT ALL. I will give you a copy of the Will to put in your safe, once you turn 18, then it will be legal. When I've had my surgery, me, you and Marie, will fuck off and leave *her*."

I heard George just agreeing to Graham. Why I was in shock, I don't know, but I just kept my eyes and ears open. I wanted the holiday out of the way, so I could make my plans.

We arrived at Tignes, the snow was perfect and the weather conditions were great, our hotel was lovely, and the kids were happy. We enjoyed the skiing and Graham was still being lovely to me, even though he was plotting behind my back – maybe he was trying to keep me sweet until he'd had his surgery, then I would look after him? This was the conclusion I had come to anyway.

The first two days on the slopes were great, and we skied to Val-d'Isère on the third day. The weather was beautiful, sun shining, so we decided to stop for a drink in one of the mountain restaurants and sit in the glorious sun for a little while. We sat and chatted about the runs we had done and the holiday so far, then the kids grew impatient.

"Come on, we have stopped for long enough now, let's get back on the slopes," George urged, so we all headed up to the chair lifts. It was now approx 2pm and the weather had changed, the sun disappeared and the snow came down. Visibility was poor, but that never put us off. Graham wanted to ski La face de Bellevarde. This was a very advanced black run; ideally it should be skied early morning on freshly groomed piste due to the steepness of it, which gives a fantastic long ride, but we skied it and loved it so we decided to go up again. As we skied down a second time, the run had become very icy, but we all skied down having great time, when suddenly, all I remember is coming round on the ground looking at the blood stained snow, and my vision was blurry. "Are you okay?" I heard a woman say. George had seen the accident and had stayed with me until I gained consciousness, then I suddenly remembered what had happened: I saw a skier to my right who was clearly out of control, I had shouted to her to move as we were both travelling at high speed, but there was very little time so I had quickly turned to my left when I was hit by another skier who had also lost control on the ice... I was fuming that some idiot had caused this terrible crash.

"Shall we call for help?" someone said.

"NO, I'm fine, I will manage."

"You are bleeding, you need first aid," the concerned woman said.

"No, seriously, I will be fine," I said as I stood up. I had a massive bump on my head and my goggles had smashed into my face. My blurry vision was a result of the blood running down my head. As I stood up I knew that I was badly injured. I was in a lot of pain around my groin and ribs; I had been winded too. I carried on and skied to where Graham and Marie were waiting, oblivious to what had just happened.

"Oh wow, are you okay, babe?" Graham said. Marie looked upset, seeing my bloodied face.

"Yes, I'm fine, I'm in a bit of pain, but I think I am just badly bruised. I will be fine."

So we skied down to the bottom. I took it more slowly to protect my wounds. As we finished the run, Graham suggested that I sit in a nearby bar, and he bought me a mulled wine.

"Me and the kids are just going to do a last run, you just chill and have your drink, we won't be long, babe," he said as they all departed to the chair lift. I just sat with my wine, nursing my wounds. It wasn't long before they finished their run. "How you feeling, babe?"

"I'm in pain but I should be okay."

"No more skiing for you then, you will have to stay in the hotel for the next three days while me and the kids ski."

I had no intentions of missing out on skiing. "Well I will see how I am in the morning, I will go to the chemist and get some painkillers and dose myself up with them and I might be okay to ski tomorrow."

"Don't be stupid, you are mad, you can hardly walk, no way can you ski tomorrow," he said forcefully.

"I'm just badly bruised and winded, I will be fine," I assured him. I took the long walk alone to the chemist for my analgesics. Graham wasn't impressed with me wanting to carry on skiing. I could see his point, and if I couldn't ski because of my injuries, then I wouldn't ski – I only suggested that I would ski if I felt better, but Graham dictated his 'request' and expected everyone to obey him. I knew I was in for a frosty reception when I arrived back at the hotel. They were all sat in the reception area with a drink and as I approached they suddenly went silent, as if I had interrupted a secret conversation...'oh here we go, another argument is brewing' I thought to myself; the atmosphere was tense.

"Listen, babe, we have just been talking, we don't think it makes sense for you to ski for the rest of the holiday, you had bad crash and you should stay behind to recover," he coaxed.

"Yes, you are probably right, I will take the painkillers and stay in the hotel," I agreed. This pleased Graham that I had agreed with him.

We got ready and went down to dinner, I limped my way around the restaurant, still in pain, but we had a lovely evening. Before retiring to our rooms, George and Marie would spend a little time with us in our room before heading to their own room. I was desperate to get into bed and rest my body. Graham and I chatted a little before we fell asleep. I slept okay and felt a lot better the next morning. We went to breakfast, the sun was beating down, it was a beautiful day, and I just wanted to ski.

"I was thinking, it's a gorgeous day and I'm feeling so much better, maybe I might test myself and ski a bit today," I said to Graham.

"I thought you were staying behind! Typical, you think you are missing out, you can't bear the thought of me and the kids having a good time without you; you are A SELFISH BITCH, it's all about YOU, YOU,YOU, spoiling the holiday because you are so JEALOUS!"

"I said I will just try. If it's too painful then I will come back to the hotel," I said.

"RIGHT, you can come but if you can't keep up don't expect us to slow down for you; we are not wasting our time waiting for you!"

I did understand why he reacted this way, and maybe I am selfish, but it was only a few years before when we had gone skiing in Italy with Jack, Lee, Louise, Anthony and Emma, and Graham badly hurt his back, and expected me to stay with him for the duration of the holiday and not ski at all – as usual double standards! He is the most SELFISH person I have ever come across.

It was difficult fastening my boots as my ribs were still painful, but I was determined. All set to go we all headed to the gondola. Graham had got over his little tantrum, or so I thought, as we decided on which run to ski. I was feeling nervous and under pressure at keeping up with them. We headed down a nice wide open run and, although I was in pain, I managed to ski OK. I only did what I felt comfortable with and after a few runs, I opted to have a break in one of the restaurants for a rest. Surprisingly Graham wanted to join me. George and Marie were happy to do a few runs together while Graham and I enjoyed a cold beer, while discussing how grown-up the kids were. It was very difficult to feel comfortable around Graham, knowing what he was scheming and plotting behind my back, but I had to stay focussed and think about getting free from him, and I could only do this by going along with everything. It was soon time to head back for dinner at the hotel. The food was lovely as always, and after our fill we went up to our rooms. Graham had received a phone call which he took in private, and when he returned he was really stressed.

"Are you okay?" I said.

"No, that was the bank, there is some kind of problem," he snapped.

This made absolutely no sense at all, but he was being so deceitful and secretive, it could have been anyone calling about anything. He was anxious and angry.

"Chill out, sort it when we get back, don't let it spoil our holiday," I said calmly.

He flew at me, grabbing my arm tightly. "Don't you patronise me." He suddenly loosened his grip but continued to shout in my face. "You have no clue about my life, do you?" he screamed.

"Apparently not because you keep it secret."

"Don't start all that shit again!" Still raging. "Right, I'm going into the kids' room and staying with them tonight," he said, then went to the safe and changed the pin code for the lock.

"What are you doing? My important things are in there," I said.

"Tough, you can't be trusted, so I have changed the code," he snapped as he slammed the room door.

I was really struggling to understand how he could fly into such a horrible rage, over what? But it was usually over nothing.

I phoned Jack and told him what had happened.

"Mum, you have to leave him, he's dangerous and getting loads worse; you can't stay with him. I will always be here to support you, but to be honest I'm sick of hearing all this, it's getting ridiculous. If you are not prepared to leave him, then stop moaning about him, simple."

Poor Jack, he doesn't want to hear all this. "Thanks, Jack, I really appreciate that, and I *am* planning on leaving, but it's not that easy," I said.

"It's simple to me: you either stay or leave."

"Yes, I'm sorting it, Jack, speak soon." We said our goodbyes and I spent the whole night trying to work out what I was going to do.

I didn't love Graham and hadn't done for many years. I was trauma bonded to him, dependent on him, caught in his trap. He had knocked all my self-esteem and confidence out of me, he was deceitful, revengeful, controlling, nasty, secretive and poisoning my kids against me; but this was now fight or flight, and I didn't feel able to do either yet.

Morning came and I was so tired. I went to the kids' room and knocked on the door. No reply. I kept knocking: no reply. I went down to reception and told them I had lost my key, got a spare then went into their room. They had all gone and left me behind. This was no surprise. I returned the key to reception and spent the day alone in my room. This was the last day anyway and I needed the rest. There was no contact with Graham or the kids all day and when dinner time came, I knocked on their door again – no reply, so I went down to the restaurant. They were all sat there laughing and chatting away. As I walked over to the table, Graham looked happy, he was laughing.

"Oh there you are, babe, where did you get to?" he teased. I just smiled sarcastically and didn't answer. "Awwwwww, did you miss us today, babe?" as he laughed loudly. George joined in with Graham and they both found it amusing that they had left me behind. I was just happy to be going home tomorrow, I needed to get back to work and start seriously saving up...

The plane landed at Manchester, and we were homeward bound. I was very quiet as I really didn't see the point of talking just to get shot down.

A few miles from home and my eye was hurting, so I pulled down the visor in Graham's car to look in the mirror. A few folded sheets of paper fell to the floor from being tucked behind the visor. I picked them up and put them back, but my eye was really irritating me now, so I pulled down the visor again a few minutes later, and the papers dropped to the floor again. As I picked them up, Graham snatched them from my hand and looked panic stricken. I looked at him without a word.

"Oh, it's just a gym membership form for me and Gaz to join, because one of the employees are off sick and she's been seen at the gym by another staff member, so me and Gaz wanted to catch her out," he spouted so fast that he didn't draw breath.

I thought for a few seconds., I knew that this was a massive LIE, but did I just accept what he said, or should I ask him if I can see the gym membership form. I opted for the latter, stupidly. "Graham, can I ask you a question?" I asked softly.

"WHAT?" he snapped impatiently, knowing what was coming. "Can I have a look at the gym membership form please?"

He slammed on the brakes. "THAT'S IT, YOU DON'T TRUST ME AND I'M SICK TO DEATH OF IT! GET OUT OF THE CAR!" he screamed, then reached over me and, after unfastening my seat belt, opened the car door then pushed me out onto the road, then sped off, leaving me crying in excruciating pain. Luckily it was only a few metres from home and I managed to crawl home in agony. I couldn't lift my left leg, I was sure that it was broken, the pain was terrible. I lay on my bed, once I was in the door. I couldn't possibly go to work tomorrow was my first thought, so I messaged work, explaining my injuries. Graham and the kids arrived home soon after and I could clearly hear Graham complaining about me never trusting or believing him, same old, same old. It was over my head, I just wanted to leave this nightmare of a life. There was very little communication between us that evening apart from: "don't worry about us, we are going to McDonald's for tea" Graham shouted as the door shut. I was just glad of the peace.

The next day I spent in bed hardly able to move. I decided to go to the doctor's the following day.

"Oh I think you have broken something, you can't put any weight on your left leg at all. I will send you for an X-ray, but you will have to go to Harrogate, as Ripon is closed now. Have you got anyone who could take you?" she asked.

"What, now?"

"Yes, you need to go straight there, I will phone them now and tell them you are on your way," she said.

"I will drive there, I drove here, lifting my leg for the pedals," I said. She was shocked at my response and insisted that I get a lift. There was only Graham, and I was doubtful that he would assist, but I rang him anyway.

"I can't, babe, I'm under a machine trying to fix it, can't you get someone else to take you?" *'Under a machine, he was probably under something, but probably not a machine!'* So I drove myself 11 miles to the hospital, and as I staggered across the car park shrieking in pain, a nurse came out with a wheelchair and escorted me to the X-ray department.

"Yes, you have a closed fractured pubis rami," said the little Asian doctor whose English wasn't good.

"What?"

"Look at the X-ray," he said as he held it up. I could clearly see the break. "You are lucky, this kind of break is usually seen from car crash victims, or any high speed activity. What did you do to cause this injury?" he asked.

I explained I had had a high speed ski crash, but then told him that I was later thrown from a car, but I didn't elaborate on that.

"Well you are looking at 8-12 weeks recovery period; the only treatment is painkillers and lots of rest," he said.

Oh great, this was terrible news, this was all I needed. I was worried about work and about lack of support at home, and worse my income – how was I going to manage?

Graham was shocked when I told him the diagnosis. "You will be off sick then, how long will you be off work?" This was his main concern; typical, he always talked about money!

The next few weeks after lot of resting, I was able to walk, albeit it was still extremely painful. I took advantage of the sunny days in the garden. Graham was being OK, he picked the kids up from school, they all sorted out meals etc until I was well enough to do it.

Chapter 27

Sunday 11th March, Mother's Day. Normally the kids would come down with a card and gifts, make me breakfast and we would have a lovely day. I could hear George and Marie in the kitchen, I assumed they would wish me happy mother's day when I got up, so I went to investigate. "Morning you two," I said to them both, but they just looked at me and sheepishly said "morning".

"You okay? What you doing?" I said, a little confused.

"Just getting breakfast," Marie replied.

"Oh OK," I said as I went to put the kettle on. Maybe they forgot it was Mother's Day, no big deal, they will remember later. The morning passed, just like a normal Sunday morning, no reference whatsoever to Mother's Day. I was feeling upset by now, but they seemed to be avoiding me.

Lunchtime came and there was a knock on the door. "Happy Mother's Day, Mum," Jack said, handing me a card, bouquet of flowers and a box of chocolates.

"Oh, thank you, Jack, that's lovely," I said, choked up because George and Marie hadn't acknowledged the day.

"Have a lovely day, Rose is in the car, we are going out so I better get going."

"Well have a great day, Jack, speak later," I said as he turned to leave.

"Who was that?" George shouted from upstairs.

"It was Jack wishing me a happy mother's day," I replied.

"Oh," George said, completely ignoring that it was Mother's Day.

While I was arranging my flowers, George and Marie decided to eat all the chocolates that Jack had bought me.

"Where are my chocolates that Jack gave me?" I said angrily.

"We ate them," Marie admitted, laughing.

The card Jack had bought me was a birthday card by mistake so he'd crossed it out and wrote Mother's Day. Graham used this to totally ridicule Jack and was laughing while showing George and Marie.

"AT LEAST HE WISHED ME A HAPPY MOTHER'S DAY AND THOUGHT ABOUT ME, UNLIKE YOU TWO!" I retaliated.

"Well that's because you spoilt Father's Day last year for Dad!" George said to me.

Wow, OMG, Graham has told them to ignore Mother's Day, how fucking vile and nasty was he. I was so upset for the kids being told to not wish their own mum happy mothers day, this was really sad.

April 2018 I was starting to move around in less pain, so began to do more, but I was still on the sick. Graham had helped out by giving me money for the grocery shopping.

It was just a normal evening at home, Marie and I sat in the living room chatting, Graham and George in the pigeon lofts. Graham came in the house.

"There's a cat on the wall," he said. I looked out of the window.

"Awww, so cute, it looks like a fairly young cat."

"I don't care how old it is, it will be after my pigeons."

"Just shoo it away then," I suggested.

He then went to shoo the cat away, or so I thought, but then I saw him and George trying to coax the cat to come to them. They caught it and Graham excitedly pinned the poor defenceless cat to the floor and told George to get a brick from the garden. Marie and I were hysterically shouting at them to leave the cat alone...

"Go inside, go inside," he said panicking.

"Not until you let the cat go," I shouted.

I ran into the house to get my phone to call the police. As I ran back to the door, I heard screams from the cat and from Marie – the cat had been bludgeoned to death, there was blood all around it. Marie and I were traumatised by this.

"I'M RINGING THE POLICE," I said, shaking with the shock.

"Don't you dare ring the police, all the support I have given you...if you dare ring the police I will fucking kill you!" he threatened.

I didn't ring the police; instead, I consoled my distraught daughter while Graham and George disposed of the dead cat. He hates cats with a passion and would often catapult and shoot them with his air rifle; this was horrifying, but my main concern was that George was so indoctrinated by Graham, that he didn't hesitate to follow Graham's brutal demands.

One evening, I received a friend request via Facebook messenger, from a friend I had worked with when I first moved to Ripon, Caroline. She knew Graham from school and had grown up in the neighbouring village. She had been married as long as I had been, but when I saw her Facebook information, I was shocked to see that she was 'single'.

I had always liked Caroline and was pleased when she got back in touch after all these years.

May 2018, we had some lovely weather and Graham would stay home and sunbathe in the garden with me; he did most of the talking, spouting loads of LIES to me about how busy work was, yet he was pleading poverty and was sat in the garden! He LIED about how much debt he had, how he needed a new van and new machines etc, etc. I just humoured him and acknowledged what he was saying. He remarked on how quiet I was, and I told him I was just constantly tired. I spent days and days watching him, listening to him, taking notes of his behaviour and generally using my time to find out the truth and what Graham had been doing. Interesting, I knew Wednesdays and Saturdays he was always uncontactable, so these two days were on my radar. I had decided to buy a tracking device and a small voice recorder. I managed to do this without Graham's knowledge. I was excited but terrified at the same time. It was difficult to put them in his car – I had to choose my time carefully. If Graham had've caught me, I dreaded to think about the consequences, and if the kids had caught me, they would tell him; but I had to do it, it was the only way to get the answers I needed. By this time, I had stopped speaking; only if necessary, I would talk to the kids but soon found out that they had been told, by Graham, to spy on me and tell him everything I said. I knew this because I had left an old phone on record in the kitchen while I was out. It wasn't always clear or complete, but I managed to get the general gist of things, so now I was living with not one but three enemies. I was close to breaking point, I had started to shake. I was a living wreck, scared of my own shadow, walking on eggshells, frightened of speaking. I became very withdrawn, I felt so alone and worthless, and once again my thoughts turned to ending my life, then I remembered Jack's words: "I will always support you no matter what, Mum." I'm not going to leave my boys, I love them so, so much; no matter how horrendous my life is, I will get free and safe.

Chapter 28

The abuse seemed to get worse the less I retaliated. I had taken away his power by showing no pain – he got enjoyment out of seeing me distraught and helpless.

In an attempt to get a rise from me, he would say to George, look at Mum's hair she is going bald, she looks like something from 'Wrong Turn' (a movie full of scary looking hill-billies on a murdering campaign). I was crying inside, biting my lip so as not to let my tears out, I sat in complete silence and didn't respond to this abuse.

"Ha-ha, look at the state of her, she doesn't know anything." They laughed loudly. "No wonder I don't want sex with her, that's what her problem is, she's not getting any sex," he said to George.

"Why did you say that to George? It's disgusting," I said, embarrassed.

"Anyway the doctor said I had to refrain from sex and any strenuous exercise with my heart condition, but you don't care about that, do you? I'm sure if you had what I have you would be the same," he said.

"Hey, you are in for one MASSIVE SHOCK, YOU ARE," he directed at me, laughing.

"Yes, I know all about it," I retaliated. "Come on then, what do you know?" he teased, still finding it very amusing.

"You have been plotting and scheming, about what to do if anything happens to you and you are going to leave everything to George."

"Ha-ha, is that what you think the massive shock is?" he said, throwing his head back, loudly laughing.

"You have received your inheritance?" I guessed.

"Haha, yes I have, and it's got fuck all to with you. It's MINE, Alisha, ALL MINE, and you are not getting your greedy hands on it. Anyway, it's ADEEMED, Alisha, ADEEMED," he said still laughing. "That's what her problem is," he said looking at George, "she wants to get her hands on MY money. You won't see a fucking penny of it, so you can get that right out of your head," he snapped.

"I'm not interested in YOUR money, Graham."

"So that's why I didn't tell you that I had it," he said, amused.

"Jack had said to me that you had received your inheritance and not told me, so I already knew."

"Anyway, that's not the shock I meant," he said, still amused.

"I'm really not interested," I said.

The abuse went from bad to worse. Graham bought a drone for 'George' and connected it to his laptop, then sent it to Lee's house to spy and intimidate him and Louise; he loves harassing them, his OWN SON, it was despicable. He had already previously sent text messages to them both, threatening to make their lives not worth living; he had stalked Louise at their home around the corner and even followed Lee to his place of employment in Wakefield.

Lee was considering starting up his own business. Jack already had his own successful building company, but Graham found out that Lee was looking for an industrial unit, and my brother happened to be selling his business which was in the same industry and he was giving notice on his unit which he rented from a local business man. I mentioned this to Lee and he approached both my brother and the landlord of the unit in the hope of setting up his own business there. Graham was unbelievably angry that Lee would set up in *competition* against him, so he contacted Lee and my brother with threatening messages, he told Lee that he would destroy him if he dare set up in business against him, and sent vile texts to my brother warning him not to get involved with Lee. Graham was so vehemently angry that he even contacted the landlord of the unit and offered him two years rent in advance to prevent Lee from having the unit. These were the lengths he went to, to stop his OWN SON from having his own business. These actions are far from normal, this was beyond cruel and evil, but Lee has gone on to have his own successful business, and both Jack and Lee are well respected businessmen, unlike their father, and I could not be any prouder of my amazing sons doing so well and being decent men despite having gone through a tough life.

There were more incidents over the next couple of months. I had gathered some recordings which consisted of Graham and the kids literally just bitching me off saying I was tight and greedy – "she always wants to be in control, we don't want her as a slave but..." – it became muffled after he said these words.

"Babe, we are going for a walk, do you fancy coming?" Graham asked me one summer's evening. He rarely invited me along, but it was a beautiful night for a walk.

"I wouldn't keep up with you, with my hip," I said.

"It's okay, we are only going for a leisurely walk down by the river, you will be okay, babe, it will do you good," he coaxed, so I agreed.

The walk started off very pleasant but after the first 10 minutes, I was feeling the pain and needed to just slow down a little. "I'm just struggling a little bit, can we just walk a little bit slower?" I said to Graham and the kids.

"Yes, no problem, babe," he replied, then I saw them laughing between themselves as they started to run off.

"Hey you lot, wait for me," I shouted.

"COME ON, BABE, KEEP UP!" Graham shouted. A couple of minutes later they were all gone.

I was really upset. It was a long walk home alone with a broken pelvis. I started to cry. 'What sort of husband tells his kids to run off and leave their mum knowing she was in pain?' I thought to myself. I became really upset.

I managed to make it home and as I walked in, "Hey babe, what happened to you?" Graham said looking very amused.

"You ran off and left me!" I cried.

"Oh, you silly sausage, no we didn't, don't be silly, why would we leave you?" Graham said, trying to make me look pathetic. He grabbed me as if to hug me while saying to the kids, "We didn't leave Mum, did we, kids? She could have easily have kept up, couldn't she?"

The kids agreed, but I could see the hurt in Marie's eyes – she knew the truth and she felt for me. I just let it drop, I didn't question him anymore.

One night in particular, I needed to go to the shop and decided to have a drive down to where Graham worked. He had banned me from going to the factory so I just drove past, then I saw his car out of the corner of my eye. I watched as he pulled into the local leisure centre car park. I turned around and followed him into the car park. He parked his car then went into the centre. Wendy, a good friend of mine, worked there and she happened to be working this night. I waited for a little while before I went in.

"Oh, hello, how are you? Your other half is upstairs in the gym," she said.

"I only came in to use the loo," I lied, then tried to get some information from her without letting her know the truth, which is that I had absolutely NO IDEA whatsoever that he was a member of the gym. "How much is it to join?" I enquired.

"£44.00 a month," she replied, "or you could get a couple's membership."

"I will talk to Graham and see," I said. I then went upstairs to the gym and the first person I saw through the double doors, was Graham on the running machine, running like he was in a sprinting race. I felt sick to the stomach, remembering him saying that he was advised not to do such activities. I heard him chatting away saying he could only do three nights a week and he would try and come more often. He then proceeded to lift weights and carry on using all the other equipment. I watched for approximately 20 minutes, I had seen enough and headed to my car before he finished his rigorous workout. I checked my phone and saw four missed calls from Marie and texts asking why I was so long and where I was, but I had had my phone on silent. I called her back.

"Mum, where have you been and why did you ignore my calls?" she said, frustrated."

"I would never ignore your calls, baby, my phone was on silent, I'm coming home now."

"I was wanting you to buy some Dr Pepper," she said.

"Don't worry, I will get some on my way home, darling." I was frantically trying to get home before Graham and get the tea cooked quickly, but I was greeted by Marie asking me lots of questions. "Let me get in the house first," I said.

She looked at me with a very suspicious face. "Where have you really been, Mum, you took ages?"

"Just took longer than I thought," I replied.

"Mmmmm," she said disbelievingly.

It wasn't long before Graham came through the door. "Did you manage to get hold of Mum, Marie?" he asked.

"She said her phone was on silent," she reported.

"It was on silent, it was just busy in the shop," I explained.

"You are a LIAR, you have been following and spying on me. She's too busy spying on me, Marie. You need to get back to work as soon as possible, you have too much time on your hands," he snapped at me.

"Hmm, I have a broken pelvis, remember," I replied.

"You are fucking milking it, there is fuck all wrong with you, you are only stood in a shop all day."

"Exactly, standing up is the worst thing for my pelvis."

"Well ask them to get you a chair to sit on. It's like this: you either get to fucking work, you lazy bitch, or I will stop paying for the food,

I'm sick of you taking the piss, expecting me to keep you while you are swanning around on the sick spying on me," he shouted.

This was so obvious now that he was getting paranoid, and had a guilty conscience, he was terrified that I would catch him out before he could execute his master plan. "How could I follow you when I don't know where you are? And why would I need to follow you? Are you up to no good and doing something you shouldn't be doing? You are being paranoid now, have you got a guilty conscience?" I replied.

"Just you get back to fucking work out of the way, your pelvis will be healed by now."

"You're not a doctor and my doctor said I need to give it plenty of time to heal, and I'm taking my doctor's advice," I snapped back.

Meanwhile, I had been in a lot of pain with my right hip. I had broken the left side but now the right side was painful. After investigation, I was diagnosed with osteoarthritis and needed a hip replacement. That was the last thing on mind – I couldn't even think of having surgery until I was in a happier place in my life.

When my sick note ran out, I went to my doctor and decided to confide in her about the domestic abuse I had suffered for many years. She was fantastic; she put me in touch with IDAS, DOMESTIC ABUSE HELPLINE. THE CRISIS TEAM.

"I really appreciate that, and I will contact them services when I'm ready," I said.

She reassured me that she was just on the end of the phone for support if I needed it. I had already been to see another doctor in January expressing how unhappy I was in my marriage without divulging too much, so they were aware of my depression.

Graham seemed very on edge and more tense than usual. I continued to track and record him, and followed him to the gym on a Monday, Wednesday and Friday nights. He also still went for his nightly walks with George – no wonder he was getting thinner. I caught him one Sunday admiring himself in the mirror and I was surprised to see just how much weight he had lost.

"Bloody hell, look at you, you have lost loads of weight and you are all toned and muscly; anyone would think you worked out at the gym," I said mischievously.

He then proceeded to make poses like Mr Universe, wow he was totally in love with himself.

"I wish," he replied. "Wish I had time to go to the gym, I'm too busy working to pay bills, never mind go to the gym," he said rather convincingly – and if I hadn't seen it with my own eyes, I would have believed his lie, like I had believed all his other LIES before.

The next couple of weeks were peppered with good and bad, but mainly bad. I was getting more and more desperate to leave, but it was looking impossible. I couldn't take any more of the constant LIES, the constant abuse, and he now had George and Marie in his 'little gang'. He would sing ♫ 'do you wanna be in our gang, our gang' ♫ and laugh, then George and Marie would join in. I felt like I had been transported to a crazy planet, things were getting more and more tense, I could feel that things were coming to head now.

"Come on, kids, let's go get a McDonald's."

So off they went. I decided to have a drive out to clear my head. I just drove onto the market square and parked up. I was just people watching, looking at families, couples and how happy they looked, I saw a man with his wife, about my age; he was talking to her while tenderly moving her hair from her face. They were both smiling, she was nodding in response to his words, he then put his arm around her waist to pull her close; they then happily walked on hand in hand. I watched happy families together, tears spilling from my eyes. I just wanted to be happy, to feel loved, to enjoy simple things; everyone but me seemed so happy. I wonder if he is horrible to his wife? I thought to myself while watching all these people just happily milling around. I felt the loneliest I had ever felt in my life. I drove to a quiet place with no-one around. I needed to scream and let all my emotions out.

I cried uncontrollably for what seemed minutes but already two hours had passed. I was in no rush to go *home* – it wasn't home to me, it was my prison, my trap, it was a place where I felt scared, unsafe, lonely and vulnerable, it was a place where I wore invisible chains; but what choice did I have? I reluctantly drove home. It had been hot in the car and I was sweating so when I arrived home I jumped straight in the shower. I heard Graham shouting but didn't know why. I finished my shower, wrapped myself in a towel, and I walked toward my bedroom.

"ALISHA, COME HERE!" Graham shouted. I went into the room where he was sitting with the kids. "WHERE HAVE YOU BEEN? IF YOU BEEN OUT SHAGGING YOU CAN PACK YOUR BAGS AND FUCK OFF!"

Wow, he really was insecure and paranoid, he was losing it big time now. He could sense that I was watching him and he was scared to be exposed. On my way into the house, I had noticed McDonald's empty cartons all over the garden, obviously left for me to clear away. "George, Marie, could you please go and pick your rubbish up from the garden, there are empty cartons all over the place."

"Oh my God, you are jealous that we have had McDonald's, you are unbelievable. Your own mother jealous of you having a McDonald's," he said to the kids. "What sort of mother are you? JEALOUS, INSECURE, ALWAYS WANTING TO BE IN CONTROL, jealous to death that we are doing something without you..." On and on and on saying the same thing over again, my own kids believing I was jealous of them.

"You are impossible!" I snapped as I left the room.

"When I have had my op, we will fuck off and leave her," he said to the kids AGAIN.

"I think we should get Mum committed, she's mental," he said to George, when he thought I wasn't listening. Now this was on another level, this was serious shit and I was terrified – he had already planted the seed with everyone, so maybe this was his plan.

Chapter 29

Wednesday 11th July 2018 it was Marie's graduation. I phoned Graham. "Don't forget, it's Marie's graduation at 10am."

"We don't have to both go, it's not that important, you just go on your own. I'm too busy, I have to fix a machine in the factory," he LIED.

Of course, it was WEDNESDAY, he was never available on Wednesdays or Saturdays, silly me. I went alone, sat waiting to see Marie. She looked at me with a very angry look on her face. I assumed it was because Graham hadn't thought his daughter was important enough for him to attend her graduation, but no, after the ceremony, while we were having refreshments, I asked Marie what was wrong.

"You know what's wrong, you are always causing stress for Dad, he has a heart condition and doesn't need stress."

And didn't we just know it, there wasn't a day went by without him sat with his blood pressure machine on, every day he would tell the kids the same thing, that he was about to die because *I* caused him stress! They were indoctrinated with this rubbish he was telling them.

After we arrived home, me and Marie were looking at the photos of the day on my phone, when Graham came home. He looked at Marie sat next to me, as if she was doing something wrong, and what she did next chilled me to the bone – she physically moved away from me and looked absolutely terrified; she stood up and walked away from me.

Graham smiled at me and said in the most evil voice in my ear...

"You have lost George for good, and you have Marie only by a thread, and if you ever, ever leave me, I will make sure that these kids NEVER, EVER want to see you again!"

I went cold, I was shaking uncontrollably, heart pounding. I started to vomit. This was like living in a real life horror movie, waiting for a slow painful death. He was right, he had successfully brainwashed and poisoned them against me.

The next morning I decided to get into Graham's laptop and listen to my recordings, which I hadn't done in a few days. I managed to guess his password, and his search history revealed that he had been looking at properties to buy here, Jersey and France. Train tickets to London, stocks and shares... a shopping channel showing his search for jet skis, windsurfers, a black negligee – clearly not meant for me. I was nervous looking on his laptop in case he came home and caught me. Graham was right: I didn't know anything about his life, I was looking at a stranger's life...I put the recorder into the USB port...

Recording #1

"Mum came to your graduation, didn't she?"

"Yes, but she was crying."

"What is wrong with her, showing you up in front of your friends, she's getting worse, the sooner we leave her the better. What was she wearing?"

"Mmmmmm she had jeans on, I think."

"Was she dressed up? Did she look nice? What top did she have on? Was she wearing high heeled shoes?"

"She had that blue tee shirt on which is off the shoulders and I can't remember what she had on her feet..."

Recording #2

"Where's Mum?"

"She went out, I don't know where."

"Did she lend Jack the camping stuff, he hasn't been round has he?"

"Not that I know of."

"She better not have lent him anything."

"She was on the phone to him for ages."

"What was she saying?"

"I'm not sure because she was outside talking to him and I was upstairs in my room," Marie replied.

"She seems to spend a lot of time talking to him, try and listen to what she's saying if you can." "OK."

This was the conversation between Graham and Marie – that's why Marie had started to follow me around a lot; it all made sense now.

Recording #3

This was recorded from his car.

Muffled voices in the background, getting closer to the car.

"Do you like my new Evoque, Evoque, Evoque? I've had it a month and haven't cleaned it yet," Graham said in a stupid, playful voice like he was talking to a child.

He got a phone notification. "It's Gaz" he LIED. (I worked out that it was actually a text from me.)

"Shhhhhhhh shhhhhhhhh shhhhhh, drip dry, drip dry" as he was showing off pretending to wash his car, with a giggling female voice in the background.

"You need to wait for the rain to do that," she said, giggling like a little schoolgirl.

"See you next Wednesday."

"AWWWWWWWW, babe, doesn't time fly though, doesn't it? Like you say, Wednesday to Wednesday seems longer than Saturday to Saturday, don't know why," he said.

"No, I don't know why either," she gushed.

"I like coming on a Saturday better, and a Wednesday, but Saturdays seem better somehow." There was a little giggle and a pathetic "yes" from her in response.

"We will have to get back to Saturdays; we will wait until after your holidays or something. Thing is, when you are on holiday, I will come different days during the week and see you."

"Yes," she said.

"OK, very good, I'm gonna drive and go pick them up, it's twenty to, I might just make it, see ya."

"Yes, bye," she said.

He then drove off.

I don't know what shocked me more, that he was ACTUALLY cheating or that I had caught him.

Everything started to fit together like a jigsaw puzzle. So I now knew that Wednesdays and Saturdays he was seeing a woman every week approximately 20 minutes away from home

After playing it over and over again to see if I could recognise the voice and to make sure that it was what I thought it was, I phoned Jack and asked him to listen to it. He and Rose both listened and came to the same conclusion as me. "Jack, he's going again next Wednesday, I will put the tracker in his car and could you follow him? The only problem is we don't know which direction the 20-away minutes is."

Jack agreed and we both decided that it would most likely be Harrogate.

15th July 2018 Marie had accidentally swallowed a pin and was admitted to hospital. I spent the night with her and it was so nice to be with her alone, even though it was in hospital. The X-ray showed the pin in her body and the only solution was to wait for her to pass it. We just sat on the bed chatting.

"Mum, you are acting differently, what's wrong, you look so sad."

"I am sad, Marie, I'm just so unhappy with Dad," I confided in her but aware of what I was saying as Graham would ask her. I held her arms, looked into her eyes. "I love you so, so, so much, Marie, I need you to know this, no matter what happens, remember that I will always love you," I said softly to her.

"I know, Mum, and I love you, but why are you saying this now, what's wrong?"

"I NEED you to know, that's all, Marie, don't worry, I just needed to say it to you."

"Mum, you are acting a bit weird, are you okay?" she said.

I smiled at her. "Yes, I'm okay, baby, I've got you, my beautiful, gorgeous daughter," I said as I held her tight.

The pin was passed the next morning, as I discovered while searching through the cardboard urine container. Graham arrived to pick us up and had George with him. They looked all official – George was carrying a black leather case, Graham had a suit on. I didn't even ask why George was off school and why they looked all official, there was no point, and I had stopped speaking unless it was in Graham's absence anyway.

Chapter 30

Wednesday 18th July 2018

Jack and I had planned the day. We decided that I would spend the day with Rose and Harry, and I would call Jack with the tracking details so he could follow his LYING, CHEATING father.

It was midday and the tracker had Graham's car parked in a residential street in Knaresborough. I forwarded the information to Jack, who drove to the destination. The white Range Rover Evoque belonging to Graham was parked outside a house. Jack took photos and waited to see which house Graham came out of. More than two and a half hours had elapsed by the time Graham appeared with just enough time to spare to pick up George and Marie from school. Graham had spotted Jack, but drove off in the opposite direction. Later that day when Jack arrived back home to me and Rose, he gave me the lowdown.

"Mum, you need to LEAVE HIM," Jack pleaded.

"Yes, you are right, but where will I go? I don't have any money or anywhere to go," I said.

"You can live here with us," Jack and Rose agreed.

My mind was racing. What about George and Marie? Painful as it was, I was in no position to support two teenagers. What about school? They were stable at home and they could come and see me anytime they wanted, I didn't want to upset their routines etc. I also thought that if I left the highly abusive situation, then it would probably help them as they wouldn't have to witness or be a part of that any more.

As we were discussing this, Graham sent me a text: "Where are you? What time will you be home, *babe?*"

It was now approximately 5pm.

"I'm just at Jack's, Rose wants me to look after Harry while she nips out for a bit, I might as well get my baby cuddles in."

"sad" was his reply.

"sad???? what do mean, sad???? don't be like that *babe* I will be home soon," I replied sarcastically.

"tell you what, why don't you stay at Jack's and he can feed your paranoia, in fact why don't you all live together and all be paranoid together! Don't worry me and kids will go out for tea."

Graham obviously knew that he had been caught with his pants down.

"Right, you can't go back now, he will be raging."

"Yes, go with your mum and she can get some of her things, Jack," Rose said. I was terrified about going back, but I felt safe with Jack by my side – he wasn't going to let that evil coward hurt me.

We arrived at the house and walked through the rear gate towards the back door. Graham and George were outside in the garden and Jack was behind me which provoked a very confused Graham.

"What are you doing? Why's HE here?" pointing at Jack.

"I'm leaving you," I said confidently.

"What do you mean? Leaving me? Why?" he asked as he had started to shake.

"BECAUSE I DON'T LIKE YOU AND YOU TREAT ME LIKE SHIT!" I said, feeling strangely empowered.

"*He's* not going in the house," he said pointing at Jack, then proceeded to intimidate him, pushing his chest out and pushing up against Jack to try and entice him to physically retaliate. "Come on, come on then, Jack, you know you want to, go on hit me," he screamed

217

in Jack's face.

Jack didn't rise to it, he just looked down at Graham and said calmly, "You're not worth it... you are pathetic, just look at yourself. I thought you had a heart condition?"

"Yes, I do and you had better get checked out because it's genetic," Graham snapped.

"Oh, is it, I thought *I* had caused it by causing too much stress?" I quipped.

"LOOK, I have just come to get a few things", I added.

"NO, NO, I don't want you in the house."

"George, George, call the police, call the police!" shouted Graham.

I just looked at him and just saw a pathetic, cowardly, little middle-aged man, shaking in his boots. I no longer felt afraid of him. It was like a huge weight lifted off my shoulders, like the sun had suddenly come out of a black sky. Graham rang the police, I can't even remember what lies he told them, but they arrived while we waited outside.

"OK, what's going on here?" the officer said.

Graham started to talk his usual crap, and they looked at me.

"Look, this is my eldest son, he has just brought me here to collect some of my belongings, as I'm leaving him," I explained calmly.

They were confused as to why he couldn't just let me in, but he insisted that they escorted me to my room to get some belongings. George and Marie were very quiet, and I tried to explain to them that I was leaving Graham and his vile abuse, I wasn't leaving them. When the police left, Graham and the kids came to the front door; he was shaking and squirming, stuttering his words...

"What's all this about, Alisha, why are you leaving?" he said in a pathetic voice.

"Well, where shall I start, let me think...you are a LYING, CHEATING NASTY WIFE BEATER," I said, very composed.

"No, I haven't lied, lied about what? ALISHA, I have NEVER cheated on you."

"Listen, you have been caught with your pants down. I had you followed and I have a voice recording on my phone with you and a woman, you were arranging to meet her on a Wednesday... '*Awwwwww, BABE, doesn't time fly, I like coming on a Saturday*'... does that ring any bells, Graham?" I mocked.

Very rarely had I seen someone panic and squeal so much as he was right now.

"Oh, what you have on your phone was a three-way conversation with Sarah the rep, she always comes to see me on Wednesday and she missed me, it was just banter when I said she had a sexy arse, it's just harmless flirting. I call EVERYONE babe, it's only a bit of fun," he stuttered.

"Nope, try again, Graham, but I now know about Sarah the rep!" Frantically trying to figure out what I had recorded.

"It must have been when I was talking to Kate, we just have a laugh, it's just sexy texts messages, that's all. Come on, why would a 6ft, 32 year old model have anything to do with me?" he said, digging himself deeper and deeper in a hole.

"I didn't know any of this, Graham, but I will ask you again... question...who...is...the...woman...you...see...every...Wednesday...and... Saturday? Simple question, Graham," I said very, very slowly to him.

"I see lots of women all the time, it will be just a customer, or female reps, I see women walking down the street all the time, we chat the pie woman up at 10am in her van every day, I might look at mannequins... Come on, babe, this is ridiculous, you are so jealous and paranoid. Here, look at my phone, you can see it's just kisses and banter," he said, trivialising it, turning it around to make me look in the wrong as usual.

"OK, where were you today?" I said bluntly.

"I don't know exactly, erm at work, probably saw some customers, I can't remember."

"It was only today, you must remember where you were?"

Now extremely agitated he said, stuttering, "Listen I don't have to explain myself to you, I'm not filling a time sheet in just because you don't trust me, you are so paranoid. Come on, this is stupid, come in, don't be stupid, let's just enjoy summer, me, you and the kids."

His emotions were erratic, he had a lot to lose if he lost me, I was his world, I was the love of his life, in his crazy head, he would have no-one to control and abuse, he couldn't lead his secret double life, and, worst of all in his eyes, I would be entitled to half of everything we owned, so he clumsily tried to talk me round. He had been caught off guard, so had no lies ready on standby.

"OK, listen, you were followed to a house where you stayed for over two hours, it was a woman who you see every week. Until you tell me the truth there is no hope whatsoever."

"I saw Jack following me today, so why would I be up to no good when my son was outside? It's a customer who lets me keep my motorbikes in her garage," he said in a clever tone, thinking he had explained himself; not the sharpest tool in the box.

"Oh, I didn't know you had motorbikes, let alone a woman who lets you keep them in her garage!" I was pleased with myself how composed and calm I had stayed. It was a refreshing change to see Graham squealing like a pig.

"Graham, I will ask you again. Who is the woman you see every Wednesday and Saturday?"

"Well, I wasn't going to tell you, but she's an osteopath, she treats my bad back," he blurted out.

Graham doesn't even have a bad back!

"I don't believe you, who is she?" I was bored by now listening to his never-ending lies, but I was getting some satisfaction watching him blunder his way out of this.

"Okay, this is the truth, I go to see a masseur twice a week, she lives in Knaresborough where Jack followed me to, I didn't tell you because I knew you would get mad and angry," he said, thinking that he was off the hook.

He was still stood on the doorstep with George and Marie (his little 'support network'), and Jack was stood patiently waiting for me. "Right are you happy now? Are you going to stop being silly and come home?" he said matter of factly. I looked at him in disbelief.

"The divorce papers will be in the post in the next few days," I said coldly.

This was the furthest Graham had seen me go, he never in a million years thought I would ever leave him, he had always teased me that I would never leave as it would break my heart to leave George and Marie. He was right, it would destroy me, I love them with all my heart – but I never imagined that he would do everything in his power to stop all contact between us forever!

"I'm not leaving you two," I said to George and Marie. "I'm leaving *him* and his abuse, I love you with all my heart," I said, sobbing. They had seen the horrific abuse first-hand, but were now becoming abusers too, on Graham's say-so. "And I'm so sorry that you have to go through this, we will still see each other, I love you two so much."

"Well, we don't love you," they said bravely in front of their abuser.

I knew they were hurting and it broke my heart walking away, these words had obviously been instilled into them by Graham, I knew that – it was only two days ago that Marie and I had told each other how much we loved each other, so I knew that this was just for Graham's benefit.

"What sort of *wife* leaves her husband in his hour of need? You are so selfish, you only care about yourself!" he said playing for sympathy.

"A *wife* who cannot take anymore suffering, Graham, a *wife* who has had enough, a *wife* who has been loyal and devoted for nearly 40 years, misguided actually, a *wife* who doesn't deserve to be treated no better than a slave; but worry not, Graham, your masseur will look after you, or Sarah the rep with the sexy arse, or any of the other BABES you know, I'm sure they will be there for you in your *hour of need*," I said as I walked away feeling liberated.

"I will see you on the street, you're NOT getting a penny out of me!" he screamed.

In his sick caveman-like head he believed that everything we had and had built up over 40 years was ALL HIS. Money was the only thing he cared about and ironically his extreme greed would be his ultimate downfall.

"Listen, can we do this amicably and civil, Graham, it will be better for all of us?" I tried to reason with him.

His reply was typical Graham style... "If you throw stones, *we* will throw rocks, won't we, kids?" typically involving our 13 and 15 year old teenagers in our divorce!

"Oh dear!" I laughed.

He then gestured very aggressively a slitting his throat motion, so the death threats had started.

"Oh, going to slit my throat now!" I said as George and Marie turned to Graham, who held his hands in the air.

"She's crazy, even imagining things now," he said to them all innocently.

No point in trying to reason with a narcissist.

"YOU ARE IMPOSSIBLE!" I said as I walked away towards Jack. We went back to his house where Rose had prepared the spare room for me to stay in.

"I can't thank you enough for this, I really appreciate this."

"You can stay here until you find your feet," they both agreed.

I was in shock. I had been with Graham since I was 16 years old, I was now 56 – that was 40 years of my life, nearly ALL my life. Now I had escaped my 'prison' I was scared; how could I possibly cope? All I could think about was George and Marie, I was desperate to talk to them away from that control freak, but that was never going to happen for as long as he drew breath.

The next day I booked an appointment with the solicitors'. After a long chat, I instructed them to draw up divorce papers based on

UNREASONABLE BEHAVIOUR. The papers were ready to pick up the following day and I hand delivered them to Graham on the Saturday morning, although there was no-one home so I posted them through the letterbox.

After speaking with the solicitors at our initial meeting I was told that I could apply for a litigation loan. Luckily I had the house from my inheritance money to put up as collateral. I believe that things happen for a reason, and because of my dad, I was able to divorce Graham, which he would very much approve of.

Divorcing a narcissist is extremely stressful and very difficult. Graham was determined that I would be destitute, and he was prepared to make this as nasty and stressful as he could.

The first few days he was texting me desperately to get me back. There was absolutely no chance that I would EVER return and endure that nightmare existence EVER again. I had done the hard part, I had left him, which, in his head, was complete betrayal and humiliating to him, but more than that, he had lost control which is unthinkable to him.

A few nights after, I arranged through my solicitor to have police escort to go to the house to get some clothes etc. Jack came with me. It was 7pm. Graham had been given plenty of notice of our arrival time. I thought he would maybe take the kids out for tea or be in another room while I just gathered my personal belongings together... but this was far from a normal person I was dealing with... There were four or five cars parked in the drive and outside the house, and Graham was stood at the front door, shouting and swearing at me and Jack. "Fuck off, you are not coming in this house."

The police escort arrived and told Graham to let us in. He was behaving like a demented freak making a complete idiot of himself; worse still as the police persuaded him to eventually let us in, it was like a scene from the Jeremy Kyle show but worse. Graham, being the absolute coward that he is, had invited three of our staff for moral support, one of the staff being Gaz, Graham's 'minder and gopher', his wife Shaz and their two young children; so Graham had his little army behind him, including George and Marie. This in itself is highly disturbing, exposing seven people to this highly personal and volatile situation.

After jack and I eventually entered the house with the police escort, Graham behaved like a wild animal screaming in Jack's face for Jack to hit him, but Jack just replied, "Dad, your breath stinks, now go and sit down, you have a heart condition."

This infuriated Graham more than ever. He then turned to me and screamed: "IF YOU LEAVE ME, I WILL MAKE SURE THAT THESE KIDS NEVER, EVER WANT TO SEE YOU AGAIN!"

"Yes, I believe you will because you are beyond evil!" I screamed back at this monster.

At this, Marie broke down in tears, but Graham refused to let me console her, screaming at me that she hated me. It was so clearly obvious that George and Marie were terrified of Graham, they were, and still are today, under his total control.

I entered my room to collect my belongings to find that Graham had destroyed my room; he had removed my clothes, my gorgeous mirror and most evil of all, my memory box of Lisa which contained personal items between me and her. I confronted him about it and he shouted:

"She was my daughter too!"

"Yes, and she absolutely despised you; it was Mum's memory box, you didn't even care about Lisa so give her the box back!" Jack shouted to Graham, who replied with disgusting verbal abuse.

As I tried to collect my belongings, Graham followed me in, immediately went into my wardrobe and pulled out an empty litre bottle of gin, an empty large bottle of Lambrini, and another empty bottle of wine, clearly planted there by him. He then paraded around the house laughing, armed with these empty bottles and shouted to them all, "Look everyone, she's an alcoholic, these were hidden in her wardrobes. Look…" He gleamed like a kid in a candy shop thinking he was clever, thinking he could convince people that I was the abuser, but this was yet another act that just confirmed to me that I was doing the right thing leaving this disturbed maniac.

"You have been here long enough now, fuck off!!" as Shaz pointed in my face.

"She will stay as long as she likes, it's *her* house," Jack replied.

Well this was enough for her and husband Gaz to threaten to kill Jack.

"Don't talk to my Mrs like that… I will end you, boy" he shouted at Jack, then Graham started to copy what Gaz had said: "Yeah, I will end you, boy." If it wasn't so serious it would actually be hilarious.

"Can I have one of the TVs seeing as there are four in the house and I don't have one?" I stupidly asked Graham, but I literally had NOTHING or NO money to buy one.

"No, you can't and we only have three now anyway!" He was intent on letting me have absolutely NOTHING.

"OK, fine, I won't take anything," I said with tears streaming down my face. I looked at George and Marie. My heart filled with agony, my babies who were under Graham's evil spell, they were only 13 and 15. I could see the pain, the confusion, the torment in their eyes; they knew, like I did, that Graham would do everything possible to prevent any contact between me and them –and nearly four years on, this has been the case: I haven't seen George and Marie since I left that summer.

"I love you both so much, I'm not leaving you, I will always be here for you, I'm leaving the abuse, I'm so sorry, I can't live like this anymore, but I love you so much," I sobbed to them.

"Well we don't love you," they said again, as though reading from a script previously prepared.

"Well I love you," I reiterated to them. My heart was ripped into a million pieces, but I had no choice – if I hadn't have left, I would most certainly be dead now and they wouldn't have a mum; it was better for them not to have to witness such horrific abuse in their lives anymore. After all, the cruel, mental "separation" from me, their mum, had been indoctrinated into them since being so young and vulnerable, that in their minds, it wasn't as painful as it was for me.

After approximately 15 minutes in this house of horrors trying to collect some belongings, I left with a handful of sentimental items, then myself, Jack and the police officer left the property. Jack then drove me to his house where I would be staying with him and his family.

The next few days were filled with panic as the realisation of what had happened kicked in. I was, effectively, homeless, penniless and had lost my kids in the process. I had absolutely no idea how I was going to survive, I just felt so blessed that Jack and Rose were letting me stay with them. They let me share their home, fed me and looked after me while I was grieving for George and Marie and coming to terms with being destitute. (I know I had the house from my inheritance, but that would be signed over to the loan company to pay for my divorce, which cost over £300k in the end.)

Only a week after I left, Wednesday morning, 8am, I went to the family home to collect my mail. I was greeted by an extremely angry Graham who immediately screamed upstairs to wake up George and Marie:

"Kids, wake up, come downstairs, she's here."

"Why would you wake the kids up, that's terrible, I just want my mail."

George and Marie came downstairs half asleep trying to open their eyes to adjust to the light – even though they were aggressively awoken from their sleep, they obeyed Graham's order.

"George, get her mail, then she can fuck off and leave us alone."

George went to get my mail and proceeded to open the kitchen window and threw my letters outside. Graham then looked at me with his ice-cold death stare and aggressively made a slicing of the throat gesture yet again with his left hand across his neck!

23/07/2018 5.16pm I received a text message from Graham:

"I have appointment with solicitor in morning at ten DO YOU REALLY WANT THIS BEFORE we start making solicitors rich ??? I not starting then turning back."

"Yes, keep your solicitor's appointment, it's apparent that this is the only way that I will get a penny from our marital pot as you clearly think all that we built up together during our 38-year marriage ALL belongs to you and that I should have NOTHING, and if this makes the solicitors rich, then that's purely down to you and your selfish GREED!!!"

I was entering terrifying, alien territory and the next two years were spent in court; it didn't seem to end, hearing after hearing...

Family court was my starting point. I needed to see George and Marie, and more importantly, they needed a mother and their brothers in their lives, so it began only after Graham delayed all proceedings for four months using his health problem to his full advantage...

'Graham cannot withstand any stress regarding divorce proceedings due to his ill health,' was the letter from the doctor.

He needed a routine heart operation, but meanwhile, he was seen out drinking with girlfriends, attending the gym, riding his secret motorbike and generally just living his life while the proceedings were successfully stayed. This had an extremely detrimental effect on me in every conceivable way possible, so I requested that I needed funds from the marital pot with immediate effect so as to survive, and our marital pot (which Graham was comfortably sitting on while I was penniless) was extremely substantial, consisting of seven properties, a business and very healthy bank accounts, so I was successfully awarded 'spousal maintenance' which was payable monthly from Graham until a divorce settlement was agreed... He fought tooth and nail, appealed and argued that he shouldn't have to pay me a penny...

"She can claim benefits" was his defence! This was quashed by the court and my maintenance was upheld. This was the disgusting attitude that Graham had his entire life, so there was no surprise that this was going to be a very nasty divorce full of his unbelievable lies.

While awaiting court hearings I was followed and stalked by Graham. I had already reported the death threats to the police, but in August 2018, I found a clear plastic folder with my name on in Graham's car while attending the house for more belongings. I opened the folder to find a stack of pages containing all my private messages from my personal mobile phone, all enumerated and labelled with the recipient's name on. I felt violated, I was shocked that the reality was he had stalked me for years. In a state of panic I immediately took these to the police to press charges. Graham, true to form, blamed the whole stalking of my phone entirely on George, our 15 year old son!

Chapter 31

August 2018

After I left Graham, I had made contact with Lee and asked if he would meet me for a chat. We had been estranged now for over two years and it had broken my heart. I wanted him back in my life desperately. He agreed to meet me and we sat and chatted over a coffee in a supermarket cafe.

"Lee, I have missed you so much, I'm so sorry about everything. I love you so much and it's been so hard, but I have left Graham."

"Oh my God, at last, what took you so long, Mum? We have been telling you to leave him for years, he's horrible."

"Yes, I know, but I had to get the strength to leave, he's poisoned George and Marie against me to the point that they were being abusive to me. He threatened to kill me and I realised that it was too dangerous to stay, he was getting so much worse."

"Mum, he's been stabbing you in the back for years, I've witnessed him telling the kids that they will leave you one day, he would spend loads of time turning them against you since George was eight and Marie was six. I confronted him one day and said that if he doesn't want to be with you then he should leave, NOT poison the kids against you. I could barely look you in the face knowing he was slagging you off behind your back. I'm so proud of you for leaving, it must have been so hard, especially to leave the kids," he said sympathetically.

"I never left the kids, Lee. I had to leave not only with my life, but for their benefit too, they were subjected to seeing so much abuse and horrific tantrums by Graham, so I removed myself for all our sakes. I will get the kids back, I'm their mum, and I will fight to the death for them. I'm so sorry for the abuse you suffered at his hands, Lee. I wish I could change it, but you are doing great, you have your own family now, a great job and a good head on your shoulders. I'm so proud of you and Jack coming out the other side relatively ok. Now that the toxic person is out of my life, I'm hoping to salvage what's left of all our relationships, especially you and Jack," I sobbed, tears streaming down my face.

We had a very long chat and arranged to meet up again soon. He explained that his wife Louise was not interested in having me in their lives after everything that had happened and I totally understood that it would take time to rebuild our relationship, but today we now have a very close bond.

25/08/2018 I had arranged to meet Lee in the local pub to discuss matters with him and inform him that I had found evidence of the stalking, and at 8pm that evening I met Lee as planned and we just sat talking. Lee then told me that earlier that day Graham had gone to Lee's house with George and Marie and had tried to barge his way into Lee's house saying he needed to talk to him urgently. Lee kept him on the doorstep to protect his wife and his two small children. Graham then offered Lee £50k to take guardianship of George and Marie if anything should happen to him and said that he had bought a four-bed house without my knowledge where he could live with the kids. Lee told Graham that he needed serious help, that he was mentally unstable and that George and Marie should be with me, their loving mother. Graham responded aggressively saying that the kids hated me, and if Lee didn't accept his offer, that he would send George and Marie to live with his elderly cousin, who is riddled with arthritis, up in Durham. All this was said in front of George and Marie, his own flesh and blood. I cannot imagine what was going through their confused heads at this time, but Graham had no interest in his kids, he just wanted to punish me.

As Lee was telling me these disgusting events from earlier in the day, Graham entered the pub with George and Marie by his side and brazenly said hello to Lee – who didn't respond. He then approached the bar to buy a drink for them. The pub had about 10 people in, but because they were all local and were aware of the situation, there was a sudden silence. Graham and the kids took a seat about ten foot away from us and proceeded to stare at us with evil looks. I could see that he was also encouraging George and Marie to join in with him. The atmosphere was extremely tense and with Dutch courage and support amongst the locals, I approached Graham's table...

"GET OUT, YOU ARE STALKING ME...GET OUT NOW!" I shouted, shaking.

"I'm not stalking you at all, Alisha," he said...but he obviously knew my whereabouts as he was still stalking me through my phone. The barmaid came over to me and asked if I was okay.

"No, I'm *not* okay, he's stalking me," I replied.

She then proceeded to phone the landlady, who arrived at around 9pm, just minutes after the incident. She was really nice and asked me if I needed anything.

I just replied, "Yes, I am being stalked by him, my ex, and I want him to leave."

She asked him to leave the premises to which his typical response was "No, I can drink here if I like".

The landlady then looked at the time and said, "Well it's gone 9pm and you have two underage children with you, so I am telling you to leave immediately."

Graham reluctantly left but decided to circle the mini roundabout in the pub car park for a while. The discussions in the pub turned to that situation with some of them telling me that Graham had been circling the pub car park before entering earlier and they thought he was mentally disturbed. Some of these people knew him when he was at school and started telling me stories of his abusive, bullying behaviour as a kid; he was known as a bully anyway. Lee and I felt embarrassed with Graham's behaviour and decided to leave, but as we went outside, Graham and the kids were parked outside waiting for me to emerge. As I was living in hiding at a secret address, I was very nervous about driving home for fear of him following me, so I stayed with Lee until I felt it was safe to go home.

The next day, I reported the incident to the police. The next couple of years were dotted with the same narcissistic, controlling, abusive behaviour which were even being extended to my friends whom he would follow, intimidate and send friend requests to on social media sites. He was threatening my friends via social media, he was reporting social workers who were allocated to helping George and Marie; it was also evident during the court hearings.

While Graham was pleading critical illness he was seen working out at the gym, riding his secret motorbike and seeing women, yet he would insist that divorce proceedings were too stressful for a man in such a fragile condition.

On 20th September 2018, while talking casually to a friend who worked in a local footwear shop, she just said to me, "Does he still have that house on Hell Wath estate?"

"What house? What house?" My heart was pounding – this was the proof I needed to present in court.

She continued to give me all the details, saying that he had purchased it in 2014, that he was renting it out after leaving it empty for two years. She was shocked at my reaction of total oblivion. I thanked her for the information and immediately contacted the land registry which confirmed this to be true. I know he had previously told Lee about a house that he had, but this was concrete evidence which I took straight to my solicitor. This house was literally around the corner from our family home, which we regularly walked past as a family on dog walks – this must have been immensely amusing to Graham, thinking he had deceived and conned me on yet another of his antics.

On many occasions Graham was seen with the kids in the local Wetherspoons and on one particular occasion in November 2018 he saw a good friend of mine, Sheryl, who was enjoying a quiet drink with her husband. Graham approached them in an aggressive manner and loudly said, "Do the kids look clean now, Shez?" then proceeded to tell her that he had read a document saying the kids were unkempt and concluded that it was her words – which was untrue. He then continued to harass her by talking negatively about me, and telling the kids, who were clearly embarrassed and stressed with the situation, to tell her lies about me poisoning my father's dog etc. The kids were reported to be emotionless with no facial expression and could have been reading from the script of Graham. This despicable behaviour by a so-called father, is a clear example of child abuse, forcing them to tell lies about their mum to people they don't know in public – shameful and highly damaging to young minds.

Chapter 32

Jack and Rose had been amazing, letting me stay with them. It was just so unfortunate that I was at one of the lowest points in my life and they witnessed my utter helplessness and distress while dealing with my situation. I was talking non-stop to the police, I had given hours and hours of interviews regarding my 40 years of domestic abuse so I was working with them closely to build my case to one day take to court. I was very lucky, the investigating detective was fantastic, she was a huge support to me throughout the investigations. She would contact me constantly to give me support and encouragement, she arranged for me to be on high alert with the police due to the death threats from Graham and I still am to date which gives me peace of mind to a certain extent. I had regular visits from the police ensuring my safety, which was immensely reassuring.

The time had come that Jack and Rose needed their life back. I am indebted to them for their unbelievable support – they picked me up when I was down, they made me laugh when all I could do was cry. My grandson, Harry, was the light of my life, he would climb onto my bed for cuddles, play peek a boo and gave meaning to my life right when I needed it most. I adore this amazing little boy so very much and would be sad to move out from a temporary life with Jack, Rose and baby Harry into the unknown world waiting for me.

I have been so very lucky having Lisa, Jack and Lee, my gorgeous daughter and sons have been my absolute saviours throughout my married life and if Lisa is up there looking down on me now, all I would say is:

"Thank you my beautiful, wonderful, strong, independent little warrior princess, I miss you more than you could ever know, but I understand completely why you left this life, you have been so instrumental in me leaving that vile, abusive life behind. I feel your strength, I hear your voice – "leave him, Mum, leave him, he's horrible" – you wouldn't have understood why it wasn't that easy for me to just leave, but I'm sure you will get it now. I had to be ready. I had been wanting to leave for years, I was living with someone I despised, then loved, then despised. I was trauma bonded, I was terrified I had no means of leaving, nowhere to go, no money, I had three young kids at the time, I wanted to make it work for my children, but how wrong I was and you made the ultimate sacrifice, Lisa, you took your life just as I had wanted to take mine many times; but I could never hurt my kids and deny them of their mum. It was a struggle after you died, George and Marie were only four and two, Jack and Lee 19 and 18; we all suffered with your loss, and still do 14 years later. You were the strongest person I knew. Thank you, Lisa Marie for being my amazing daughter for 22 years, 8 months and 23 days and for being a loving sister to your brothers. I will love you forever and ever, all my love your heartbroken mum xxx."

Jack said he would help me look for a place to live, he offered to lend me money until I got on my feet, but I was determined to do this without his very kind offer, so I spent my time searching for properties to rent in Harrogate, so I could be close to Jack and Rose. Within hours I had earmarked three flats to view. The first one was in a lovely, quiet part of Harrogate. I asked Sheila to come and view it with me; she was nearly as excited as I was, so I arranged to view the next day. As we drove up to this very impressive house, I was overwhelmed by the huge windows and the hexagonal design of this house which looked more like a former building of importance, so I was eager to view. The agent arrived, and we stood behind him, and as the front door opened we could see the space was great, a massive staircase which served three floors to the right, lots of doors all around us, but the smell was damp and dirty. The further we looked the more grim it became; it looked like squatters had been living there; it was so sad to see such an amazing house in such a bad state of repair. I quickly declined the room I viewed, and left feeling despondent.

"Don't give up, this is the first one you have seen," Sheila said. She always put a positive spin on everything but my self-esteem was on the floor and my emotions were delicate.

My phone rang a few hours later. "Hi Alisha, Jean here just to confirm a viewing this evening." I had totally forgotten about another viewing I had that day. I went along and was pipped at the post by a girl just before me for the best room in the house. I didn't want a house share, but beggars can't be choosers, can they? Jean saw my disappointment.

"There is a lovely apartment on Duchy Road that you might be interested in."

"Duchy Road? I couldn't possibly afford to rent anything in that area, Jean, it's so expensive, but thank you, I will continue my search," I replied.

This was a very affluent part of Harrogate; only in my dreams could I imagine living in such a leafy, beautiful part of this lovely town, so close to gorgeous beauty spots and only a short walk into the bustling town with miles of lush green parks etc...but what happened next was unbelievable...it was just as though Lisa was looking over me and making this happen. It was the most bizarre experience...

It was Thursday 13th September 2018 7pm. "Follow me, Alisha, we are going to look at this apartment, I know you said you can't afford it, but maybe you could get someone to share with you, but I want to take you to see it."

I agreed but didn't want to get my hopes up. I followed behind in my car down leafy streets with the most gorgeous houses all set back in large grounds, then we pulled up outside this impressive house. Just the location alone was out of my reach.

"Right, Alisha, just follow me, it's a garden flat just up here," Jean said, very upbeat.

I followed her to this gorgeous apartment and stood looking at the front door, tears running down my face. The feeling was unreal, it was as if the apartment was waiting for me. I heard Lisa's voice in my head …yessssss, Mum, this is your sanctuary, this is yours, take it…

"I love it, Jean, I want it, I just love it," I said as the tears rolled down my face.

"You haven't seen inside yet!" she said, laughing.

"I don't need to, this is going to be mine."

Jean opened the door and led the way into what would be my haven, my sanctuary, my freedom, my life… I followed Jean into the very long galley kitchen which looked brand new, all furnished with a country farmhouse style table and six chairs, all appliances included; it was perfect. Upstairs led to a very cosy living room, ideal size, again included was a cream leather sofa, timber floors throughout, sheepskin rugs. The bedroom had a new double bed, the bathroom, much larger than average, with a new white suite, large walk in shower and again just perfect; this was made just for me. I cried, "Jean, I really want this, I love it but I just cannot afford it, I'm gutted, this is perfect for me."

"Let me have word with the landlord. How much can you afford to pay?"

I felt embarrassed giving her a figure £145.00 lower than the asking rent price. "He isn't going to drop that much, Jean."

"Leave it to me, I'm going to speak to Mr Charlesworth right now. You have another look around, I won't be long." She was less than 10 minutes. "OK, I have spoken to Mr Charlesworth and he's happy to let you have the apartment for £145.00 less than the asking rent. Also ALL the bills are included in the price, and all the furniture, so it is ready to move into immediately – what do you say?" she said, beaming.

I just hugged her and cried, "I can't actually believe it, to be honest, I'm so happy, thank you so much. I know it's Thursday today, but can I move in on Sunday as my son Jack can help me? I will pay you the bond and a month's rent in advance on Sunday when I sign the agreement," I blurted out.

"Great, shall we meet here at 11am on Sunday?" asked Jean.

"Yes, can't wait," I said, still in shock. How did that happen? I was thinking to myself on the way back home to Jack's. It was the most bizarre experience, although I had had previous ones which I won't share in this book, but all I can say is that from the minute I left Graham, I felt I was being helped and guided, so many 'coincidences', 'opportune moments' and things that extraordinary just fell into place, I was sure that Lisa was helping me and giving me her amazing strength.

I arrived back at Jack and Rose's to tell them my good news and they were so happy for me, but I'm sure they were even happier to get their house back to themselves. They both came with me on the Sunday to help me move in and they were amazed at my little gem of a find – and I was still not far away for any babysitting duties required from me. A few hours later they left for home and I was stood in my new apartment, alone, when suddenly I started to sob uncontrollably. I had fallen to the floor and just cried and cried, I just realised that this was the very first time in my life, at 56 years old, that I was on my own. I had lived with my parents and siblings until I was 17, I then moved in with Graham until I left on 18thJuly 2018, then lived with Jack until 16th September 2018. Now suddenly I was on my own and didn't know how I would cope. I suddenly felt vulnerable, alone, scared, lost and my heart was breaking missing George and Marie so much. The texts between me and the kids were consistent of language that Graham used, the grammar and spelling was far inferior to George and Marie's standards – Graham is practically illiterate, his spelling is atrocious and his grammar is non-existent, so the messages I was receiving from the kids' phones were indicative of Graham's language, which told me that he had control of their phones, like he controlled every other aspects of their lives. The text messages were very abusive, full of anger and hate, wishing me dead, very disturbing content, and knowing that these vile messages were his doing, I was becoming immensely concerned about the situation at home for them living with such a hateful, vengeful abuser. During the next couple of months Graham had made it impossible for me and the kids to have any contact at all, he continued to transport them to and from school, and boarded the letterbox up to prevent them receiving mail; his control was worse than ever.

I had been given advice by the police to contact domestic abuse helplines, IDAS, Cafcass, Women's Aid and others. I had started to have panic attacks and horrific nightmares, so I went to the doctors, who knew of my history regarding the domestic abuse and were very supportive, they referred me to counselling and signposted other bodies for support of domestic violence. I was also given anti-depressants which I was reluctant to take at first, but ended up being grateful that they did take the edge off my trauma. The mental health team came to give me support at my new home and when they felt I was ready to try to get back into work, my best friend, Sheila, got me a job one day a week working alongside her where she was the manager of a large gym. I didn't realise at the time just how valuable this would be for me. I was receiving so much support which definitely gave me the confidence to integrate into 'normal' life.

Chapter 33

One day in September I needed to retrieve an important letter, so I went to the family home to find that it was completely empty. The house was trashed as if it had been burgled, but I soon realised that this was actually how Graham had been living with the kids. It was deplorable beyond words, it was filthy with rubbish spilling onto the floors. I was not actually that shocked as he had always been very dirty with no hygiene standards, and it was me who had worked like a slave to keep the house clean and tidy, as well as working full time jobs. He was happy in his pigeon lofts knee deep in pigeon shit, dreaming of winning big races abroad; I was the one who made a home for me and my kids – he didn't even know how to turn on the oven!

I entered George's room to find clothes strewn on his floor, then Marie's room which also looked like she had left in a hurry. I immediately phoned the police to report them 'missing'. Graham had always threatened that they would all disappear and I had no clue where they were. This sent me into a deep panic knowing how mentally unstable Graham was. The police said they were looking into it but Graham was declining all his calls as predicted. My only hope was the school so the next morning I rang them. "Sorry, George and Marie are absent today," the receptionist reported after checking with their respective classes and they hadn't received an explanation from Graham. I was very anxious and telephoned Social Services regarding my concerns. As the days passed, Social Services were working alongside the police and the school to support the kids – they had apparently moved into the 'secret' house that Graham had bought years earlier. He had practically thrown his tenants out so he could live there in 'secret'; he refused to divulge his address to the school, but George and Marie were attending albeit under his control.

There was a social worker allocated to support George and Marie, but Graham was fuming at what he saw as an intrusion. It soon became apparent to Jo, the social worker, that the kids were, in fact, being controlled by 'dad' talking to her as if reading from a script, living in a house which she described as soulless with no love. She picked up on the fact that there lacked closeness between them and 'dad'. Her report went on to say that she had concerns for the kids. I was elated – at last it was recognised that there was abuse. Graham was obviously livid with her findings, so reported her to the powers above. There were two more social workers appointed to support George and Marie, but again when they started to ask questions regarding why there was no contact between me and them, Graham became aggressive and reported them also to have them removed from our case. This was becoming a regular pattern when Graham saw that they could recognise abuse, then he would report them for misconduct or some lie.

On 11th October 2018, there was a court hearing at Harrogate court which was to award me financial relief. The order was made that Graham was to pay me spousal maintenance immediately so I was at least receiving enough money to pay off my credit cards, pay my son back, put food in my mouth and a roof over my head.

His ludicrous offer of £30,000 settlement was so ridiculous, it wasn't even worthy of a reply, so the only way forward was to find the money to fight for my rightful share of our estate, and this is where I had to apply for a litigation loan. This was extremely scary for me and very risky, but what choice did I have? This was about principle now, about Graham abiding by, something he kicked against all his life, being accountable, being told that he was WRONG, and being told to do the right thing. I had faith in my solicitors and my barrister, they were a huge support to me emotionally and they became my "family" throughout these very harrowing court hearings, of which there were many.

Family court was extremely stressful and lengthy. I was fighting a losing battle against someone who had indoctrinated George and Marie to such an extent that they were echoing the words of Graham, saying they didn't want any contact with me, or their two brothers. The only conclusion now was for the judge to make a 'NO ORDER' order, meaning that all doors were left open for direct and indirect contact between me and the kids, that there was NOTHING in place to prevent any contact between George, Marie and myself, but I later learned that Graham told the kids that there was a court order in place to prevent me from communicating with them! George and Marie believe his lies, they have never been told the truth throughout their whole lives so they believe that a judge has made an order against me which is a complete LIE … Hopefully when they do learn the truth, they will then realise how abusive, controlling and evil their father is, then run a million miles from him just like Lisa, Jack and Lee did.

I am still fighting to see George and Marie to this day and have been since the day I left in July 2018. Graham has managed to keep complete control of the kids by boarding up his letter box so no mail can be received without his permission, giving them phones which he tracks, removing them from school and keeping them prisoners at the family home under his watchful eye, cameras installed to check on them constantly, denying them friends and freedom; they are completely ostracized from the world, and because he's brainwashed them into telling all the authorities that they are happy living like hermits under his control with no connections to family, friends, education, work or freedom, then the police, social services etc are saying that they have to listen to a 16 and 18yr old and cannot do anything to help them. This is a CRIME.

It's the worst kind of child abuse ever. George's friends are driving their own cars, working or at university, have girlfriends and boyfriends, they have a social life, go on holidays and days out with their friends, yet George is being denied all this because of his father. I see Marie's school friends clothes-shopping together, socialising together, most have boyfriends and a life, but again, Marie is living behind locked gates and closed curtains, denied a normal life...this is surely a CRIME!

As their mum, I am completely helpless. Graham has tried to completely delete me from their lives, even removing all photos of me from the family home. This individual surely should be sectioned under the mental health act?

Meanwhile, in between all these hearings, I was managing to enjoy my life as much as I could. I spent more time with my very best, beautiful, loyal friend of many years (35 years to be precise) Sheila; she was my confidante, she was my great support network away from Jack and Rose. We spent some lovely times lunching and shopping, being girls having fun, I would be invited out with her and her partner and we were making up for lost time and were at last enjoying times which were previously forbidden to me.

One night while out in a local bar, I bumped into a friend who I had worked with 40 years ago who I hadn't seen for a long time, Deena. She was with her friend Vi, we got chatting and the subject of ski holidays was brought up. "Well, I won't be gong skiing again now that I'm single, I don't have any one to go with," I said to Deena.

"Why not come with me, I'm hoping to go in January with Vi; it will be great, we will have a good laugh, it will do you good," she said excitedly.

This was music to my ears. I couldn't believe how happy I felt, it was like my life was opening up in all different directions. I had been so isolated from real life, and this was truly eye opening for me.

"You will have to come over one night and we will arrange it," she said as she texted me her number.

Jack and Rose were trying for another baby. We were starting to move on.

I was active on the dating sites, which were a bit daunting at first, but I was so shocked to match with the majority of the dates – after all I had been told daily that I was fat and ugly, so the many compliments I received from men who were saying the opposite, were alien to me. I met many lovely men, and had some amazing memorable dates. It was so refreshing to meet men who were so far removed from what I had been used to for 40 years, I had doors opened for me, I was treated with respect and kindness, I was paid compliments and ALL of them wanted to see me again; this was the boost I needed and I am still in touch with a few of them now, so not ALL men were narcissistic, vile control freaks, only the nutter that I married. I was also in touch with a lovely man who was a long standing customer of ours, Burt, who lives in France. He invited me over to stay with him as he was aware of my situation, he said the break would do me good – "I have a very large house and you can have your own floor with your own bathroom, don't worry, there is lots of space if you need time on your own." He had really thought this through, but I was very hesitant and thought about it for a while. I needed to push my boundaries and live a little so after a lot of persuasion I decided to go. I stayed for four days and it was the best time I had had in ages. Burt and I laughed until we cried, I met all his lovely friends, he showed me the sights, took me to lovely restaurants, we had the best time ever and I will treasure the memories of that holiday always. We have remained very good friends and always will be.

I made lots of friends, reconnected with old friends, went on holidays with groups of girls, the first one being with my old friend Jay. I knew Jay from when our children were about six years old, her son Kayden and my daughter Marie were in the same class at primary school. We lost touch, then became reacquainted when I walked into my divorce solicitors where she was working on the switchboard. We immediately picked up where we had left off, she was a huge support to me, and we became very, very close. I would spend endless nights with her at her rural cottage, I felt safe there and she looked after me while I was going through hell and back. She introduced me to two of her close friends Anna and Lyn, and we soon became the four musketeers, holidaying and going out together.

Carolyn sent me another message. She had just come out of a 40-year marriage too, so we met up for a drink after a rocky start. She was single and requesting me as a friend, so I texted her asking why suddenly she wanted to be my friend. She explained that she was living back in Ripon and was contacting old friends, of whom I was one. I explained my situation to her and it took me a little time to fully trust her, but our friendship became closer and closer, we spent a lot of time together, socialising and supporting each other, we were both dealing with divorce proceedings at the same time, both had been married for 40 years and both needed support. Carolyn and myself have become very good friends over the past few years, and I introduced her to Deena, and Vi who had another friend called Lucy, we all formed a very strong bond and spend a lot of time together. We have ski holidays together, we went to Majorca on holiday which was amazing, have Xmas outings, days and evenings out and they all were a massive help and support to me while I was dealing with the horrendous court hearings alongside our times together.

We are all a good support network for each other, and I personally feel blessed to have them in my life.

Chapter 34

Christmas Eve 2018

After asking Lee if I could buy presents for his kids Ryan and Rhianne (I knew they had a baby girl born in January 2017, but sadly I had never seen her), I dropped them round to his. As he opened the door to me, there were his two gorgeous babies looking up with their big brown eyes, dressed in their Christmas pyjamas, sat on the stairs. I was instantly in love. I said hello to them and said to Louise how adorable they were. She told them to say hello to me, and this was to be the beginning of a slow rebuild of our relationship, I doubted that we would ever be as close as we were and she was doubtful that I had left Graham for good, knowing that I had previously left and gone back to him, so she was quite rightly reserved.

The relationship between me and Lee was becoming closer, and I was eager to reunite Jack and Lee, so I organised evenings out for us three and life was starting to pan out a lot better. But George and Marie were never far from my thoughts – my heart ached for them missing a huge part of their lives.

Family court, York, the first hearing took place 6 November 2018, four months after I had left, but due to Graham's delay tactics where Graham hadn't attended, this was the third one so far. We were called to a small room. Graham entered, swaggering in looking like the cat that got the cream in his long black trench coat, his tongue in the side of his cheek, forcing his face to smirk and laugh. It made my skin crawl just seeing him, he knew that I had caught him with his pants down, I knew that he had lied and cheated and led a double life for many years, so the forced, pathetic smirking, was, in his eyes, laughing at me not knowing what he was doing behind my back, during the hearing. My barrister alerted the judge to Graham's sanctimonious behaviour, which quickly wiped the smirk from his face.

I just wanted to see George and Marie, but it proved impossible. Graham had successfully alienated them from me and their brothers. This was recognised by a judge further down the line of hearings that:

"THIS IS A CLEAR CASE OF PARENTAL ALIENATION AND THIS IS A VERY SAD CASE THAT GEORGE AND MARIE HAVE BEEN ALIENATED FROM THEIR MOTHER AND SIBLINGS, I WILL MAKE SURE THAT THEY ARE REUNITED WITHIN TWO WEEKS AND I WANT TO KEEP THIS CASE."

Sadly, this did not materialise. Graham was adamant that he kept control of the kids by constant brainwashing and manipulation of their young minds, they were terrified of their father, and he did everything to ensure the kids didn't ever have contact with me or their brothers again.

In short, without detailing the many hearings that followed, Graham spun a web of lies to the judges, pleading poverty, asking his friends to issue fictitious invoices for the purchase of racing pigeons to the total of £30,000, saying he had lost thousands of pounds at the horse races and casinos; he hid £80,000 in accounts in George and Marie's names, he paid off the mortgage outstanding on the secret house of £182,00, so he was telling the courts, not only had he spent his inheritance of £480,000 but he had to close the family double glazing company on 13th December 2019 due to it "haemorrhaging" money.

So there he stood in court, under oath, in front of the judge spinning his lies, but what he didn't realise is, that judges see people like this in court all the time.

Throughout the whole proceedings spanning over two years, the most SICK, disturbing, vile, unbelievably cruel, disgusting thing of all, was an invoice raised by Graham's 90 year old mother, to our deceased daughter LISA, for £2,000 for damage she caused in Graham's mother's flat seven years before Lisa died. This was obviously the work of Graham hiding behind his very elderly sick mother. Graham also paid his mother £10,000 cash plus £2,000 from LISA...

Who invoices their dead daughter to hide £2,000? This is the work of an immensely sick, mental individual. The whole court, especially the judge, was utterly sick to the stomach hearing this invoice being read out in court.

Christmas Day 2018

Jack and Rose invited me to have Christmas in Durham with her family. I took Harry's presents round on Christmas morning, to Jack and Rose's and watched Harry open his presents. I had bought him his first slide which be loved and lots of other toys; he was my world, I absolutely doted on this gorgeous little boy. We set off up to Durham mid-morning. Rose's mum and grandparents had been really busy putting on the most gorgeous spread, I got on really well with Rose's family, they were so friendly and welcomed me with open arms. Christmas was amazing. I stayed until Boxing Day and had the best time.

The judgement made by the judge in Harrogate court, in November 2019, ruled in my favour of a 55%/45% split. The judgement was perfected on 31st January 2020. Graham was fuming and did not accept this ruling, so proceeded to appeal and take this judge to the high court.

18th February 2020 I was elated: my decree absolute was granted. I was divorced from this horrendous person who had destroyed so many lives, mainly his own children's lives, and continues to do so, but I was so happy to be free after 40 years.

14th May 2020, a date I won't forget: Lee's 31st birthday and the date of the final hearing of the FDR (Financial Dispute Resolution), I was awarded 55% as per the hearing previous, so effectively he lost the appeal. This was finally the end of the court hearing, this was a massive relief for me now ... because of Graham's stubbornness, this divorce cost, between us, over £300k, yet he was the one supposedly *"not wanting 'to make the solicitors rich'..."*

Deadlines were made, Graham was given seven days to sign over all the properties to me, he retained the family home and the "failing" business. I promptly signed my half of the family home to him. It was such a relief to finally receive my fair share of OUR estate, I could now plan my life as I chose.

June 2020 I now had a rental income from the properties awarded to me from the divorce and would now start my new life.

Chapter 35

Covid-19 came along in March 2019, and this was just the perfect screen for Graham to further his control and abuse; he had the ideal excuse to remove himself, George and Marie from society totally and it was accepted because of this pandemic!

From this moment on, my energy was spent in close contact with Social Services, Cafcass, IDAS, the Police and all other authorities who could help free George and Marie from this horrendous isolation they faced – the letter box at their home was still boarded up, the gates were constantly locked and the curtains drawn permanently. George and Marie were, and still are, denied contact with family and friends. He removed them from school in February 2020, they missed over two years of education – is this a caring father? Or an extremely controlling, revengeful abuser hellbent on punishing me?

I was constantly told that the law says children over the age of 12 were heard and if a child of 12 was saying that they did not want to see a parent or their siblings, whether it was as a result of being poisoned and brainwashed against that parent, it didn't seem to matter. But the system needs to wake up and recognise that parental alienation is a serious form of child abuse. I believe the law needs changing. I understand that there are genuine cases where it is not appropriate for them to see the other parent, but in my case and many others I know of, parental alienation is largely used purely to punish the other parent after a spilt up.

On 6 May 2021 Lisa's anniversary, I went to try and see George and Marie while Graham was out. Many people in this area are aware of the situation and have kept a look out for George and Marie, but no one has seen or heard of them for nearly two years. Some people even questioned whether they actually lived in the house, so I went to find out myself. This was extremely risky for me but I seized the opportunity while I could. The drive was clear so I knew Graham was not home. I knocked on the door but no one came to answer. I stepped back and saw an unfamiliar face at the bedroom window above, he had shoulder length hair, and looked like Jack. He opened the window and looked terrified, his voice was deep, and he had grown and changed since I last saw him – it was George. "Wow, he's a man now, a good looking one, but why the long hair?" I thought.

"Fuck off, fuck off, I will ring the police, FUCK OFF YOU BITCH" he screamed from the window, then Marie ran to the window. "Fuck off!" she screamed. People walking along the street turned to look in disbelief... This was very disturbing.

"I just wanted to see you, I love you both so much," I quickly said, shaking on the spot, aware that George was on his phone, probably to alert Graham, so I had to leave and quickly. This scene just confirmed to me that these two teenagers were petrified, they behaved like caged animals. George had probably been denied a haircut due to the horrendous control of Graham. My heart broke for them. I didn't want to cause them stress or grief from Graham, I just wanted to see if they were actually still alive and to tell them that I loved them.

Graham had done a very good job poisoning them against me, but it's not me that I'm concerned about, it's what damage this has caused to George and Marie. Their behaviour was extremely disturbing and indicative of abuse, but no one will listen because Graham has successfully brainwashed them into saying they don't want to see me or their brothers. This is by far a clear case of child abuse.

Chapter 36

Where my story lies today:

I am trying to raise awareness of this horrendously damaging abusive act called PARENTAL ALIENATION. This is obviously a recognised act by the authorities, yet not investigated thoroughly enough for it to be stopped.

I am trying to raise awareness that DOMESTIC ABUSE goes on in every walk of life behind closed doors, and people need to be aware of their neighbours, friends and family and look out for the signs. I am a lucky survivor of domestic abuse as many victims lose their lives, but I truly believe I narrowly escaped being just another statistic.

I am still fighting to free George and Marie from their isolated, controlled environment and I will fight until the day I die. I made a public appeal on social media to let them know that, what they have been told about me by their father, is nothing but lies in a revengeful attack on me for daring to leave him and his abuse.

My video appeal can be seen on Facebook:

https://m.facebook.com/story.php?story_fbid=918374952439680&
id=100028015518201

The words he screamed to me when I left, just proves my point... "IF YOU LEAVE ME, I WILL MAKE SURE THESE KIDS NEVER, EVER WANT TO SEE YOU AGAIN."

No child should ever have to hear those words, my heart shattered into a million pieces right there.

I feel blessed that I am surrounded by my amazing sons Jack and Lee, and my fantastic daughters-in-law, Louise and Rose, my precious four grandchildren and my many close friends, because without this support, I really wouldn't be here today.

Every single day, I thank myself for leaving and feel proud of myself for gaining the strength to walk away from abuse.

My fight continues and my pain is horrendous, but I know that one day my kids will see the truth and I will be waiting with my arms wide open.

Lisa Marie, my angel in heaven, I love you forever and miss you beyond belief, but you gave me this strength to keep on fighting until the end...

Jack and Lee, you are my absolute world, my heroes, my life, and I love you both so much. I would not be here today if not for you two, you have both been extremely instrumental in me writing this book and I'm bursting with pride for you both.

This book arose because of you. ♥

I love all my children with all my heart.

It is possible to break free from abuse, there is lots of support out there, it's extremely painful and difficult to get the courage to leave domestic abuse, especially after many years in that trap, but anyone reading this book who thinks it's not possible, please believe in yourself, you can do this... I am living proof and not only did I leave, but I have managed to carve out a great life for myself. I don't want a man in my life again, I am a strong, independent woman and most of all I'm a survivor. I have learned to like myself and am proud of who I am. In my heart, I have faith that George and Marie will learn the truth and want their family back in their lives very soon.

Cry Wolf by *Moa Drugge* (released August, 2022):

https://sptfy.com/CryWolf

This is NOT THE END.

The government have published my petition to criminalise parental alienation, I need as many signatures as possible to get this petition passed in Parliament. Please could you use the link below or visit my Facebook page and sign this petition with thanks.

https://petition.parliament.uk/petitions/615816